The Complete Guide to Raising Chickens

Everything You Need to Know
Explained Simply
REVISED 2ND Edition

By Tara Layman Williams

THE COMPLETE GUIDE TO RAISING CHICKENS: EVERYTHING YOU NEED TO
KNOW EXPLAINED SIMPLY REVISED 2ND EDITION

Library of Congress Cataloging-in-Publication Data

Williams, Tara Layman, 1972- author.
  The complete guide to raising chickens : everything you need to know explained simply / by:
Tara Layman Williams. -- Revised 2nd edition.
    pages cm
Includes bibliographical references and index.
ISBN 978-1-62023-016-9 (alk. paper) -- ISBN 1-62023-016-X (alk. paper) 1. Chickens. I. Title.
SF487.W715 2015
636.5--dc23
                              2015011932

  10 9 8 7 6 5 4 3 2

EDITOR: Melissa Figueroa • mfigueroa@atlantic-pub.com
FRONT COVER DESIGN: Meg Buchner • megadesn@mchsi.com
INTERIOR DESIGN: TL Price • tlpricefreelance@gmail.com
BACK COVER & INSERT DESIGN: Jacqueline Miller • millerjackiej@gmail.com

Printed on Recycled Paper

Printed in the United States

Reduce. Reuse. RECYCLE.

A decade ago, Atlantic Publishing signed the Green Press Initiative. These guidelines promote environmentally friendly practices, such as using recycled stock and vegetable-based inks, avoiding waste, choosing energy-efficient resources, and promoting a no-pulping policy. We now use 100-percent recycled stock on all our books. The results: in one year, switching to post-consumer recycled stock saved 24 mature trees, 5,000 gallons of water, the equivalent of the total energy used for one home in a year, and the equivalent of the greenhouse gases from one car driven for a year.

Over the years, we have adopted a number of dogs from rescues and shelters. First there was Bear and after he passed, Ginger and Scout. Now, we have Kira, another rescue. They have brought immense joy and love not just into our lives, but into the lives of all who met them.

We want you to know a portion of the profits of this book will be donated in Bear, Ginger and Scout's memory to local animal shelters, parks, conservation organizations, and other individuals and nonprofit organizations in need of assistance.

– Douglas & Sherri Brown,
President & Vice-President of Atlantic Publishing

Table of Contents

Chapter 3: To Own or Not to Own — Considerations Prior to Purchase 33

Chapter 4: Blue Ribbon Chickens — The Best Breeds 43

Chapter 5: Home to Roost 87

Chapter 6: Picking up Chicks: Shopping for Your Flock 113

Chapter 7: Hatching Eggs 133

Chapter 8: Health and Anatomy of a Chicken   151

Chapter 9: Breeding Chickens   175

Introduction

Welcome to the fabulous world of chickens. You, too, can be the proud owner of healthy and productive poultry, choosing from among hundreds of chicken breeds. After you make up your mind to purchase birds, you may be unsure about owning a flock or may not know where to begin. Should you start with eggs or chicks? What type of equipment do you need? How much land should you have? What are the zoning laws in your area? You have many questions, and rightly so.

Owning livestock is a commitment and responsibility. These birds will depend on you for their physical and emotional well-being. They need to be fed and receive fresh water daily, and you need to keep their housing clean and safe. Chickens are very sensitive to their surroundings and are susceptible to stress, so you will want reduce the amount of stress in their environment to keep your birds healthy. Disease can spread quickly among a flock, and it is imperative to inoculate your birds to increase their immunity. Taking them to your veterinarian for annual vaccinations will ensure their physical well-being.

Having chickens of your own provides you with many benefits. First, chickens produce an abundance of wholesome eggs. Fresh eggs with sunshine-colored yolks that sizzle when you crack them into a frying pan will be available right outside your door day after day. If you raise your chickens for meat, you have the peace of mind of knowing your poultry is free of chemicals, hormones, and antibiotics. Your family can enjoy free-range chicken with more flavor and less processing. Or, perhaps you decided to raise chickens because you would like to show them. Show birds come in colorful varieties: Some have sleek feathers, such as the Spanish Andalusian, or you may prefer the fluffy silkie breed. Whatever your desire, you are sure to find a chicken breed that will meet your needs.

Chickens are categorized as pure breeds, hybrids (egg-laying and mixed), and bantams. **Pure breeds** are chickens bred from members of a recognized breed, strain, or kind of chicken without a mixture of other breeds over many generations. **Hybrids** have a mixed lineage, often bred to accentuate or eliminate certain qualities of a particular breed. **Bantams** are mini chickens. They can be any breed but are typically half to one-quarter the size of an average bird. Bantams make great pets, especially in residential neighborhoods, because they are petite and require less space. They have the same characteristics as their full-size counterparts, but are just smaller.

This book is a thorough manual on how to raise chickens, explained in its simplest form. From breeding to butchering and everything in between, you will find the answers to your questions here. Case studies from farmers and laypeople are distributed throughout the book with advice on how to care for your flock. To assist you further, the appendices include resources on where to purchase chickens, coops, equipment, and feed, along with organizations that can provide current information, support, and networking with fellow chicken owners.

There are several things you will need to do to ensure your flock is healthy and happy. Here is a checklist of everything you need and are advised to do to get started with your flock:

- Permission from local council
- Communicate with neighbors

- Space and location
- Coop (blueprints and equipment, or pre-constructed)
- Bedding
- Nesting boxes
- Roosts
- Feeders
- Waterers
- Manure boxes
- Feed (age-appropriate)
- Incubators (if hatching eggs)
- Probe thermometers
- Storage containers for food and scoops
- Heater for chicks
- Heater for water
- Fertilized eggs, chicks, pullets, or cockerels
- Egg baskets to collect your fresh eggs

Having your own brood of chickens is a rewarding experience. Planning and preparation will give your new additions a successful start and set the stage for a fulfilling relationship with them. If you decide at a later date that you have too many chickens for your coop and want to downsize, or if you are unsure what to do with older chickens, this book will provide you with humane options. This guide will teach you how to raise chickens from start to finish while making the journey as enjoyable as possible for both you and your flock.

Chapter 1:
Chicken Scratch: A Little Bit of Chicken History

What came first: the chicken or the egg? There are several theories. Some scientists agree on the theory that chicken eggs developed as dinosaurs evolved into birds, thus reptile eggs came first. Others believe the chicken came first based on a protein found in both eggs and chickens. But whatever the case, chickens originated in India and Thailand from the single Red Junglefowl breed and evolved through the centuries into hundreds of breeds as they were carried from continent to continent.

It may be hard to imagine, but sketches of chickens found on shards of pottery and on cave walls suggest that during the Roman Empire, these birds were worshipped. Long before being considered a menu item, they were used as sacrifices to Roman and Greek gods. The Romans, who were a superstitious people, believed slaughtering a chicken could help them make decisions in battle. "The Keeper of the Sacred Chickens" was a position in the army and a title one of the soldiers held. Romans carried a cage of sacred chickens with them when they went to war. They would throw food and crumble at the bottom of the chicken cages when the troops needed assistance, such as when they should attack. If the chickens ate, it was a sign that everything was fine. If they did not eat, then something was wrong and the soldiers were to take caution. In this particular battle, when the keeper of the sacred chickens fed the birds, they did not eat. The Roman general Publius Claudius Pulcher was headstrong and ignored the birds, tossing their cage into the sea. He said they could drink if they did not want to eat. The Romans then lost their battle, the Battle of Drepanum. In Greek culture, the Greeks would offer chickens as sacrifices to the gods to try and appease them or in the hopes of receiving something they wanted.

So how did hens and roosters get from Asia and Europe to America? History suggests Christopher Columbus carried chickens with him on his ships from Italy during his second voyage to the New World. With today's ever-changing technology, scientists still search for more specific answers and are conducting DNA testing on remnants of chicken bones found in North and South America. These bones may pre-date Columbus, indicating the birds were there before he landed on the continent. If this is the case, a breed of chicken may have developed in the Western Hemisphere from another breed of bird, or another explorer may have brought chickens with him.

From 1500 to the 1900s, chickens were raised on small farms and in family backyards, primarily for producing eggs. America's poultry industry did not come to fruition until 1923 when Celia Steele, a housewife in Sussex County, Delaware, had the foresight to see that chickens also could be sold as broilers and not just layers. A **broiler chicken** is raised for meat, and a **layer** lays eggs. She saw the profit potential and purchased 500 chicks, intending to sell them for meat. At the time, poultry was a delicacy and was not typically sold for meat, so Steele's first flock sold for 62 cents per pound. Later in 1924, the birds sold for 57 cents per pound, which is the equivalent today of close to $15 per pound. Homemakers and restaurant owners discovered the versatility of preparing chicken (frying, broiling, roasting, and as stew meat), causing demand to increase.

By 1926, Steele's flock increased to 10,000, and less than ten years later, the prospering Steeles owned seven farms. Even today, Delaware, the birthplace of the broiler chicken industry, remains one of the country's biggest chicken producers, delivering millions of birds each year.

Industrializing a Farm-Based Industry

The 1940s saw the integration of the chicken industry. Prior to that time, feed mills, farms, processing operations, and hatcheries worked as separate entities, according to the National Chicken Council. The integration of these made the chicken industry more efficient and streamlined — the feed mills loaned money to the farms to buy chicks from the hatcheries. When farmers sold the flock to the processors, they used the money they received from the processors to pay back the feed mills. This practice became more common and regulated as chicken consumption increased. Refrigeration also helped the industry because it allowed consumers to store their meat longer. Factory farming produced more products for less money, and raising chickens that scratched around in the backyard became less popular and not as lucrative.

In the 1950s, production increased to meet the needs of the Baby Boom. Vertical integration — when one company controls all processes from marketing to production in an effort to reduce costs — helped manufacturers afford new technology, which increased sales and profits. Entrepreneurs with vertical integration systems controlled most of the chicken industry at this time. In the 1960s, marketing expanded to television and print, making poultry brand names more recognized and popular than ever.

Automation technologies of the 1970s helped producers meet consumer demands. Regulations and laws became more focused on production as people became more educated on the poultry's nutritional values, diseases associated with chickens, and the process of speeding up chicken growth. The government and the public scrutinized the cleanliness of chicken plants, the environments the chickens lived in, and the way the birds were killed. Poultry was not the only industry with stricter regulations; the United States overall was setting higher standards and fine-tuning its food markets. Regulators' eyes were open to the potential harm of unsafe practices, and they closely monitored the progress of food production. Demand was steadily increasing, and chicken producers enhanced chicken growth to meet these needs because faster-growing birds meant more poultry available in a shorter amount of time, which increased profits.

Chicken — The New King of Meats

In the 1980s, demand for poultry expanded further when fast-food restaurants added chicken tenders and nuggets to their menus. Fast-food giant McDonalds, which was famous for its burgers, introduced Chicken McNuggets in 1983. By the end of the year, the chain was the second-largest chicken retailer in the world, second to Kentucky Fried Chicken in the fast-food market. This chicken sensation helped increase poultry sales overall. In 2003, the amount of chicken nuggets sold in all restaurants increased to more than 200 percent of the amount sold in the 1990s. McDonald's is credited with introducing the nugget into the American way of life. It was not just a fad; the chicken nugget became a staple that appeals to all age groups.

By 1992, chicken sales surpassed beef sales for the first time. In 2001, U.S. exports of poultry to other countries reached $2 billion, an all-time high. Not only were poultry broilers booming within America, they were also increasing globally.

Stricter laws developed in the past six decades to ensure the safety of the birds produced for consumption, and the U.S. Department of Agriculture (USDA) enforces these rules. These laws became necessary after animal-handling practices were deemed inhumane and factory conditions were ruled unclean. Because of the new rules, birds are less expensive than they once were. More birds are currently available, which drives the cost down. The birds also have more meat on their bones because they are given special feed to plump them up quicker. They are produced in cleaner, safer environments than they were in the past. Although debate continues over the humane treatment of these animals, government regulations aim to achieve the best possible conditions for both the workers and the birds.

Feathered Friends

The broiler industry devised a system to grow and sell chickens more rapidly, making more of them available for consumption. But chickens are more than just an industrial moneymaker. They are versatile animals that can provide food, companionship, and a hobby for you. Flock owners will attest to these animals' uniqueness and the benefits of owning poultry. Chickens are curious animals with different personalities and are rewarding animals to own.

CASE STUDY: BACKYARD BIRDS

Charlene Lindsey

Charlene Lindsey grew up on a farm in Beech Grove, Arkansas. Depending on the time of year, Lindsey's family had 15 to 50 chickens scattered across their backyard, scratching and pecking and providing food for her and her family. White rocks, Rhode Island reds, and dominikers made up their flock.

"We hatched our own eggs and sometimes bought baby chicks in the springtime," says Lindsey. "You could get them from a farmer's co-op or directly from other farmers, but we would get ours from mail order."

Lindsey's coop was homemade. She explains, "Basically, we made a building just tall enough to stand up in. We put nests on one side and a place to roost on the other. You do not really need windows because the hens like it dark to lay their eggs and to sit on them. Make sure you have nesting boxes. We filled them with straw and also put some straw on the ground. The only challenges were collecting the eggs every day and keeping the coop clean. Sometimes predators would get in. Dogs, foxes, and opossums were the worst."

When asked what advice she would give to a novice chicken owner, Lindsey says, "Start with just a few and make sure you have plenty of room for them to run."

Sidebar:

A small poultry flock is relatively inexpensive, requires less space than most animal enterprises and doesn't require much time. In addition, raising a small poultry flock is also a good way to introduce youth to animal agriculture (for food or fiber) and to help build a sense of responsibility

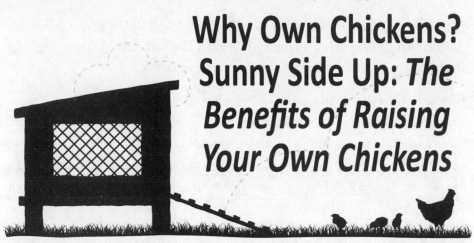

Chapter 2:
Why Own Chickens? Sunny Side Up: *The Benefits of Raising Your Own Chickens*

Are you toying with the idea of owning chickens? There are many considerations to take into account. These quirky birds provide humans with not only food, but also companionship, entertainment, and a hobby. This chapter covers all the benefits of owning and raising your own chickens.

Reasons to Raise Chickens

As pets

Although chickens may not seem like the first choice when selecting a domestic pet, you will be surprised how interactive they can be. If you raise your chickens from the time they are chicks, they will learn to respond to you and even let you hand-feed them. Some breeds are more inclined to allow this, such as the Cochin because they are so docile and friendly, but other breeds, such as the Ancona, are more skittish and may not take to eating from your hand. The best way to develop a relationship with your birds is to talk to them every day. When you bring them a treat, use the same call each time to train your flock to come when they hear your voice. As a treat, give them white millet, a nutritious grain found in most birdseed mixtures that is found at feed stores. Giving your birds treats also will help forge a bond between you and your flock. Chickens can eat almost anything, but keep their diet balanced, especially if you are selling them or their eggs. Kitchen scraps are fine, too, but make sure they are fresh and do not contain excess salt.

Chickens will follow you around and watch your movements. You can pat them on the head and hold them like other pets, but do not pick up an aggressive bird or one that is not familiar with you. Holding a chicken correctly will help keep the chicken calm and less stressed, but incorrectly holding a chicken can aggravate or scare it. Make sure your movements are gentle so you do not to frighten it.

Chickens also have the ability to be trained. If you are keeping your chickens as pets, you may want to train them to follow commands, such as coming when called. Training is essential in teaching your rooster or hen to do something they did not know before you taught them. It is easier to start with chicks that are socialized and comfortable with people. However, it is not difficult to work with older chickens, or chicks that are not socialized. It takes routine practice, a safe environment, and lots of treats to successfully train a chicken.

For their eggs

Chickens are not only great pets, but they also provide food. The average hen lays approximately 260 eggs per year. Some breeds of chickens, like the Rhode Island red are better layers than others. Even if you have a small flock — say, for example, you own six chickens — you can expect to reap 1,560 eggs, which can mean a lot of omelets for you and your family. These eggs are better quality than store-bought eggs because they go through less processing. Commercially processed eggs come from chickens with manipulated diets and levels of nutrients. Many commercial facilities will also induce molting in their flocks to increase egg production. In layer facilities, eggs are either immediately processed, or wait in a cooler 12 to 14 hours before processing. Either way, once ready to be processed, the eggs are washed in a detergent solution that removes soil, visually inspected, and then graded to be packaged accordingly.

Egg grade is determined by a standardized set of qualities determined by the USDA. The grades you see in the grocery store — AA, A, and B — are determined by inspection of the inside and outside of the egg.

According to USDA standards, egg grade is decided by these factors:

- AA Quality — The shell must be clean, unbroken, and practically normal. The air cell must not exceed 1/8 inch in depth, may show unlimited movement, and may be free or bubbly. The white must be clear and firm so that the yolk is only slightly defined when the egg is twirled before the candling light. The yolk must be practically free from apparent defects.

- A Quality — The shell must be clean, unbroken, and practically normal. The air cell must not exceed 3/16 inch in depth, may show unlimited movement, and may be free or bubbly. The white must be clear and at least reasonably firm so that the yolk outline is only fairly well defined when the egg is twirled before the candling light. The yolk must be practically free from apparent defects.

- B Quality — The shell must be unbroken, may be abnormal, and may have slightly stained areas. Moderately stained areas are permitted if they do not cover more than 1/32 of the shell surface if localized, or 1/16 of the shell surface if scattered. Eggs having shells with prominent stains or adhering dirt are not permitted. The air cell may be over 3/16 inch in depth, may show unlimited movement, and may be free or bubbly. The white may be weak and watery so that the yolk outline is plainly visible when the egg is twirled before the candling light. The yolk may appear dark, enlarged, and flattened, and may show clearly visible germ development but no blood due to such development. It may show other serious defects that do not render the egg inedible. Small blood spots or meat spots (aggregating not more than 1/8 inch in diameter) may be present.

When you raise your own eggs, the natural diet of your chickens will result in the best quality egg possible. The eggs your chickens produce can go from the nest to the frying pan in a matter of minutes, which is the freshest type of eggs available.

For meat

Some people raise chickens primarily for their meat and consider eggs an added bonus. Certain breeds of chicken are meatier and will give you a hearty portion for your meal. If you prefer not to kill the birds yourself, you can take them to a butcher. But if you would like to know how to do it yourself, the step-by-step process is in Chapter 12. Chapter 12 also provides resources on where to take your chickens for someone else to butcher.

For breeding

Breeding chickens for sale or for show allows you to keep the same bloodline or create a breed that has the qualities you desire, such as a particular size or egg color. You can find out more information about a particular breed of bird from a breeder who specializes in producing that breed, in books, or online at websites such as My Pet Chicken (*www.mypetchicken.com*). This website is full of information on every breed of chicken, and it also sells chicks and supplies for your birds. You also can inquire at your local co-op, a group of individuals who are interested in raising chickens and sharing their expertise, or visit a nearby farmer or avian (bird) veterinarian.

You can also crossbreed purebred chickens to result in hybrid chickens until the birds have the characteristics that you desire. If your flock is growing and you do not want to keep the chicks that result from your attempts at creating the perfect hybrid, you can give them away, sell them, donate them to a local farm, or put up ads online at websites such as Best Farm Buys (*www.bestfarmbuys.com*). This is a free site where you can post products and services for sale or shop for them. Enter your ZIP code to find products close to you.

Even amateurs can successfully breed chickens. Most breeds are fine to crossbreed, but if one of your birds has a problem — for example, it is weak or does not have a full coat of feathers — change bloodlines, or switch to a bird from a different lineage, and do not breed that particular bird. To have a perfect flock, breed only robust, healthy birds.

For selling

You may opt to sell your excess chickens. Check with your local government office, department of agriculture, or City Hall to see whether any laws prevent you from selling your birds or eggs. Put your birds up for sale online on websites such as eBay Classifieds (*www.ebayclassifieds.com*) and USFreeads (*www. usfreeads.com*). Another option is to put ads in the classifieds of your local newspaper, or set up a booth at a flea or farmer's market. Sell only healthy birds and be honest with your buyers, because you want to have a good reputation for selling in your community. When selling, it is best to let buyers know the chicken's breed, age, the kind of egg they produce, how often they produce eggs, and health.

Most chickens cost about $1 to $5 each. The price of a chick depends on its sex and breed. Females tend to be more expensive than males, and a rare breed will cost more. More expensive are pullets, which are young hens that recently started to lay eggs. Pullets usually cost around $15 to $25. If you are unsure how much to charge for your birds, browse current advertisements to see the prices other breeders are charging. If you have an abundance of chicks or if your chickens are getting old and unproductive, you can price them for less than average or offer a package deal such as five birds for $5. Do not sell your birds if they are sick or weak. Most of the time, you can tell just by looking at a chicken whether it is healthy. Its eyes should be clear, its breathing should be clear and not wheezy, and its coat should be full and shiny. If in doubt, do not sell the bird, but instead take it to your vet.

Showing chickens

Many birds are used for show at county and state fairs. You can show birds as a hobby, and competitions often offer prizes, which could include money, ribbons, or medals, for the top birds. Showing birds can give you an opportunity to meet with other chicken owners and discuss your flocks and other similar interests. There are competitions you can take your chickens to throughout the year, including opportunities to show your birds at county and state fairs that usually take place during the summer.

Nutrition and Quality of Life Concerns

Chickens can be classified as commercial, free-range, organic, or pastured poultry cage free. The differences in the way chickens are raised will affect their quality of eggs and meat and the quality of life the chickens experience. It is important to know the differences among commercial, free-range, organic, and pastured poultry cage free because they affect the way a chicken is raised. This can affect you as well if you consume the meat or the eggs. It also will affect your customers if you decide to sell your birds or eggs. People are more aware now than ever before about where their food comes from and the long-term effects it might have on their health.

Commercial Chickens

Commercial chickens are raised in mass quantities with the intention of selling the meat and eggs. To meet the increase in demand of chicken meat that occurred in the past century, machines and technology are evolving. Birds are de-feathered and slaughtered simultaneously, which processes them more efficiently. The birds are growing faster, too, through added hormones, which the Food and Drug Administration (FDA) approves.

Production complexes that are comprised of a feed mill, hatchery, chicken farm, and processing plant developed as a result of vertical integration. With this system, contract farmers raise chicks from the hatchery, housing them in climate-controlled chicken houses. These buildings are typically 500 feet long and 50 feet wide and house approximately 20,000 chickens. The overcrowded conditions stress out the birds, which affects their health. Sickness spreads quickly, so the flock is inoculated as early as the **ova stage** while the birds are still in the shell.

The chicks raised for meat, as opposed to the egg layers, are moved to a **grow-out house** where they are usually caged and fed until they plump up. The chickens remain there around six to seven weeks until they weigh enough for slaughter; this weight ranges from 1 to 7 pounds, depending on the breed of chicken, but on average they weigh around 3 to 4 pounds. Hormones accelerate the birds' growth, plumping up breasts and thighs, so it takes less time than a natural growth cycle. When the time comes for the birds to be slaughtered, they are conveyed through a stun cabinet where they are transported through water and stunned with a light electrical current. This process calms them for the slaughter so they are not flailing about. Then they are moved to an automatic neck cutter. The birds are washed, sanitized, and inspected to ensure that the meat is safe to package.

Reasons to avoid commercial chickens and raise your own flock

Mass-produced chickens may come from crowded environments that cause them to peck each other. They are stressed, which causes them to produce toxins in their bodies and weakens their immune systems. Weaker chickens suffer because they are trampled upon and pecked at incessantly, which causes open wounds and sores.

Mass-produced chickens are exposed to hormones, antibiotics, inoculants, and chemicals, and you may not want to ingest these substances through your food. Synthetic chemicals that are added to food, even in small doses, can cause serious illness. A food can be natural, such as an apple, but that does not mean it is organic unless it has a certified seal. Natural foods can contain additives, pesticides, and preservatives, as opposed to organic foods, which are chemical-free. Although the Food and Drug Administration approves the use of pesticides or preservatives, the more organic food we consume, the healthier we will be.

Animal cruelty is also a concern for commercial chickens. In the past, some production complexes used a practice known as **debeaking,** which removes or trims the beak to discourage pecking and cannibalism. Scientific studies revealed that this prevents the birds from preening properly and causes them pain. In the 1990s, many commercial chicken companies ceased this practice as many people consider it inhumane, although it is still in practice. Critics also consider the method of slaughtering chickens to be cruel. The electric current used to stun the birds is accepted by the industry but still worries animal advocates. Overall, you do not know the history of the bird you purchase if you buy it from a commercial chicken company.

Free-Range and Organic Chickens

Free-range chickens, or free-roaming chickens, are not caged. Although this term evokes the image of chickens meandering on green pastures, this is not always true, and there is no guarantee that free-range chickens are treated humanely. In fact, it does not mean they are even allowed outside; it just means that they are not caged. Even commercially grown chickens can be labeled free-range if they are never placed in a cage. If you are purchasing free-range chickens because you believe they are chemical-free and healthy, the terminology may be misleading you.

Free-range birds mostly are found on farms. You can raise free-range chickens in your own backyard, and while they will always need a coop, they should have the mobility to wander in and out of it for most of the daytime hours.

For a chicken to be considered free-range and organic, here are the standards that should be met, according to the USDA National Organic Program:

- Chicks should be under organic management from the second day of life.

- Housing for the birds should be clean, and bedding and the coop itself must not be made of pressure treated lumber.

- Protection from predators and shelter from the elements is required.

- Antibiotics are not to be used. If a bird or flock gets ill, they should be treated, but the treated animals cannot have the organic seal after treatment.

- Vaccinations are not permitted. Instead, preventative measures regarding healthcare are recommended, including natural food, good nutrition, and a healthy and safe environment.

- Growth hormones are not allowed.

- Feed needs to be natural, and the addition of vitamins and minerals should only be given for overall health purposes. All feed must be organically produced. Animal byproducts from mammals and poultry should not be used. This applies to fishmeal and crabmeal, too, unless it is certain they are organic.

- The land the chickens live on must have shade, shelter, and palatable, sustainable vegetation. Living conditions must be as close to a bird's natural environment as possible. Temporary confinement is permitted for special care or traveling, but continuous cage confinement is not acceptable. The birds must have access to outdoors and direct sunlight.

- Beak and claw mutilation is not permitted, unless necessary for the welfare of the bird.

- If you are selling your chickens or eggs and the amount of your sales are less than $5,000, you do not need to be certified organic to claim your birds are organic, providing you abide by the guidelines. If your sales are over $5,000, you can go to the USDA website to find information on your state and how to be certified organic.

Organic food and grocers are more popular than ever. **Organic chickens** have the same standards as free-range chickens but are fed only organic grains and live in a completely organic environment. On organic farms, no synthetic products are allowed, including pesticides and fertilizers. The land the chickens eat from must even be organic through long-term management of soil, and there must be a "buffer zone" between an organic farm and surrounding, nonorganic land. These birds are raised in a healthy and comfortable environment and may or may not be caged. A bird that is not caged is considered free-range. The difference between organic chicken and free-range chickens is that free range chickens do not have to adhere to the strict organic guidelines. You can purchase organic chickens for consumption in most large grocery food chains, farmers' markets, and fresh-air markets. Organic chickens will have a label, certifying that they meet the standards. Organic Ecology (*www. organicecology.com*) has a page where you can enter the barcode from your purchase to verify it is certified organic.

Pastured Chickens

Pastured poultry, according to the USDA National Organic Program, is regulated by the same standards as organic chickens: No chemicals or antibiotics are added to their food, and the birds will grow at a normal, natural pace to the intended size for their breed. Unlike other organic chickens, pastured birds have access to outside and greenery — not just gravel or dirt — to eat. This is the ideal environment for your livestock.

Egg layers — hens that lay eggs — raised in this manner will produce more consistently, and birds raised for meat will have more flavor and substance. Organic and pastured poultry will produce eggs that not only have brighter yolks and are more appetizing, but also have more nutrients. Research shows that organic eggs have less cholesterol and taste better. Their eggs have twice the omega-3 fatty acids, triple the vitamin E, seven times more beta carotene, and two-thirds more vitamin A than "regular" eggs. Pastured organic eggs also have one-third less cholesterol and one-quarter less saturated fat.

Raising pastured chickens will offer you these advantages:

- The chickens can grow chemical free, at their own pace, the way nature intended.
- The stress level of the chickens is lower than those of chickens in commercial environments.
- There is control over which pets or other animals are exposed to your chickens, and you can protect the birds from other animals.
- The chickens help control pests in gardens by eating bugs.
- The waste chickens produce makes great fertilizer and compost, leading to a more sustainable way of living.

Chickens will enhance your life. They will give you a chance to escape from the hectic pace of the day-to-day grind and step out into your backyard and watch over your flock. They will provide you with fresh food, companionship, and a sense of pride. They are curious and unique creatures, and once you own them, you will find a whole new appreciation for them and for the world around you.

CASE STUDY: CHICKENS IN THE ROARING 20s

Grace Shotwell

Grace Shotwell grew up in the 1920s during a time when raising chickens meant you raised them for food, sharing, and trading meat and eggs with your neighbors. Families worked on the farm during the day and sat down to supper together each night. Their farm had fruit trees, a large garden, and a river nearby where they could fish as the chickens scratched the ground and sunbathed on lazy afternoons.

Shotwell's family had about 10 to 20 chickens, including breeds like Plymouth Rocks, wyandottes, leghorns, and a variety of bantys. Their meat and eggs helped to feed Grace, her eight siblings, and her parents, as well as her neighbors. They lived a sustainable life on their farm.

The coop was made by hand by Shotwell's dad. It was a basic structure with a shed with roosts on one side and nests on the other. The coop was safe from predators, like foxes, and secure for the flock.

Shotwell tells a story she remembers from when she was in school. One summer her uncle gave her older brother some baby capons. She also had a 4-year-old younger brother who used to watch as their father would wring their chickens necks to kill them for supper. One day the baby brother came running into the house excitedly. He said proudly to his mom, "I wringed and I wringed and I wringed their heads off!" Sure enough, he wrung four of the capons. It was sad, but it was also funny to see how excited her baby brother was to be just like his dad.

Chapter 3:
To Own or Not to Own — Considerations Prior to Purchase

If the benefits of owning chickens are attractive to you, it is time to think about if you and your family are ready to own your own. It is important to weigh whether or not you are ready to undertake the time and monetary commitment that comes with owning chickens. Besides time and money, do you have the space for birds? Are you legally allowed to have chickens on your property? Are you willing to get a little dirty taking care of the daily maintenance chickens require? This chapter lays out considerations you need to make before you delve into the world of chicken owning.

Zoning for Your New Addition

Now that you decided you want to keep some poultry of your own, the next step is to check local zoning laws and ordinances to confirm that you can keep poultry. Do not assume you are allowed to keep livestock because you live outside city limits or because your neighbor has some. Check for yourself at your local government office because laws can change. Even though a neighbor has been raising chickens for years, this practice may have been grandfathered in, which means the neighbor had chickens before the laws existed and is now permitted to keep their birds. Or, perhaps nobody in that jurisdiction noticed your neighbor is breaking the law. You can discreetly own a few chickens if you have enough property, but breaking the law is not acceptable. It is also smarter and safer to do a little research before buying chickens because the government can fine you for breaking the law. For example, in Orlando, Florida, it is illegal to keep chickens in residential areas. If caught, you have to get rid of the chickens and owe fines of $1,000 a day if you do not adhere to the laws.

The Planning Board, County Clerk, City Hall, Department of Agriculture, or in some areas the animal control department will have the laws concerning keeping livestock. Get the information in writing in case you have questions later on. If you plan on building a coop, check for any restrictions on constructing buildings on your property with these departments; also consult your neighborhood's board or covenants for rules regarding buildings and livestock. If zoning laws prohibit owning chickens in your neighborhood, do not be afraid to appeal these laws. The regulations may be outdated, and if nobody has approached the local government in a long time, there may not have been a reason to change them.

Because laws vary greatly, it is difficult to find a comprehensive collection of every law from each state on one website. Not all counties, towns, and villages have current websites, so the best solution is to inquire in person or by phone at your local government office. If they do not have the specific information you are looking for, they can point you in the right direction.

Where to House Your Chickens

City living

Once the zoning issues are taken care of, assess the space you have available on your property. Owning chickens is not just for rural homeowners; designer coops and chicken diapers exist so that city slickers can satisfy their yearning for country living. Omlet (***www.omlet.us***) offers a coop aptly named the Eglu for its igloo-like shape. With the Eglu, the coop where the chickens sleep and lay eggs is on one end, with a covered run, or pen, attached. These coops can be used in areas as small as 20 feet by 30 feet and can house two to four chickens. Although space is limited in city living, keeping a chicken does require some room for the birds to roam, and this type of coop is compact and light for easy care. If you decide to raise your chickens in the city, your main concern will be ensuring you have some space for your birds to run. You can make your own patch of grass for them to forage in by planting some grass seed in a 24 inch by 24 inch plastic or wooden planter about 2 inches high. Put some soil in it, plant some grass seed, and let your chicken play in it. You can add some worms or slugs to the dirt and your bird will love to forage for the treats.

If you want to keep your pet chicken indoors, chicken diapers might be a good option. These diapers have straps that wrap around the wings and legs, and offer a lined pouch to collect the manure. It may sound silly to have a chicken in a diaper, but it will help keep your house clean. Also, the waste collected in the diaper makes excellent compost and fertilizer for your gardens.

Two websites that provide chicken diapers are:

- My Pet Chicken (*www.mypetchicken.com*) — This site offers five sizes, in assorted colors and designs, and lined for extra support.

- Chicken Diapers (*www.chickendiapers.com*) — You will need to provide your chicken's measurements to ensure a snug fit; the diapers on this site come in assorted colors and patterns.

All you really need to own chickens in a city or urban setting is a place for your bird to run, roost, nest, and sleep. For your own quality of life, a coop is recommended so the bird will have a place to feel safe and so you will have an area where you can secure your chicken. Homemade coops are just as handy as store-bought coops, and your chicken will not know the difference as long as its needs are met.

Country chickens

If you live in the country, you probably have more space available to build a bigger coop. When you are building a coop on your land, include some type of fencing around your yard to keep predators like raccoons, coyotes, and skunks out and your chickens in. Your fence only has to be 2 feet to 3 feet tall, as most chickens will fly up to perch on something but do not fly a long distance. If you are in an area with predators that can jump fences, such as cats or mountain lions, consider building a fence about 8 feet tall.

You will need some type of coop to protect your chickens from the elements and provide comfortable housing for them to sleep and lay eggs in. Coops should offer 3 to 4 square feet of space per chicken and need to include nesting boxes for egg laying, roosts for perching, a feeder, and a water container. Coops should have a door or hatch that you can lock at night with your birds safely tucked inside. The bigger the coop, the more comfortable your birds will be.

More land gives you the opportunity to expand the size of your flock. If you plan on adding to your brood at a later date, plan your coop accordingly so you do not have to renovate it later.

Caring for Your Chickens

Chickens are relatively easy to care for and require minimal time and attention. Feeding takes only about 15 to 20 minutes per day, but chickens do need to get out of their coop for fresh air and sunshine. Most chickens prefer to stay outside all day unless it is raining. If you travel extensively with your job; work more than one job or work excessive hours; or if you work and attend school, you may want to reconsider owning livestock unless you have someone you know and trust to help you care for them. As with all pets, your birds need to be fed and watered daily, and their coop needs to be kept clean. Clean the coop about once a week, but if you have a larger flock, you may want to do this more frequently. Chickens defecate frequently, so keep their bedding and coop area clean. Birds are social creatures and enjoy your attention and nurturing. Lots of people have just one chicken, but chickens enjoy being part of a flock.

You should also think about other pets and how they might get along with your birds. Most chicken breeds co-habitate with other animals quite nicely, but your cats or dogs may have other ideas, especially if they have not been exposed to chickens before. Keep your chickens in a safe coop and supervise your pets' interactions until you are completely sure no harm will come from leaving them alone.

If you plan on raising chickens from eggs, expect to devote extra time in your day to the eggs. Chickens are delicate in embryo form and require someone to check the temperature and humidity level in the incubator about once an hour, especially if the incubator is homemade or not self-regulating. Baby chicks, either in the egg or a few days old, demand a lot more attention than a full-grown chicken. If you are hatching eggs, you will need to monitor them and turn the eggs daily. Baby chicks and chickens should have a fresh supply of food throughout the day and you do not have to worry about them overeating because chickens only eat when they are hungry and need to. Fill feeders early in the morning. Checking the feed on a regular schedule will keep your birds happy and less stressed, and will also prevent against moldy food being left in feeders.

As treats, chickens love watermelon, cooked eggs, seedless grapes, carrots (raw or cooked), apples, cooked grits, lettuce, kale, cooked pasta, peas, raw pomegranates, cabbage, asparagus, bananas, and the list goes on and on. Some chickens may be more finicky than others. Chickens love eggs, but it is best to feed them only cooked eggs. If you give them a taste for raw eggs, they may not let you collect them in the morning, as they may beat you to it. Also, seedless grapes are better for chicken's digestive systems.

Items you should not feed chickens include very salty foods, such as pretzels, potato chips, or salted French fries, as this can cause salt poisoning in small bodies. Candy of any sort, especially chocolate and sugar filled candies are bad for their systems, as with any pet you may have. Raw green potato peels can create a toxic substance called salanme if you feed it to your flock. Avocado skin and pits are also not recommended for poultry, as they contain low levels of toxicity and can be very harmful to your chickens.

Chickens are easy to care for and they can eat almost anything. Keep in mind, though, that if you are raising your birds for meat or eggs, the food you give to your birds may eventually be ingested by you or your family and friends. Be selective to keep your bird's health at an optimum. They will appreciate it and they can be trained through the use of food. By all means, give them treats, but be aware of the foods you give your flock.

Clipping wings

There is something so restricting when you imagine a bird with clipped wings — it seems unnatural to alter what comes natural to birds by preventing them from taking flight. The truth is, though, when owning chickens, some breeds are able to fly, and if your fence or surroundings are not built to keep them secure, clipping their wings may be one solution. Because the neighbor's dog or a two-lane highway may be within their reach, clipping their wings can keep them safe and keep them alive. In some cases, clipping a bird's wings helps to keep the bird free-range because you do not have to keep it enclosed most of the time.

If this is your first time clipping a bird's wing, you may want to enlist the help of an experienced friend. If you do not know of anyone who has chickens and has done this before, find a friend or family member that can help you hold the bird during this process.

Clipping your chicken's wing should not hurt the bird. It is like clipping your dog's nails. Most often, the animal is afraid of the process. For birds, the vibration from the actual clipping of their stiff feathers scares them. There should be no blood or very minimal blood. If you clip your chicken's wing, and the bird starts to bleed, use your first aid kit to stop the bleeding. If the bird is bleeding heavily, call or visit your vet immediately to treat the bird.

You can clip a chicken's wings when its adult feathers are grown in. Even if a chicken has its adult feathers, it is advisable to wait until flight becomes a problem. Do not cut pinfeathers, which are the tips of new feathers on a bird's body. Clipping one wing is enough to prevent the chicken from taking flight; it throws the bird off balance and still allows it to fly, just not very high. Some chicken owners prefer clip both wings to keep the bird balanced. The wings will grow back, just like people cut their hair and it grows. There are tutorials of how to clip wings posted on YouTube (*www.youtube.com*) by chicken owners. Go to the website and type in the search "How to Clip a Chicken's Wings."

To get started, you will need:

- An assistant
- Very, very sharp scissors
- Old towel
- Rubber gloves to protect your hands
- A first aid kit (just in case of injury)
- Treats for when the task is complete.

1. First, decide who will clip the wings and who will hold the bird.
2. Gather your chicken. Be calm. If you cannot get hold of the chicken, it is not advised to chase it around. This stresses the chicken. Try again at another time or try to gather another bird.
3. Hold the chicken by the legs. Support its body by keeping your hand underneath its body. Your palm should be open and flat. Leave either the left or right wing free.
4. Talk to it in soothing tones.
5. Spread the wing. Display it in its entirety.
6. The first 10 feathers from the outside of the wing are flight feathers; these flight feathers are usually longer than the rest and often a different color. Cut just beyond the edge of the next layer up. This is approximately 3 to 5 inches.
7. Quickly clip the bird's wings. Use very sharp scissors. Dull blades may hurt the bird.
8. Give your bird a treat.

Chickens molt annually, so you will need to clip your chickens' wings each year with its new growth of feathers.

Cost of Your Chickens

Having your own livestock means you will have your own eggs and meat, but how much money will this save you? How much will it cost to get started and then maintain your new hobby? If your budget is small, the good news is the cost of chickens can be minimal. You can get extravagant if you want, but it is not necessary.

Budget for these items when you decide to start your flock.

- **Chicken coop:** Anywhere from free to thousands of dollars. Your budget will determine how much to spend. Using recycled materials to make your coop will not cost you a dime.

- **Egg incubators:** These devices that hatch fertile eggs will cost you between $40 and $50.

- **Chicken feed:** $7 to $10 for a 20-pound bag. Commercial feed varies but most types of feed consist of grains, wheat, barley, rye, and ground corn.

- **Chicken feeder:** Approximately $3 to $20. Chicken feeders can be automated or non-automated and hold food for your chicken to eat from. This helps with mess, as chickens tend to scatter their food. If you choose to feed your chickens by hand, you will not need to purchase this item.

- **Chicken waterer:** This container offers water similarly to the type of water bottle a gerbil or hamster uses. Chickens can use this type of bottle even though they have beaks. This will cost $3 to $20.

- **Nesting box:** This place where a hen feels inclined to leave her eggs costs approximately $20.

- **Heater for coop:** You will need this if you live in a cold region, and it will cost approximately $40.

- **Annual veterinarian costs:** These costs will vary, but budget $150 to $1,000 based on a small flock of relatively healthy chickens.

Purchasing a dozen eggs in a grocery store costs around $1 to $4.99 for store-brand or organic eggs, and cut-up, fresh, boneless chicken breast can cost $4.29 to $6 per pound. If you consume eggs on a regular basis, then you and your family will find that in the long run you will save money and time by raising chickens. If you purchase one dozen organic eggs per week at $4.99 per dozen, you would spend $259.48 per year for 624 total eggs. If you had just one prolific egg-laying chicken, you could get 250 to 300 eggs per year, which means you could save about half that money. As an added bonus, the eggs from your chicken would be nutrient-rich and chemical-free.

Considering the Neighbors

You have one more factor to think about: your neighbors. This includes anyone who lives close enough to your home to hear or smell your birds. Even if the zoning laws permit livestock, which you can find out by checking with your local government or animal control office, it is a kind gesture to communicate to your close neighbors and inform them that you are buying chickens. Even if someone objects, it does not mean you need to abandon your plan. You did your part and made them aware that you will be a new bird owner and that your new additions may be heard crowing from time to time.

Why is it so important to keep your neighbors informed? Unhappy neighbors may complain to the local government about the noise and smell of your pets. Keep your coops and yard clean, follow local ordinances, and communicate with your neighbors to prevent hassles down the road. If you are abiding by the rules and neighbors still complain, unfortunately there is not much more you can do. But fresh eggs and chicken meat may be a way to win them over.

Owning chickens will enrich your life because chickens will provide you with food, companionship, and a sense of sustainable living. To fully understand the importance of organic living for your chickens, you need to understand the conditions of commercially produced, factory-raised chickens. Their lives are considerably different, and the birds are treated as a commodity.

CASE STUDY: A LEARNING EXPERIENCE

Kari Martin

Kari Martin wanted a project the whole family could take part in. Her girls were young and she wanted to instill in them a sense of responsibility. After much thought, she decided to get some chickens and start a small flock in her backyard in Seabeck, Washington. Her neighbor kept chickens and she got five young laying hens from them. This provided a perfect opportunity. Her girls could learn to care for the birds, and they would also have fresh eggs daily.

Martin's husband built a small coop in their backyard. It offered five nesting boxes and a run for the hens. There was a gate to get in and out for her and the girls to collect the eggs. They made sure the coop was child friendly so her daughters could independently feed the birds and collect their eggs. The family named their chickens and painted the names on the side of the coop. One hen in particular, Daisey, would always come when called, which gave the girls a thrill.

"Make sure you are willing to make the commitment to be there every day for your birds," says Martin when asked what advice she would give a new chicken owner. "It was easier for me, being a stay-at-home-mom. But they do require time and attention. It is worth the effort, though. It is really cool to feed and care for the chickens and get such wonderful results!"

Chapter 4:
Blue Ribbon Chickens — The Best Breeds

Shopping for your new, feathered friends is fun but can be overwhelming with all of the choices available. To help you decide which breed is best for you, figure out your primary reason for keeping birds. Owning birds to show in competitions or for ornamental purposes is one reason. Some people own chickens primarily for eggs, some for meat only, some for both eggs and meat (these birds are referred to as dual), and some for pets. In this chapter, you will find the best breeds in each category.

First, it is helpful to know the terminology of chickens in each stage of their life. (*A full glossary can be found in the back of the book.*)

- A **chick** is a baby chicken.
- A **hen** is a mature, adult female chicken.
- A **rooster**, or cock, is a mature, male chicken that has not been castrated.
- A **pullet** is a female chicken under 1 year old.
- A **cockerel** is a male chicken under 1 year old.
- **A capon** is a castrated male bird.

You do not need to have a rooster for a hen to produce eggs. The eggs will not be fertilized and will not hatch into baby chicks, but your flock will be more docile without a male. Roosters can be aggressive, especially when mating with a hen. If you have a male, you can still eat eggs that the rooster fertilizes as long as the embryo has not started to form. An embryo can only form under specific conditions that your refrigerator does not mimic.

Best Breeds for Exhibition

Attend county fairs or local exhibitions to take a gander at the popular breeds that participate in these events. Any purebreds can be used for show, and some shows also allow for hybrids. One of the most prestigious organizations chicken owners can join is the American Poultry Association (APA) (*www. amerpoultryassn.com*), which uses a point system to classify its members. For example, if you participate in a state meet or any APA-sanctioned show with 750 to 1,499 birds, you receive ten points. The more points you receive, the higher your standing in the association. The association has various levels, including Master Exhibitor, Grand Master Exhibitor, and Hall of Fame Exhibitor. Once you reach each level, you receive an award, such as a plaque and recognition in the APA yearbook. Join the APA through their website, where you also can find more information on where meets are located and how to register.

Start with small, local shows before traveling to larger regional shows with your birds. This will give you an opportunity to learn from more experienced chicken fanciers and see how the shows operate. When you are ready to show your chickens, be sure they are in top condition. Follow the guidelines the judges give, which should be outlined for you when you register. Ask a representative if you do not receive them. Even a small detail that is not followed could disqualify your bird. To avoid disappointment on show day, be prepared ahead of time and make sure you understand all of the rules.

Below is a list of birds that are visually impressive and are good breeds to choose should you want to show chickens. Most anatomical terms will be identified here, but if you are unfamiliar with the function, size, or variation of a particular feature, you will find it in detail in Chapter 8.

Silkies

This bird originated in China and Japan and arrived in America in the 1800s. Their feathers do not have the barbicels that hold a normal feather together, which means silkie feathers look like hair, giving the birds the illusion they are fluffy. Their feathers are similar in texture to fur and are not like the smooth feathers other chickens have. They typically have a **topknot,** which is a poof of feathers on top of their head, or their faces can be completely covered with feathers, similar to a shaggy dog. Silkies come in a variety of colors: red, buff, white, black, splash (a chicken that is one color with a splash of another color highlighted typically on its head and back), cuckoo (barred or striped with another color such as black and white), and lavender, with blue/black skin and black bones. Their earlobes are blue or turquoise, and their eyes are brown or black.

The **comb** is the fleshy growth on top of a chicken's head. It is a thin piece of skin that comes in different shapes and is either red or purple. Some chickens have thicker combs. Silkies have walnut-shaped combs that should be wider than they are long. Some Silkies have **pea combs,** which are low combs with three ridges, or a thin **single comb** that attaches to the beak along the skull with five or six grooves and stands up. This type of comb probably would be disqualified from a show because it is not the ideal comb for a pure breed. Whereas most chickens have four toes, silkies have five, which just adds to their uniqueness.

Male bantam silkies weigh approximately 36 ounces. A **bantam** is a miniature version of a full-sized chicken, usually about ¼ the size. The female bantam weighs about 32 ounces. The weight of standard-sized silkies is approximately 6 pounds for the male and 5 for the female. These birds are not proficient egg layers and lay only 50 to 120 eggs per year. Their eggs are a dark cream to brown color.

Silkies are a docile breed, which makes them a great choice for novices. They also make wonderful pets. Because their feathers are not webbed, they cannot fly. Silkies, like all chickens, require a protective coop to keep them safe from predators. Hens and roosters of this breed are known for their parenting skills. The roosters often call to the chicks when food is found, which, with other breeds, is usually the hen's responsibility.

Showgirls

Showgirls are a cross breed between silkies and the naked neck turken. They are an ornamental breed that looks like a miniature version of an ostrich. They come in a bantam size. These little birds have both male and female genders, but both are call showgirls, which is sometimes confusing.

They have five toes on each foot. They come in white, black, buff, blue, lavender, and splash with dark skin. A full crest of feathers sits on top of their heads, but their necks are bare. Their bodies are fluffy and their legs are feathered. Like the silkies, their comb is walnut-shaped.

Showgirls are gentle and friendly, and are perfect birds for new chicken owners looking for a docile breed that is easily handled. They bear confinement well, and they weigh approximately 3 pounds. They do not require much space.

They have a relatively high production rate when it comes to laying eggs. Their eggs are small and range in color from creamy white to light tan. When breeding showgirls, it is best to mate a showgirl rooster with a silkie hen. The naked neck is a dominant gene, and will always come through. Mating two showgirls lessons the quality of their feathers and immune system.

These birds make great birds to show. Their look is very unique, and their demeanor is very gentle. They are a crowd-pleaser and a judge favorite.

Andalusian

This breed had its start in Spain and was further developed in the United States and England. The andalusian lays white eggs. Colors seen in this breed are blue (which is the required color to show this breed of chickens), black, white, or black and white. The adult blue chickens have slate blue feathers with a narrow ridge of dark blue. This breed is an active forager, keeping feed costs down during warm weather when the chicken can remain outside. However, the bird is so active that it can run very fast, making capturing quite the event.

Cochin

This Chinese ornamental breed is a favorite for poultry shows. They have feathered feet and come in a variety of colors. It is a very heavy breed, with roosters weighing up to 11 pounds. The hen only lays medium-sized, brown eggs for a short period of time, but makes an excellent mother. She will even become a foster mother to chicks of other breeds.

American game

These feisty birds were originally bred for cockfighting, which is now illegal in the United States. Although they are not used for fighting, they still have a natural instinct to be territorial, so adult cocks should be separated to avoid fighting. Despite being aggressive birds, they are easily handled by humans. Today, many breed these chickens for exhibition because of their strong physical and gameness traits. The American game is known to be a hardy bird because of their good flying and foraging skills. Hens of this breed lay medium-sized eggs that are white or cream colored from mid-spring to late summer or fall. The American game comes in virtually every color and can have pea, straight, triple, or a combination comb.

Clown face, also known as Spanish, white-faced Black Spanish, and Spanish white-ear

Their name says it all. They are white-faced with a black body. They are fancy birds, but proficient egg-layers as well. Originating in Spain, clown faces are the oldest of the breeds from the Mediterranean.

They have gray skin, a clean leg with dark shanks, a single comb, and their eggs are white. Clown faces are slow to develop, and their white faces take about a year to completely develop mature features. These birds tolerated confinement and bear the heat very well; however, they are prone to frostbite, so in cold climates or in cold weather it is important to take good care of them, and keep them in warm surroundings.

Males weigh about 6 pounds. Females weigh about 4 to 5 pounds. Bantams usually weigh around 2 ½ pounds. These beautiful and unique birds are also good pets, as their temperament is docile and they are good exhibition birds.

Houdan

A French ornamental bird, Houdans, were developed from Polish, Crevecours, and possibly Dorkings breeds. Houdans were commonly raised on small farms around the towns in Normandy, France. Considered to be dual-purpose birds, these birds are raised for their fine, tender, and juicy white meat with delicate bones, as well as their ability to produce an ample amount of eggs each year. They come in two varieties: mottled and white. Mottled is a blended mixture of two colors. In this case it is typically black and white. The chicks are a fluffy ball of black and white markings with the beginnings of its trademark crest just starting to flare out. The white variety was created in America.

Houdans have a V-shaped comb. Their legs are clean and they have 5 toes. Four of the toes are at the bottom of the chicken's leg, and the fifth toe is higher up on the leg. Their crest, which is a puff of feathers atop the head, is their most noted feature. As with all crested breeds they need to be checked for mites and lice daily. The roosters weigh 8 pounds, the hens weigh 6½ pounds. Houdan bantams are a delicate bird at approximately 3 pounds. The standard hen lays medium, white, eggs regularly totaling approximately 100 eggs yearly. Bantam hens are sporadic and are not proficient layers.

Houdans are easy to handle as they have a very gentle nature. They are a good show bird. They make good pets, too. They are available at most hatcheries or online. Even though they are flighty birds, they bear confinement well. All they need is some room to run and a roost at night to be content.

Brabanter

The brabanter chicken is thought to have originated in the Netherlands. The breed was nearly extinct in the early 20th century, but was recreated from German breeds to become the chicken that we know it to be today. Brabanters are largely ornamental birds. They have a crest that is tight and pointed forward, which means that it does not block their vision. Brabanters also have muffs, which are feathers that protrude from the sides of the chicken's face, and some have a beard.

Brabanter bantams are a cross between the bearded Polish bantam and the standard brabanter. They weigh about 3 pounds, with the standard rooster weighing around 7 pounds and the hen weighing around 5 to 6 pounds

There are several varieties of the brabanter breed of chicken, including cream and the gold colored, both of which are found in the United States. Outside of the United States there are other varieties, including self black, white, blue laced, cuckoo, golden black half moon spangled, silver black half moon spangled, yellow white half moon spangled, golden blue half moon spangled, and lavender. This breed is gentle and friendly and would be a welcomed addition to your flock or family.

Frizzles

This bird is from Southeastern Asia and gets its name from its feathers, which curl outward. Frizzles' colors include red, black, white, blue, silver-gray, splash (spotted), and buff, and their eyes are red. Although frizzle here refers to a breed of chicken, the term "frizzle" is also a way to describe a bird that has fuzzy-looking feathers.

Frizzles have a single comb on top of their heads and a clean leg that does not have any feathers on it. The standard weight for the rooster frizzle is 11 pounds, the hen is about 8 1/2 pounds, and the bantam for this breed is 4 to 6 pounds. Not only are they popular show birds, but also they are proficient egg layers, laying more than 200 eggs per year. Their eggs are cream or tinted in color and of a medium size.

Frizzles have a friendly demeanor and docile temperament, making them excellent additions to your family. They are easy for novice chicken owners. Their feathers do not fare well in wet weather, so they need a dry coop. They do not mind being confined, so you could keep them indoors.

Polish

Also called a Padua or Poland, this chicken is most known for the tall, starburst-shaped crest engulfing its head. Polish breeds are available in several colors and markings. Solid colors are typically white, black, blue, and cuckoo (also referred to as barred). Some birds have lace markings and are gold, silver, and chamois. The crests can sometimes cover the chickens' eyes, so they can be startled easily. Use a special waterer, such as a nipple drinker, so the crest stays dry and clean. Their comb is V-shaped or horn-shaped.

Polish roosters weigh about 6 pounds, and hens weigh 4½ pounds. Bantams are approximately 3 pounds for males and 2 pounds for females. Care for this fowl requires more work than other breeds because of their coat. They are partial to mites because of the thickness of their topknot, which is another term for crest. One way to prevent mites is to use a spray insect repellent, being careful not to get it in the bird's eyes. The birds should be kept dry because their thick feathers will hold moisture longer. Polish hens are good layers and produce 150 to 200 white eggs per year. They are not good sitters, though, and have been known to abandon or destroy their eggs. You can use a hen that is **broody** (meaning in her fertile cycle and instinctively wants to sit on eggs), or use an incubator for the eggs this breed produces.

Yokohama

This is a striking bird with a long tail that can grow up to 2 feet in length. They are white and red, saddled, or red shouldered, meaning the feathers that cover their shoulders and upper back are a strikingly different color than their body feathers. Their skin is yellow. These are ornamental birds, and are not good layers or typically used for meat because they are not fleshy, nor are they tender to eat. Their combs are single and thin or walnut-shaped and red in color.

Yokohamas require a taller coop and higher perch than most breeds because of their magnificent tail. The cock of the breed weighs about 6½ pounds, and the hens weigh about 5½ pounds. The bantam Yokohama weighs approximately 3 pounds for a male and 2½ pounds for a female. The males tend to be aggressive and dominating. This breed is not recommended for a novice, but as you gain more experience they are an excellent ornamental breed to show.

New Hampshire red

With its bold, red, and orange body and black tail, this bird is a classic vision of a chicken. It is an American breed derived from the popular Rhode Island red. Originally, these birds were bred for laying eggs, but their hearty bodies make them good meat providers. Their eggs are brown and typically classified as large. Their red single combs have five points, and their eyes are red. They make great show birds because of their colorful coats. This is one of the easiest breeds to raise, and they are versatile to show or to use for egg laying or meat producing.

New Hampshire reds are great for beginners because of their friendly nature and tame attitude. They are not aggressive or as flighty as other breeds and are easy to handle. Roosters weigh about 8½ pounds, and hens weigh about 6½ pounds. The bantams weigh about 5½ pounds.

Japanese bantam

This bird is a true bantam, meaning it does not have a large counterpart. The color varieties are white, black, black-tailed white, black-tailed buff (buff is a rusty color), barred brown red (meaning they have a red body with brown stripes), grey, and wheaten (a creamy tan). They have a single red comb, red earlobes, and black eyes. Their legs are short and clean with four toes.

The most notable feature of this bantam is its tail. The body is petite, but the tail is large and often reaches over the chicken's head. The males sometimes are disqualified from competition because their tails are **rye,** or fall to the side rather than standing erect. The females have profuse tails, but not as large as the males'.

The Japanese bantam is not a proficient egg layer, and the eggs they lay are tiny and rare. They make good pets because they are easy to tame and gentle on landscape, and they are social birds that will interact with people.

Black or blue Sumatras

The black and the blue Sumatras are beautiful, ornamental birds that have long tails. The black Sumatras, both the hen and the cock, have chocolate brown eyes and no wattles, which are the flaps of red or purple skin under a chicken's chin. Their legs are clean, blueish in color, and have multiple spurs, or sharp protrusions. Their faces are deep purple and their black plumage has a green sheen to it.

The males have long, flowing, tails that hang down. They are a beautiful breed of chicken with black skin and bones. They are bantams, with the rooster weighing 5 pounds and the hen weighing 4 pounds. Although the hens lay about 100 eggs per year, the birds themselves are used mostly as a pet or show bird and not for their egg laying ability. Their eggs are white, and the chicks are often born yellow with splashes of black.

Black and blue Sumatras are believed to be derived from the jungle fowl and possibly crossed with another species of bird, such as a pheasant or pheasant cross breed. They were imported to the United States and Europe in 1847 from the island of Sumatra, which is located in the far South East Asia.

Although somewhat a rare breed of bird, many hatcheries have the black, blue, and a splash variety for sale. There is a white Sumatra, which is hard to find. Although this breed is mostly used as a show bird, they are beautiful birds to own and care for as pets.

Dutch

The tiniest bantam of all, the Dutch chicken, weighs only 1 pound. It is a true bantam chicken with no large counterpart. The petite bird is somewhat docile in the female gender, but the male has been compared to a snapping turtle. They are lively and active, but tolerate confinement well. These little birds are perfect if you do not have much room for your flock to roam.

Dutch chickens come in several colors. They are silver, light brown, blue, black, white and blue- light brown. They have a clean leg, with white skin and white or blue shanks. Their earlobes are white. Dutch hens produce approximately 100 tiny eggs per year.

These birds were originated in Holland where they are still popular today. They were introduced to the United States shortly after WWII but did not catch on in popularity. In the 1970's they were reintroduced once again. Dutch bantams are an exhibition favorite.

Appenzeller spitzhauben

The Appenzeller spitzhauben's origin is in Switzerland. This breed of chicken forages well and loves to roam the mountainside and roost in trees. It is a fairly rare breed but a beautiful bird with crested feathers on top of its head.

Spitzhauben means pointed bonnet, which is what the crest looks like. It is available in blue spangled, black spangled, gold, gold spangled, silver spangled and barthuhner.

The rooster Appenzeller spitzhauben weighs around 4 ½ pounds and the hens weigh around 3 ½ pounds. Their comb is V-shaped, except in the barthuhner variety. They have a rose comb and no crest. The Appenzeller spitzhauben has a clean, blue leg, with four toes. Their eyes are brown. Their eggs are white and medium in size. They are average egg layers laying approximately 155 eggs yearly.

These birds are very active and do not bear confinement well. They love to roam and forage for insects. They require very little food and are easy to maintain. If you want an Appenzeller spitzhauben, be sure you have lots of room for them to roam and make sure their run and coop are secure. They like to take flight as best as they can. Their nature is overall friendly, docile, and calm. They are good in all climates. Their combs and wattles are relatively small, which means in cold weather there is very little skin that is susceptible to frostbite.

Although Appenzeller spitzhaubens are fairly rare to find in the United States of America, they are popular in Europe. They are not recognized by the American Poultry Association.

Aseel

Aseels are a somewhat rare bird and one of the oldest breeds of chickens. They originate from India and were developed to be an aggressive, belligerent bird. The instinct to fight is a dominant gene that has been bred into them. It is said that even chicks that are just a few weeks old will start attacking their own mother. More than one rooster should not be in your flock because they are very aggressive. Although, owners claim that these birds are docile towards people and easy to care for at home.

The aseel's feathers are short, hard, and glossy. Aseels have strong, curved, necks and short beaks, making their face is almost predator like. Their eyes are pearl colored, and set fairly close together. The skin and legs are yellow, and they have a clean leg with 4 toes. This bird does not have a wattle or a crest. Their pea comb is small.

Aseels are kept as pets or used as an ornamental breed. They are available in black breasted red, dark, spangled, white, and wheaton. They bear confinement well, and are fine in any climate. Hens weigh 4 pounds, while roosters weigh between 5 and 6 pounds. Bantams are 2 ½ pounds. The hens are low producing egg layers. They lay light brown eggs of a medium size.

Crevecoeur

This beautiful, yet very rare breed, was originally meant to be a table bird, which is a bird meant to eat, but its striking coat and crest make it a popular ornamental bird used for show. Crevecoeurs hail from Normandy, France. Black is the only color that is recognized, but some variations are blue. Since their feathers are delicate, they are best suited for climates with warmer weather, and cold and wet regions are hard on them. They do well in confinement, but are active and need room to run during the day.

These chickens have a clean leg, which means featherless, with four toes on each foot. They are friendly, quiet, and the hens are seldom broody. Under all of those black feathers is white skin and they have dark shanks. Crevecoeurs have a V-shaped comb and a long wattle. The roosters weigh about 7 to 8 pounds and hens weigh about 6 pounds.

The eggs of the mother hens are medium size and white. They lay approximately 2 eggs per week, or around 100 eggs a year. Overall, the Crevecoeur can provide plenty of eggs, it is a good size for a table bird, friendly enough to be a pet, and it has unique features for showing and competitions. It is an endangered bird, but can be found at various hatcheries online. It is sure to be the perfect bird.

Sicilian buttercup

This Mediterranean class of chicken was discovered in 1892 in Italy. It is named buttercup because its comb is a perfect buttercup comb with 5 points. The rich colors of the roosters and hens of this breed attracted the attention of Americans who show birds. The males are a rich, orange-red bird with black spangles in their feathers. Their lustrous black tail has a green sheen to it. The female buttercup is a deep gold or amber, and all of her feathers are accented by black spangles. Their shanks and toes are olive or yellow green, their skin is yellow, and their earlobes are white.

Buttercups are foragers by nature and prefer to be free-range. They do not bear confinement well, and owners claim that their birds are friendly but restless. Most typical characteristics of this breed is that they tend to be a bit wild and do not prefer to be social with people.

The hens are seldom broody, and they have a low egg production. The eggs they do produce are small and white. Even though they do not provide an ample supply of eggs, they are attractive show birds that will surely please the crowd. A small bird, the buttercup weighs around 4 to 5 pounds.

Pekin bantam

The true bantam, Pekin bantam, from China circa 1830, is an ornamental breed with an uncertain history. There are several theories surrounding this breed. One rumor is that the first Pekin bantam was stolen from the Chinese emperor in 1860 from his private collection. Another theory is that the breed was brought from China to Queen Victoria as a gift and then bred with other breeds, which explains the breed that we know today.

These light birds are great for show. They are extremely gentle and make for great family pets as well. Children will delight in fact that Pekin bantams are lively and active, yet very docile and well adjusted. They are so petite that they require very little room. They love to forage for garden bugs and other pests.

Malay

From Eastern Asia comes the Malay chicken. This aggressive chicken is not recommended for novice chicken owners. The breed stands tall; some are reported to be close to 3 feet tall. The Malay is also a heavy breed with roosters weighing 8 to 9 pounds and hens weighing about 7 pounds. Flighty and wild, Malays do not tolerate confinement. With their long legs, slanted eyes and tight feathers, this breed looks intimidating.

Malays have a clean leg with four toes. They have a long life expectancy. They come in black, white, spangled, red pyle, black breasted red, and weaton for the female only. The comb is strawberry.

Malay hens are poor egg layers. On average, they lay one egg per week, and the hens are not broody. Malay chickens should have lots of room to run, roam, and forage. Cold weather does not suit this breed well because their feathers are hard and do not provide much insulation. Softer feathers, like down, hold body heat and protect the birds from the cold. Malays are best kept as an ornamental bird.

Best Chickens for Egg Laying

A good egg layer will produce 150 to 250 eggs per year. Hens usually start to lay eggs around 4 to six months and will continue to lay eggs into their teens. As a general rule, good egg layers should have deep, full abdomens. Eggs come in different colors but taste the same, and a hen will always lay the same color egg. If you are a novice owner and would like to get chickens primarily for eggs, you will need only about four birds to get started, which will give you 20 to 28 eggs per week.

Araucana

Not only is this bird a good layer, but also the eggs she produces are blue-green or turquoise. Some varieties of this chicken also lay pink eggs or brown eggs with pink hues. These eggs are perfect for Easter decorating, gifts for neighbors, or just to add some variety in your egg basket. The chickens come in partridge (black stripes that meet at the middle of the feather then move outward), silver-blue partridge, yellow partridge, fawn, wheaten (creamy tans), white, black, and lavender.

The roosters of this breed weigh about 5 pounds, and hens weigh about 4 pounds. Bantams of the breed weigh 28 ounces for a male and 26 ounces for a female. Araucanas can be tailed or **rumpless,** meaning without a tail. They have a pea comb that it is low to the head with three ridges, and they have a clean leg without any feathers. A unique feature of these birds is the tufts of feathers they have by their ears.

Araucanas are a good choice for novice bird owners because they have high energy, but it is okay to pen them. Their home should offer fresh green grass every day, so a mobile coop or free roam might be best. They will provide you with approximately 200 eggs per year.

Cream legbar

The legbar breed of chicken has 3 varieties: gold, silver, and cream. The gold and silver varieties are a type of leghorn, and lay cream colored or white eggs. The cream legbar, though, is an autosexing, blue egg-layer, meaning you can tell the sex of the chick by the color of its feathers. Cream legbars are very popular for their egg laying abilities. They lay green and blue eggs.

This breed is a mix of barred rock, brown leghorn, and Araucana breeds. Through much trial and many generations of mating, the cream legbar was developed. The process began in the 1930s. If you were to cross your own chickens of the aforementioned breeds, you will mostly not have the same result. Through the generations of breeding, the ideal hybrid was developed with the dominant genes presiding to ensure colorful eggs.

Cream legbars have a yellow beak, a smooth, red, face, red comb and red, long and thin wattles. The comb is a single erect comb with five to seven even spikes. The comb is smaller in males than it is in females. The earlobes are a pale blue on both the male and female. They have a crest on the back top portion of their head. Their skin is yellow with a clean leg. Cream legbars have four evenly spaced toes on each foot. Their shanks are typically strong, clean, and rounded.

The roosters are muscular birds with a long, feathered necks and a tail that sits at a 45-degree angle. The females are decent egg layers, producing about 180 eggs per year. The temperament of both genders is fairly flighty. They are considered to be noisy birds with cackles are similar to those of the Araucana. They are hearty in any climate, but do not bear confinement well. They are non-broody, but very nervous. If you are looking for a bird to provide you with a colorful array of eggs and you are able to tolerate the noise, this may be the breed for you.

Ancona

Originating near Acona, Italy, this breed is black with white-tipped feathers. They are a smaller type of chicken that lays small, white eggs. Although smaller in size, they lay around five eggs per week. This breed can be flighty. This trait combined with their darker color helps them to avoid predators.

Holland

This often-overlooked breed has a high productivity of medium, white eggs. This breed does well in all climates, even extreme cold. However, their single comb might become frostbitten in the winter. As a calm and hardy breed that forages well, these birds are able to adapt to virtually any surrounding. They are known to be quiet, friendly, and calm chickens, and hens of this breed seldom become broody.

Sussex

These birds, which originated in Sussex County, England, are also known as speckled Sussex in America. They are plump birds, available in white, silver, red, brown buff, and speckled. Avoid exposing this bird to excessive sunlight because their coats have a tendency to become brassy. The speckled variety gets more speckled with each molting, making it an attractive bird.

Sussex chickens have a single comb and a clean leg. They are a heavy breed, weighing around 9 pounds for the male and 7 pounds for the female. The bantam variety is approximately 4 pounds. The earlobes and eyes are both red, and their skin is white. They are proficient egg layers, laying 240 to 260 eggs per year. They are also plump enough for meat. Their eggs are large and are a cream to light brown color.

Because they are alert, curious, and docile, these chickens make great pets. They can be free-range or penned. This is a hearty breed that will lay eggs even in the coldest part of the season, which is not typical in all breeds.

Leghorns

In America, the colors of the Leghorn range from white, black, red, Columbian (mostly white body with a black tail or black wing tips on tail), partridge (black stripes meeting at the middle of the feather then moving outward), brown, silver partridge, and black-tailed red with white skin.

Their combs are large and can be single or **rose,** meaning almost flat on top and very fleshy with small, round protuberances. They have red eyes and a clean leg without feathers. White earlobes are a trait of the Leghorn, indicating a good egg layer. Hens will produce about 200 white eggs each year.

Roosters are somewhat aggressive, and the breed in general can be excitable and noisy. Leghorns like to take flight. Ideally, they need large, tall coops that allow movement but are secure. It is also a good idea to have trees with branches for the birds to perch on, as this will help satisfy their desire to fly. The bantams are calmer than their larger counterparts. The rooster weighs typically 6 pounds and the hen 4 ½ pounds. Bantams of this variety are about 1 pound.

Rose comb brown

The rose comb brown is a variety of the Leghorn chicken breed. The male weighs about 6 pounds, the female weighs around 4 ½ pounds, and the bantams weigh in at about 3 pounds.

The Leghorn varieties, including rose comb buff, single comb silver, single comb white, single comb black, and single comb dark brown are all proficient egg layers. Most of the white eggs found in grocery stores are all from Leghorns.

They are an economical bird to own to produce 200 plus eggs a year. The rose comb brown produces white eggs. Some varieties of the Leghorn breed produce brown eggs.

Their homes should be tall and large coops as they are flighty birds like Leghorns. They are easy to care for as they are independent and are good foragers. They make great pets, lay almost an egg a day, and are good for meat, too. They are a great value.

Friesian

This ancient breed of chicken originated in the Friesian Islands. Their unique and dazzling markings make this a great ornamental bird as well as a good layer. The Friesian's feathers come in chamois penciled coloring, silver penciled, and gold penciled. Although this breed has been around for over 1,000 years, it is relatively new to the United States of America, being introduced in the 1980s.

Friesians are not only known for their beauty. They lay about 230 white eggs per year. They are a small breed with roosters weighing 6 pounds, hens weighing 5 pounds, and bantams weighing between 2 ½ and 3 pounds.

The temperament of this breed is extremely nervous. These birds are flighty and not easily kept in a confined space. If you have lots of room for these chickens to forage and want an egg layer this may be a good bird for you to own. They are beautiful and serve many purposes.

Australorp

These chickens have white skin and feathers that are black and blue with a beetle-green sheen that sunlight enhances. Their combs are single and bright red. The eyes, beak, and earlobes are dark. Their legs are clean and are slate blue, except for the toes and soles of the feet, which are white.

The australorp weighs up to 10 pounds for a rooster and up to 8 pounds for a hen. The bantams weigh between 28 and 36 ounces. Their temperament is quiet and gentle, making them perfect for children to handle, and the neighbors will not even know they are there. They produce brown eggs, and owners should expect about 200 eggs during the laying season, which ends when the weather gets cold. Australorps do not fly and tend to stay grounded because they are heavy. Their home and run do not have to be especially secure to keep them in, just secure enough to keep predators out.

Catalana

This bird is popular in South America and Spain but is available in North America. They are hardy birds and good egg layers. They are buff in color, and some have a black tail. They are a large breed, with males weighing 6 to 7 pounds and females weighing 4 to 6 pounds. Bantams are approximately 3 pounds. They have a single comb with six points, and the male's comb stands erect. They also have a clean leg and four toes. Their wattles are red, and their earlobes are white.

The hens lay medium-size eggs, which are creamy colored or sometimes tinted pink. Although these birds are not aggressive, they are very active and flighty. They do not particularly like confinement and would prefer free-range living with lots of room to move. The males can be aggressive toward each other. This breed fares well in the heat and hot environments.

Hamburgh

Hamburghs or Hamburgs derive from Holland. They come in silver-spangled, golden-spangled, golden-penciled, silver penciled, and black and white. This breed is typically a small bird, with the adult male weighing 5 pounds and females weighing about 4 pounds. Bantams weigh in at 1½ pounds.

They have clean legs with 4 toes, and their comb is a rose comb. Their skin is white with slate blue shanks. The hens are proficient egg-layers and lay about 200 small white eggs yearly. They fare well in the winter months. Hamburgs are alert, active birds that do not do well in confinement. They fare better as free-range birds. Hamburgs tend to avoid human contact and are not as friendly as other breeds. This chicken breed is spritely, though and will not disappoint if you want an egg-layer.

Fayoumi or Egyptian Fayoumi

The Egyptian Fayoumi dates way back to B.C. originating in the area along the Nile River in Egypt. The roosters walk tall with an impressive posture. Their carriage is almost vertical, giving them a long, lean look. They are flighty birds and known to be excellent escape artists if you keep them confined. Fayoumi's mature quickly, and the males will try to crow as early as 5 or 6 weeks old. They continue their enthusiasm for crowing as they grow. Your nearest neighbor may not be a fan of the early morning ritual of the male rooster so be sure you are prepared for a robust crowing with this animated bird.

Fayoumi's weigh in at 4 pounds for the male and 3 pounds for the female. The hens can start laying eggs as early as 4 months of age. They lay small, white eggs. Fayoumi's have rose combs, white skin, and slate blue or willow green shanks. If you live in a warm climate, these hardy birds endure heat well. They are economic eaters and are fairly inexpensive to raise.

Lakenvelder

This chicken is a sight to behold. The lakenvelder's head and tail are a deep black color. Its body and breast are snowy white. The comb, wattle, and eyes are bright red. This breed is a classic chicken. They have a high carriage. That combined with the striking colors of their feathers make them a great show bird as well as a proficient layer. Lakenvelders are a light breed, too. The rooster weighs 5 pounds and hens weigh 4 pounds.

Lakenvelders come from Germany. They are not aggressive towards other chickens. Although they tend to take flight, they adapt well as free-range birds or confinement. These birds tend to be shy and not very social toward people, but they are a hardy breed, and can live in a variety of climates. Underneath their feathers, lakenvelders have white skin and dark shanks.

The hens have a high production rate for laying eggs. They lay about 200 eggs a year. The eggs are small and white.

There are different versions of the lakenvelder. There is the golden lakenvelder and the more common silver lakenvelder. Bantams are the Vorwerk variety, with a black, gold, black, combination. Lakenvelder is said to translate from Dutch to mean "shadow on a sheet."

Gingernut ranger

The gingernut ranger is a cross between a Rhode Island red and a light Sussex. These docile, yet friendly birds are proficient egg layers with hens laying approximately 150 to 200 large, brown eggs per year. This breed of chicken has a deep breast, an upward pointing tail, and wings that give the appearance of being neatly tucked to the sides.

Their legs are clean and yellow, and each foot has four toes. The comb and wattle are both medium in size. The face is smooth and red. Hens weigh 5 to 6 pounds and roosters weigh 7 to 8 pounds.

This gentle bird is a great forager and would be happy to wander throughout your garden in search of slugs, bugs, and other treats. They manage well in confinement. Overall, gingernut rangers are an easy bird to start out with for new chicken owners.

Easter eggers

Easter eggers are, by far, the most fun variety of chicken to own. Easter eggers are not a breed, but rather a variety of chicken that does not conform to any breed. It does not belong to a class, and therefore cannot be shown in a competition. However, Easter eggers lay colorful, extra-large eggs that make them that much more fun to keep. These birds tend to be super friendly and social. They lay eggs from blue to green to aqua and pink in different shades of those colors.

Easter eggers bear confinement well and are hardy so they can endure hot, cold, wet, or dry climates. They are very docile, and make for a wonderful family pet. Children will marvel at the different colored eggs — and adults will, too.

These birds have a clean leg, with four toes on each foot. They are a large fowl but have a bantam counterpart. Roosters weigh 7 pounds, hens weigh about 5 to 6 pounds, and bantams are about 3 pounds. Hens lay about 200 eggs a year, but some have been known to lay 6 to 8 eggs per week. This would give you close to 400 eggs yearly. They are well worth the investment.

Easter eggers are fairly easy to find. They are a very common mixed breed. Often, they are mistakenly labeled Araucanas or Americaunas. Both of these breeds produce colorful eggs and are most likely crossed with the Easter egger, but Araucanas and Americaunas are both recognized breeds.

Best Chickens for Meat

Chickens not only provide fresh eggs, but also they can provide meat for your family. Some owners get very attached to their flocks and do not think they can slaughter a chicken for food, but as long as it is performed in a quick and humane manner, killing a bird for food is an honorable way to end its life.

Dorking

This British breed has been around for about 2,000 years, and its specific purpose is to be a plump, meaty bird able to feed a family. Its colors are red, silver-gray, and white. The combs of silver-gray and red birds should be single. The combs of white birds should be rose, which means they are fleshy, flat and broad on the top with a curved surface with small and round protuberances.

The rooster weighs between 10 to 14 pounds, and the hen weighs 8 to 10 pounds. Bantams weigh up to 3 pounds and are also good for meat. Their legs are clean, short, and white with five toes. Their earlobes are red, and their eggs are white. Dorkings will lay about 3 eggs per week.

These birds are docile and easy to handle. They do not like confinement much and will be happier free-range. You need sufficient space for them to forage for insects and wander. Dorkings take up to two years to mature, and they live up to seven years. Chickens overall have been known to live up to 20 years, although eight to 10 years is the average chicken's life span. Feed that is balanced and provides proper nutrients will give you a meatier bird.

Langshan

China is where the Langshan originated and was discovered in the 1800s. The Langshan was very popular in late 19th century America because of its qualities. They can tolerate all climates, are meaty, and are adequate egg producers. They also have a gentle temperament. They are blue, black, and white, with a single comb and white skin. The blue and black birds have a green or purple sheen to them in sunlight. Green is a more desirable color and represents a more prestigious bloodline. Their eyes are dark or black. Langshans have long, clean legs with four toes. Some varieties have lightly feathered legs. By today's standards, these birds are big but are not as meaty as some commercially produced chickens. These chickens stand tall, about 20 to 24 inches high, and their tails can be long, about 18 to 24 inches, and are erect and carried at a high angle.

These birds are medium egg producers, providing about 140 to 150 eggs yearly. The eggs they lay are light to dark brown, and in some cases plum-colored. These are not as common but are the most desirable color. Langshans are a good choice for new chicken owners because they are gentle and docile.

Cornish

Cornish chickens were developed primarily for meat in Cornwall, England. This breed's trademark is its muscular body and excellent carcass shape. They have yellow skin, and their feathers are short and close to the body, ranging in colors that are dark, white, buff, and white-laced red. Their eyes are reddish-brown, and they have a single pea comb. Their legs are clean, and they have four toes.

The roosters of this breed weigh around 10 ½ pounds, and the hens weigh 8 pounds. Bantams weigh about 3 to 5 pounds. Cornish chickens are the standard breed for grocery stores because of their meaty bodies. They have skyrocketed in the industry to become the top-selling fryer or broiler chicken.

These birds are not proficient egg layers, but they do produce brown eggs. They are not friendly poultry so they are not the best choice for a pet. Cornish chickens tend to be noisy. They do well in confinement, but they need exercise to help them keep their muscular, meaty shape. They are also energetic birds that are always on the move.

Brahma

The name of this bird comes from the River Brahmaputra in India. Brahmas are sometimes referred to as the "King of Chickens" because of their large size. They come in an assortment of colors, including buff Colombian (meaning they have black tails or black-tipped feathers on their tail), gold, and white. Their coats can be light or dark in color. They have red eyes and a small, single pea comb. Their legs are feathered.

Brahma roosters are docile, even somewhat submissive compared with other breeds, and they weigh between 10 and 12 pounds. Hens weigh 7 to 9 pounds, and bantams weigh about 38 ounces for a male and 32 ounces for a female.

Brahmas are fairly good egg layers and produce approximately 140 brown eggs yearly. Although they are large birds, they are gentle and easy to handle. They take up to two years to mature. Brahmas need a dry environment, but they can fare well in hot or cold climates. They do not fly and are content behind a 2-foot fence.

Faverolles

This chicken is a crossbreed developed originally to produce hearty, plump birds. The lineage of the Faverolle is most likely a mixture of several breeds, including Houdan, Dorking, Malines, white-skinned light Brahma, and the common five toed fowl. The colors are black, buff, laced blue, salmon, white, and ermine (a light-colored bird). They have light red eyes and a single comb.

The weight of the male bird is 9 to 11 pounds, and the female is 7 ½ to 9 ½ pounds. Bantams are about 2 pounds. Their legs are lightly feathered, and they have five toes. They are productive egg layers and lay about 100 light brown eggs each year, even through the winter months. These are active birds that are always on the go and need room to roam. They are gentle and sometimes can be bullied by more aggressive breeds, such as the Cornish, old English game, or modern game chickens.

Cubalaya

This hearty bird comes in white, black, black-breasted red, or blue wheato (having a dark blue body with a rusty coat on top). They are good egg layers, producing cream-colored and tinted eggs, but are raised primarily for their meat. They are a beautiful, ornamental bird with long tail feathers that curve downward, known as a **lobster tail.** They have bay-colored eyes, red wattles, and a pea comb. They are fairly rare in the United States, as they originated in Cuba and are not a popular breed here.

The birds weigh 6 to 7 pounds for a male and 4 to 5 pounds for a female. Bantams are approximately 3 pounds. This breed is friendly and can be trained to eat out of your hand. They can endure any climate and do well in confinement.

Scots Dumpy

Scots dumpy is known by several names, including bakies, cralwers, and creepies. This breed was developed in the Highlands of Scotland and is now a very rare breed. Their most striking trait is their short, squatty legs. Scots dumpy should have legs that are a mere 2 inches long from the ground. They are a heavy bird with a lot of meat on their bones. The roosters weigh in at 7 pounds, and the hens weigh 5 ½ to 6 pounds. Bantams of this breed are approximately 3 pounds.

This breed's legs are short, white, and have no feathers. Each foot has four toes. The eyes, comb, wattle, and earlobes of the Scots dumpy are a bright red in color, and its beaks are also white. Especially in the roosters, this breed's tail is long and flowing.

Scots dumpys are docile and gentle birds. They come in a variety of colors to include black, cuckoo, white, brown, and silver and gold. Although their legs are white in most varieties, in the black Scot dumpy, its legs are slate grey or black.

Hens of this breed are considered to be ideal mothers. They care for their young and are very attentive to their needs. They do have a habit of going broody, though.

Best Chickens for Eggs and Meat

Some chickens can provide both meat and eggs for your family. If you want to keep your flock small or stick to one breed of chicken, you may want to begin with one of the breeds listed below. Chickens that are proficient at laying eggs and providing meat are known as dual-purpose birds.

Rhode Island Red

This bird is well known throughout North America and is one of the most popular breeds because of its gentle nature and multi-functionality.

These chickens are easy to care for, great pets, excellent egg layers, and good meat providers. They are a deep red color, with some varieties having black on their tail or wings and yellow skin. Their comb is a single or rose that is broad and solid with protuberances that are small and round. They also have a clean leg.

These birds are proficient egg layers and produce 250 to 300 brown eggs per year. The roosters weigh about 8 ½ pounds, and the hens weigh 6 ½ pounds. The bantams of this variety weigh approximately 4 pounds. Roosters tend to be aggressive in this breed, but overall Rhode Island reds are quiet and amicable. Long exposure to the sun will cause the color of their coats to fade. They are content with a standard pen and coop.

Plymouth Rock

These chickens were bred for both meat and eggs, and their colors vary. The barred is a striking bird with white feathers and black, horizontal striping. They also come in white, buff, multiple penciled (a feather with several types of lines or markings), triple laced (having several layers of a contrasting color around the edge of the feather), penciled partridge (several lines or markings), multiple penciled silver partridge, Columbian (white with a black tail or black-tipped feathered tail), buff Colombian, and blue lace (meaning the feathers have a border of a contrasting color around the edge). Their skin is yellow, and their legs are clean. The eyes are bay-colored, and they have red earlobes. A single medium-size comb sits on top of their heads.

Plymouth Rocks will lay approximately 200 cream- or brown-colored eggs in a year. They are a hardy bird and will lay eggs throughout the winter. Roosters weigh approximately 9 ½ pounds, hens weigh about 7 ½ pounds, and bantams are between 4 and 5 pounds.

Marans

This breed of chicken was developed in France in the 1920s around the town of Marans. This versatile bird is fleshy for meat, a good provider of eggs, friendly enough to make a pet, and suitable for breeding. Their eyes are reddish-orange, and their comb is single with up to seven serrations. Their earlobes are red, and their bodies are black, dark cuckoo, golden cuckoo, and silver cuckoo. Their legs are typically clean and are a light color, but some variations have lightly feathered legs. They have four toes.

Roosters of this breed weigh about 8 pounds, and hens weigh 7 pounds. Bantams are about 30 ounces. Marans are most noted for their eggs, which are a rich chocolate brown color. This breed does best free-range because they are busy bird, constantly moving about. Although friendly, they do not particularly like to be handled. Take this into consideration if they will be around small children who may want to hold them.

Wyandotte

This heavy bird is a great layer of cream- or white-colored eggs, laying around 150 to 220 eggs per year. They are fast-growing and have at least 14 color variations in America, including silver laced golden, white, black, buff, Colombian, partridge, silver penciled, and barred. Their skin is yellow, and their color patterns make them a popular breed for show.

Wyandottes have rose combs, red earlobes, and red wattles. Their legs are clean with four toes. They like to take flight, so they should live in a covered run or have their wings clipped. This fowl has a good disposition and is typically calm in nature, but the males can be aggressive. They will naturally have their own hierarchy among the flock, and more than one rooster can bring out their aggressive nature.

Roosters weigh about 8 ½ pounds, and hens weigh 6 to 7 pounds. Bantams weigh 4 pounds. Keep the pale-colored varieties away from excessive sunlight because they are sensitive to it.

Barnevelder

This chicken is not one of the most popular breeds, but they are easy to care for and great for a novice chicken owner. Their colors are black, double-laced, double-laced blue, and white. They have red single combs, wattles, and earlobes, and their eyes are orange-brown. Their legs are yellow and clean with four toes.

The roosters weigh 7 to 8 pounds, and the hens weigh 6 to 7 pounds. Bantams are about 4 pounds. A healthy hen will produce approximately 170 brown eggs per year. The color of the eggs will lighten as the hen gets older. The double-laced varieties are noted to be the prolific egg layers.

Barnevelders are quick growers, meaning their frame and build fill out in a relatively short time compared to other breeds, making them good to raise for meat. Their temperament is docile and friendly. They are prone to bullying if living among other breeds. They do well in confinement and are not fliers, so a low fence will keep them corralled.

Chantecler

This is the first chicken breed to originate from Canada. Developed from crossbreeding several other types of chickens, the Chantecler was created by a Trappist monk who realized that Canada did not have a chicken to call its own. This is a large bird, with the males weighing 7 to 8 pounds and the females weighing 5 ½ to 6 ½ pounds. Bantams are about 2 pounds. They come in two colors: white and partridge. Their skin is yellow, and their legs are clean with four toes. Their wattles and pea combs are small and red. They were bred this way to help them weather harsh Canadian winters because birds with larger wattles and pea combs are more prone to frostbite. Smaller body parts are easier to keep warm and prevent from freezing. Overall, a larger bird is heartier and can survive the severe weather.

Chanteclers are a quiet and docile breed. They are proficient egg layers, with hens laying approximately 210 brown eggs per year. They are used for both meat and eggs. Although a hardy breed, they are somewhat rare.

Java

Java chickens thrived in the United States between 1850 and 1890. They are an ideal farm bird as the hens are ample layers and the birds are tender and juicy table fare. Java chickens come in black and mottled colors. They were very popular in New York and New Jersey in the mid to late 1800s because their black pinfeathers could easily show consumers if the birds had been plucked correctly. As the chicken industry grew, chicken entrepreneurs decided they could conceal white feathered birds more easily if the plucking was sub-par. This practice nearly caused the Java to be driven to extinction.

Despite this, the breed persevered, and small farmers raised the Java because their dual purpose suited their needs. Even today, the young cockerel makes for a good roaster and the rich brown eggs provided by the hens are tasty and bountiful.

Java roosters weigh approximately 9 ½ pounds and Java hen's weigh approximate 6 ½ pounds. They are easy to care for and their docile nature makes them a pleasant family pet. These birds have a clean leg, yellow skin, and dark shanks. They have a single comb and red earlobes. This bird will provide you with plenty of food and companionship.

La fleche

Originating in France in the 1600s, the la fleche chicken comes from the Valley of La Sarthe. This breed has been around for centuries. They come in white, cuckoo, and blue lace, but black is the most common color and it is the color they are most known for among chicken breeds.

La fleche is a hearty table bird. Males weigh 8 to 9 pounds. Hens weigh 6 to 7 pounds. Bantams weigh in at 3 pounds. Though their coat is a deep black color, this breed has remarkable white meat as a table bird. If you are looking for a proficient egg layer, the la fleche hen lays 180 to 200 large eggs each year. Their eggs are white to light brown in color. This breed is seldom broody.

As a pet, la fleche are not very people friendly. They are somewhat shy, yet docile. They are active and thrive as free-range birds because they enjoy foraging for food. La fleche are active and like to roost in trees. You can train them to return to the coop each night by feeding them at the same time each day. They will be hungry and will learn that feeding time is in the evening. This is the easiest way to gather your flock at the end of the night.

La Fleche have a long, v-shaped wattle and their comb has dual spikes or horns. They have even been referred to as the "Devil's Head" because of their shape. Their earlobes are white, and their legs are clean with 4 toes.

Ixworth

The Ixworth breed of chicken made its appearance in 1939, originating in Suffolk, England. It is a dual-purpose bird, meaning that is proficient at egg laying and also provides sufficient meat to be considered a good table bird. These chickens were created from a mix of the white varieties of the following birds: Old English game hens, Sussex, Minorca, Orpington, and Indian game birds.

Their comb is a pea comb. They have clean legs and light to white legs. Their eyes are orange-red. The male weighs about 9 pounds and the females weigh about 7 pounds. There was a bantam version of the Ixworth, but it faded out in the late 1930s to early 1940s. This is considered a rare bird. The hens tend to go broody, but they do lay about 200 eggs per year.

Vorwerk

The Vorwerk breed shares its name with a vacuum cleaner. It is a likeable breed of chicken that is docile and bears confinement well. This breed comes in black bluff black in the United States. In Holland, though, it comes in blue bluff blue, and white bluff white. The breed is rare because of a small gene pool.

The Vorwerk is very similar to the lakenvelder, but it is a different breed. It comes in a standard and a bantam size. Male standards weigh 5 ½ to 7 ½ pounds. Female Vorwerk's weigh 4 ½ to 5 ½ pounds. Bantams weigh 27 ounces. Their skin is slate gray and their eyes are orange red. Their coat is black on the head and tail and buff on the body and the breast. Their wattles are red and medium in size.

The hens are proficient egg layers. They lay 150-200 eggs per year and they are brown, medium sized eggs. Vorwerks are suitable to live in all climates. They are good table birds and provide ample amounts of eggs. They make good pets due to their docile personality and do well as a show bird. If you are looking for a multi-purpose bird, this one is for you.

Buckeye

Originating in Ohio, this duel-purpose breed is thought to be the only chicken breed to be developed by a woman. These are hardy birds that can withstand both cold and hot temperatures because of their pea comb and tight feathering. Hens are good layers and lay medium-sized, brown eggs throughout the year, and weighing in at 9 pounds for a rooster and 6 ½ to 7 pounds for a hen, they make a good table bird. They are known to have nice yellow skin, good thigh meat, and a large breast. The buckeye is an active breed that is well suited to being free range. They can be vocal and noisy, the roosters are known to be territorial, and hens of this breed tend to be very friendly. Note that this is an endangered breed.

Best Pet Chickens

You may want to keep chickens for a pet, as a hobby, and for companionship. Eggs are an added bonus. The following breeds are easy to raise, gentle, and attractive. They are not necessarily good egg layers or good for their meat.

Jersey Giants

This bird is large and needs lots of space to move about. They were originally bred for their meat, but their slow-growing nature deters chicken owners from this purpose. The plumage is a dark black with a dark beak and an angled tail. Some varieties are white, blue, and splash (having one solid color with a splash of a darker color on top). The single comb is red, as are the wattle and earlobes. They have a clean leg that is dark in color.

Despite their size, Jersey giants are calm and easy to handle. They are alert and interactive, which makes them good pets. Roosters can weigh up to 13 pounds, and hens can weigh up to 10 pounds. Bantams are not typical of this breed because their main trait is their size. They do fairly well laying eggs, producing up to 180 brown eggs per year. They also have a gentle crow so the neighbors should not mind. Their home should be large enough to house the flock comfortably. You will know they have enough space when the birds have room to move around, perch, and sleep.

Orpingtons

This chicken makes a great choice to raise in the backyard because of its docile and cuddly nature. They have small heads on hearty bodies, and they come in black, blue, buff, and white. They have a single, red, serrated comb and an elongated wattle. The earlobes are small and red, and their legs are short and clean with four toes. The dark-colored birds have darker eyes, and the lighter colors have red eyes.

Orpington roosters weigh about 8 pounds, and the hens weigh about 6 to 7 pounds. Bantams weigh about 4 pounds. They are decent egg layers, producing 160 brown eggs per year. Some varieties produce a pink-tinted egg. They do well in confinement but enjoy the chance to wander free and forage for insects. This poultry is easy to handle and makes a great family bird.

Red star

Red star chickens are hybrids. They make good pets because they are quiet, docile, and petite. Hens are prolific layers and produce more than 200 brown eggs yearly. They have a red buff color, single red comb, red earlobes, and clean legs with four toes. Some varieties of the star breed come in black.

This bird is approximately 6 pounds for a female and 7 pounds for a male. Bantams are about 4 pounds. They are a hardy bird that can withstand colder temperatures and will lay eggs in winter months. A standard coop will make a fine home for them.

Sebright

Sir John Sebright from England developed these little birds in the 1800s, and this breed of chicken is beautiful and makes for a good pet or exhibition bird. They bear confinement well, and they are bantams, with the males weighing 22 ounces and the females weighing 18 ounces.

The colors of the Sebright are gold and silver with black lace. They have dark red eyes, red rose combs, clean legs, and four toes. They are not good egg layers, producing about 52 tiny eggs yearly. It is difficult to raise these birds from eggs, as they have a high mortality rate and their embryos are delicate and small. They are popular show birds because of the black lace markings on their coat.

Booted bantam

This bird is also known as the Dutch booted bantam and is popular in Germany and the Netherlands. It originated in Asia and was brought to the United States in the early 20th century. They are ornamental birds with attractive coloring that can be black, porcelain, self blue, and white. They have profuse plumage, their tail is angled upwards, and their eyes, wattles, and earlobes are red. They have a single comb with five points. Their legs are feathered, as are their feet, and they have four toes.

The booted bantam is one of the few breeds that is a true bantam, and the males grow to about 2 pounds and the females to about 1 to 1 ½ pounds. Their nature is gentle, and they are known to follow their owner around the yard. They make great garden birds because they forage bugs but are very gentle around the plants. Soft bedding is recommended for them to tread upon because of their feathered feet.

They are fair egg layers, producing two to three eggs per week. These bantams lay small cream-colored or tinted eggs and produce mostly in the summertime. This docile bird is sure to be a loveable addition to your flock.

Delaware

This is a relatively new breed of chicken developed in the 1940s. The breed was originally called "Indian Rivers." They are a rare breed — a cross between barred Plymouth Rock roosters and New Hampshire red hens — produced to provide ample amounts of both eggs and meat. Their eggs are brown, and an average hen will produce four per week.

They are friendly and calm birds that make great pets. Male Delawares grow to 8 pounds, and the females grow to 6 pounds. Bantams are approximately 4 pounds. They are mostly white with some barring markings and have a single comb, a clean leg, and four toes.

Seramas

Seramas are a relatively new breed of bantam chicken, being developed in the past 15 to 20 years. It is a smallest and lightest bantam breed that does not remain true to their color or size when bred. This means that any eggs you hatch can be one of 2,500 documented color varieties. Hatch day is a treat if you are raising your flock from eggs. Also, the chickens can be one size bigger or smaller than the parents. Cocks weigh about 8 to 10 ounces and hens weigh about 6 to 10 ounces.

These birds are only 6 to 10 inches from the ground to the top of their comb. They are ideal pets for people with little space. A pair of Seramas can live comfortably in an 18- inch by 24-inch cage enclosure. They are "people" birds. They love attention and interaction with human beings.

Seramas come from the jungles of Malaysia and are used to temperatures of 90 to 100 degrees. They tend to get stressed if they are in climates with temperatures below 40 degrees, so it is in their best interest to keep them indoors if you live in a cold climate.

This breed has a clean leg with four toes. Its wattles typically have 5 points. The hens are known to be good breeders. Because this breed has a variation in size and color, no two birds tend to look alike.

Campine

Campine chickens originated from Belgium, but never became quite popular in the United States. They are an ornamental bird that can be used in shows as well as being a well-adapted pet. Campines can be a bit wild and prefer to be free-range as opposed to caged, but they adapt well in confinement and can be quite friendly. Chicken owners claim that Campines can be trained to eat out of their owner's hand.

These birds weigh about 5 pounds for the male, and 4 pounds for the female. They have a clean leg and a large, single comb. Their skin is white and their shanks are blue. Hens lay white eggs that are medium in size. They are average egg-layers, producing about 150 eggs per year. They are economical eaters.

Campines are not docile birds, but can be tame. They attempt to fly and love to be on the go. The best environment for these chickens is a place with lots of space to roam and forage. Campines are active, lively, and not broody birds. They are fun to watch and care for as pets.

Miss Pepperpot

How can anyone resist this charming little hen with a name like Miss pepperpot? Only available in the female gender, it is a cross between a Maran and a Plymouth Rock. Their feathers are black with a green sheen to it. On their chest, they have red and gold feathers. They have a black beak and clean legs that are slate grey. Their thick plumage protects them from severe weather. They can survive in a hot or cold climate, and in wet or dry weather, as long as they have the proper care.

Miss pepperpots are an adequate layer of large brown eggs. They are more popular in Europe than in the United States. These hens are a fairly modern hybrid with gentle and friendly personalities. They will enhance your flock with their demeanor and will certainly be a conversation starter when you mention to your friends that Miss pepperpot moved into your home.

Sultans

Rumor has it that all sultans can trace their family tree back years and years ago to one crate of birds that was brought to England from Istanbul. These gentle birds were a favorite among Turkish royalty. The breed is all white, with a topknot, muff, and beard. Sultans have vulture hocks and a feathered leg with 5 toes. They have a v-shaped comb. Outside of the United States, other variations of this breed exist, such as a blue variety.

Sultans are super docile, and make great pets for children. They tend to be a delicate bird, so harsh climates and cold weather is not suitable for them. Sultans can be easy prey for predators. Take extra care if they are a free-range bird. This chicken is a good forager. They make great garden wardens.

The standard breed for this bird weighs in at 6 pounds for the rooster, and 5 pounds for the hen. Bantams weigh about 3 to 4 pounds. Hens are poor egg layers. They lay small white eggs but not very frequently. All in all, this breed is a great family pet or a beautiful ornamental breed used for show.

Picking Your Ideal Breed

If you want a chicken, there is sure to be a breed suitable to your needs and environment. The breeds listed in this chapter are just some of the many varieties available. If you find one you like, do a little research to make sure it will do well in the setting you can provide. Some birds are better in colder or warmer climates than others, so that should be one important consideration. Also, if you do not have lots of space to offer, bantam breeds are petite and require less room to roam.

Some excellent websites that offer details on a variety of chicken breeds are listed below. Each one also offers products for sale to care for your chickens.

- Backyard Chickens (*www.backyardchickens.com*) — This website provides information, pictures of chickens, and contact information if you have questions. Novelty items can also be purchased on this website.

- My Pet Chicken (***www.mypetchicken.com***) — This website provides advice, pictures, charts, and information on all breeds of chickens. You can purchase chicks and supplies here.

- Ompet (***www.omlet.us***) — This website provides limited and unique items for sale, as well as live birds to buy and information on different breeds.

Selecting your breed should be fun. You can even get a mixture of breeds so your flock is diverse and interesting. Once you find the breed you want, you will need to prepare your home for you new additions. The first step is getting a coop.

```
CASE STUDY:
A DIVERSE BROOD
```

Cherranie Terbizan

At her home in Valdosta, Georgia, Cherranie Terbizan cares for her flock of 70 chickens. Her brood consists of gold and silver bantam seabrights, welsummers, Rhode Island white, bantam Millie Fluer D'Uccles, Araucanas, Cochin bantams, silkies, dominiques, cornish game, Easter eggers, gold lace wyandottes, silver laced wyandotte, black cooper Marans, Polish, Campines, among others. Terbizan keeps her chickens for eggs and as pets. She started with mostly chicks, but did purchase some grown chickens and hatched two from eggs.

Terbizan recommends getting started with chicks or eggs from friends, on Craigslist, or through the website Back Yard Chickens. "Back Yard Chickens is one of the best websites you can be on if you own chickens. You can also get your chickens from [the site]," she says.

Out of all the expenses involved with raising chickens, Terbizan says the coop and the run are probably the most expensive. "The food, oyster shell, and scratch is pretty cheap. But the coop and run can cost a pretty penny," she says.

Her coop was built by her husband. Its dimensions are 16 foot by 20 foot by 6 foot, and it is covered with a tarp. It is made out of 2 x 4s and lined with chicken wire backing. Half of the siding is plywood. The coop does a good job of protecting her birds from predators. There are not many predators Terbizan worries about, except a pesky neighborhood dog. "He thought my chicken was a squeaky toy that you did not have to throw! Well, let us just say when the toy quit squeaking he left it in my driveway."

Terbizan's advice to new owners is to always keep your birds in a clean environment, make sure to always have food and fresh water. "Pretty much, treat them as though they were your own child," she adds.

## Chapter 5

Home to Roost

Chickens are easy to care for, but because of inclement weather, predators, and just for their overall well-being, chickens need a structure that will keep them safe and dry and give them a place to sleep at night. Hens also will require a safe place to lay their eggs. The coop can be almost anything that you want it to be, but any standard coop needs to meet certain requirements.

Characteristics of Good Coops

Coops can be any size, shape, color, or material. The size of your flock will determine how large your coop will need to be and how much material you need to get started. You can purchase materials for your coop at lumberyards, hardware stores, online, thrift stores, and flea markets, or you can find recycled materials from Habitat for Humanity (*www.habitat.org*) stores. Habitat stores have lumber and other items like doors and windows that you can recycle. It just takes a little creativity. To find a local Habitat store, go to the organization's website, and type in your ZIP code. If you plan on using recycled lumber, do not use wood that is painted or has been chemically treated because the chickens peck at everything, and these can be hazardous to their health. Regardless of the type of coop you use to house your chickens, it needs to have the following elements:

- Sound structure
- Bedding and flooring
- Nesting boxes
- Runs
- Roosts or perches
- Feeders and waterers
- Lighting for both chicks and chickens
- Ventilation
- Insulation
- Protection from predators and weather

Sound structure

The rule of thumb is to allow 3 to 4 square feet of space per chicken and 2 square feet for bantams to keep from overcrowding. Find a space on your property that adheres to any zoning laws (such as keeping fowl 50 feet from your nearest neighbor) and has enough room for you to build your coop. It should be in an area that gets enough sunlight and drainage. Ideally, it should be on a gently sloping piece of land that would allow heavy rainwater to dry quickly. If this is not possible, elevate the building to avoid water problems because your coop will need to stay dry.

A solid roof will be the best protection for your flock. Aviary netting or wire will work, too, but a solid roof offers added protection from the elements. You can use metal panels, wood, or roofing shingles. Some predators, such as raccoons, can pull apart chicken wire, so use welded wire fences that you can purchase at feed stores and lumber yards.

You can make a basic coop from a shed with fencing around it. Include the other requirements, such as ventilation, perches, and bedding, and you will have a safe, simple home for your chickens in just a few hours. Check every angle of the coop to ensure it is secure from predators and the elements.

Runs

A chicken run is an enclosed area where chickens are allowed to move around. The run should have 10 square feet of space per chicken, but the bigger the run, the better it is for the chickens. If you have trouble with predators, or anticipate having trouble with them, cover your run with wire mesh. The windows and doors on your coop need locks to secure the birds at night or when unsupervised. Some predators, raccoons especially, are very clever and can break into even the most secure runs and coops.

Bedding

The floor of the chicken coop can be concrete, wood, linoleum, or vinyl (the last two are easier to clean), but it should be covered with wood shavings, wood pellets, hay, or straw. Pine wood shavings are the best choice because they hold up well and smell good. Never use cedar because it can be toxic to your birds. Sawdust is not recommended because it can cause respiratory problems. Hay and straw can attract mites, lice, and rodents; you can still use it but you will need to clean more frequently and check daily for infestation.

The **deep litter method** is the most popular bedding method because it takes little time and also provides compost. This method requires layering 4 to 8 inches of wood shavings on the coop floor; you will need to rake the shavings every day to spread them evenly. Your chickens will help do this naturally, and you can throw corn on the floor to encourage the birds to scratch through the shavings, keeping the bedding even and aerated. Raking the shavings helps aerate the wood, which will decompose on the bottom. After it mixes with the chicken manure for six months to a year, the shavings will become compost, and you can spread it in your garden or lawn for fertilizer. You need to clean out the coop only once or twice a year; if your hen house starts to smell, you will know it is time to clean.

To clean the coop, shovel out the wood shavings and remove feeders, waterers, and anything else that can be taken out. Put on some rubber gloves and mix one part bleach, one part dish washing liquid (antibacterial), and ten parts water. Scrub the coop from top to bottom with a scrub brush and rinse it well with a hose. Wait until the coop is completely dry before putting fresh bedding down and allowing the chickens back in. Moisture can cause mold and mildew, which can cause illness in your flock.

It is perfectly acceptable to clean your coop weekly or monthly if you do not like the thought of doing it only twice a year. If you choose to do this, only 2 or 3 inches of wood shavings or hay is necessary to use at one time. You can make the shavings thinner in the summer months and thicker in the winter. Mesh wire can cover part of the floor to catch manure, but it is not recommended for the entire floor because it is not healthy for the birds' feet and it makes the floor too cold in the winter. Chickens also have the need to scratch, and wire does not give the same opportunity to scratch that wood shavings do. Scratching is a natural behavior chickens exhibit as they search and forage for food and also explore their surroundings.

Nesting boxes

Hens need nesting boxes to lay their eggs. The standard size is 15 inches long, 15 inches wide, and 12 inches deep. Some chicken owners get creative and use baskets or something similar for the boxes. Hay and straw are best to use as filler, and these boxes should be changed monthly to prevent health problems. The amount of nesting boxes depends on how many chickens you own; one box for four to five hens is adequate. Keeping the boxes at a slant will help to ensure the birds do not roost on top of each other.

For laying hens, the need to nest arises 24 hours after a hormone fluctuation that is a result of ovulation. A hen — both domestic and wild — will naturally find or build a nest where they can lay an egg as a result of this fluctuation. As this behavior is purely biological, it is essential to provide your hens with the materials they need to nest. According to the Humane Society of the United States (HSUS), a hen with no way to nest will suffer from frustration and distress.

Lighting

Good lighting is essential in the coop because it promotes maximum egg laying and stimulates egg production, especially in the fall and winter months when the days are shorter. If the coop is not designed to let in much sunlight, even artificial light will help stimulate egg laying in hens. Using two 65-watt bulbs will be sufficient for a coop that is 8 feet by 10 feet. Lighting also can synchronize pullets to start laying at the same time. FarmTek (*www.farmtek. com*) has a good website with a variety of lighting fixtures designed specifically for poultry, and it offers everything from solar lighting to light bulbs to infrared heat lamps.

You should regulate how much light your chicks receive. Guidelines are:

- Chicks up to seven days old should have light 24 hours a day.
- Chicks one to six weeks old should have light eight to 12 hours a day.
- Chicks six to 19 weeks old should have light 12 hours a day.
- Chicks 20 weeks or older should have light 12 to 16 hours a day.

Lighting can induce early egg laying in pullets, so it is necessary to monitor how much they are exposed to each day. Lights provide warmth for the birds, and you can use timers to regulate how much light your chickens receive each day.

Ventilation and insulation

Good ventilation may seem obvious, but it is important not to overlook this when you are preparing your coop. Ventilation allows fresh air and oxygen into your coop, as well as the release of carbon dioxide. Without it, potentially toxic carbon dioxide can build up in the coop and harm the flock. A simple way to create air passageways is to drill several holes in the top of the walls and cover them with mesh. If you prefer, you can have windows in the coop. Although windows can help keep your birds cool in the summer, you also will need a good vapor barrier and insulation to keep them warm in the winter. Be sure the ventilation and insulation work together to achieve the most comfortable environment. Keep in mind that the insulation inside your coop will need to be covered so your birds do not peck at it.

Roosts or perches

It is a natural instinct for chickens to want to perch off of the ground to protect themselves from predators, especially at night. The birds sleep shoulder to shoulder on an elevated roosting bar if they have a coop or will sleep in a tree if they are free-range. The number of roosts in the coop depends on the size of your flock. If you have more than one perch, do not situate them directly on top of each other, so that the birds can freely go to the bathroom without hitting another bird.

Arrange your perches in a ladder style, sloping toward the back of a wall. You can even use an old ladder for your roost. Perches should be across from the nesting boxes so you can collect eggs without having to walk through bird feces. Do not structure perches above the feeders or water containers to prevent bird droppings from contaminating them.

Wood works better than metal or piping when constructing roosts or perches, and a broom handle or dowel will work well. Perches should be 2 inches in diameter for chickens and roosters, 1 inch for bantams, and the edges need to be smooth and rounded for better gripping. Space the bars about 12 inches apart because if there is enough space for chickens to roost, it is less likely they will perch on feeders, waterers, or other places not meant for perching.

The floor beneath the roosts will collect the majority of the bird poop, and this area will need to have easy access, which you can attain by opening a window or shutter on the wall behind the coop. Some coops have manure boxes under the perches that are several inches high, filled with bedding, and covered with moveable screen lids. You can take the manure from these boxes every day or once a week and use it for composting and fertilizer. You also can clean the screen lids when you remove the manure. You should be able to move the boxes so you can do a deep cleaning from time to time. If you do not want to use the manure boxes and your coop does not have a window, you can put in an easy-to-clean floor, such as linoleum, under their roosts. If you plan on using linoleum on the entire floor, sprinkle bedding across it except under the roosts so the chickens can scratch and walk around without hurting their feet.

What's pastured poultry?

A common way to raise pastured poultry involves putting 75 to 100 three- to four-week old meat chickens in movable pens during the growing season. These floorless 10' by 12' by 2' pens are moved daily by sliding them along the ground, providing fresh pasture. Chickens also receive a grain-based ration. At 8-14 weeks, the chickens are butchered.

Feeders and waterers

You also will need to find a space for feeders and waterers in your coop. Waterers can be placed both inside and outside, but food should be kept strictly inside the coop to prevent luring outdoor critters to your chickens' home. Feeders come in different sizes, shapes, and prices, but deep feeders will prevent excess waste because chickens will not spill as much over the sides.

If you decide to use a trough feeder, fill it only one-third full to help reduce waste. Automated feeders are available at feed stores and co-ops. These feeders have a timer and will release food for your birds if you are not available to feed them yourself. You also can make homemade feeders from buckets and recycled household items. Go online to sites such as Banty Chicken Domain (*www.bantychicken.com*), and join chicken-owner forums to find other creative feeder ideas from fellow chicken fanciers. As long as the feeder is secure and holds enough food, it will work.

Chickens are messy eaters, and one way to help control the mess is to elevate the feeder so it is about the same height as the back of the chickens. This keeps their feet out of the feeder, helping avoid some of the mess. If you would rather not purchase a feeder, you can toss seed to your birds. This requires a few extra minutes each day but will help you bond with your flock.

You also will need to purchase water containers for your flock. Remember when you are selecting a waterer that baby chicks require special attention. If you must use an open bowl, place stones in it so if a chick falls in, the stones will prevent it from going completely underwater. A nipple-type waterer is similar to the water bottles hamsters use and is designed to keep water clean. You also can find water cups that attach to cages. You can purchase a water bowl heater to prevent freezing in cold weather. This product is not necessary, but will ensure that your birds have water available even in frigid temperatures.

Preparing for Your Coop

Once you know what your coop will need and you have the location and the equipment, you are ready for the coop. You can design your own plans or find blueprints online. Prices vary, but some are free. Select a design based on your skill level and ability to read the plans as well as your flock's needs. Here are some websites that can help:

- Green Roof Chicken Coop (*www.greenroofchickencoop.com*) — This website offers plans for sale, pre-cut coop kits, and assembled coops that you can order.

- Build Eazy (*www.buildeazy.com*) — This website offers a variety of build-at-home projects. You can access free, step-by-step instructions on how to build a coop at home, and the instructions will include a list of materials and photos of what your project should look like.

- Brain Garage (*www.braingarage.com*) — This website provides free plans for a chicken coop, along with a variety of building plans for other projects. This website offer tips, designs, and some plans you can download free of charge.

Because no one wants to look a shabby building, paint or decorate the outside of your chickens' home. However, paint is not necessary on the inside of the coop. Chickens like to peck, and the chemicals they ingest will be passed on to the eggs they lay that your family will eat. Also, paint could be toxic to the flock.

Tractor coops and urban coops

If your brood is small, you may want to consider a mobile coop called a **tractor coop.** These are bottomless coops that are mobile, and they are designed for chickens to scratch and graze. These potable coops are on wheels, and you should push them around your yard so your birds have fresh pasture and so your yard will have the chance to produce new grass over the used patch of land. Do not use a chemical pesticide where your chickens will be grazing because that can be toxic and the pesticides can pass through to the eggs. Plus, your birds will nibble up any pesky insects, so you do not need chemical control.

For city dwellers, an urban coop such as the Eglu can be purchased online from Omlet (*www.omlet.us*). A 20-foot by 30-foot space is all you need to set up an Eglu. They come in several sizes and colors and are offered in an egg shape or as a cube. The egg shape looks like half of an egg and provides shelter for your birds. One end is enclosed, and the open end has fencing that extends from it, which is the run. The fence is enclosed on all sides and on top, keeping your chickens inside and predators outside. It has a hatch to let your birds in and out. The Eglu sits directly on the ground and does not have wheels. It is designed to house two to four chickens.

The Eglu Cube sits off of the ground on wheels with a ladder extended from the doorway to the ground for the chickens to enter and exit. The actual coop is rectangular, and you can order it with a run that is also rectangular and attaches to the coop. The run is available in different sizes to fit your needs. The cube option also has a hatch to allow your chickens out.

Both the Eglu and the Eglu Cube are designed to keep your chickens warm in the winter and cool in the summer. They are easy to clean, with a removable panel underneath the coop that pulls out. Nesting boxes and perches are inside, and you will have access to reach in and collect eggs. They are stylish, and prices start at $495. You can also order chicks with your Eglu on these websites:

- Omlet (*www.omlet.us*) offers coops for sale as well as chicks. This is an informative website with information about breeds and products.

- My Pet Chicken (*www.mypetchicken.com*) provides coops and products as well as chicks for sale. It also has information on caring for chickens and descriptions of different types of chicken breeds.

If you do not have the skills or time to build a coop, you can buy standard-size coops at co-ops, feed stores, supply stores, and online. Other places you can peruse are farmer's co-ops and flea markets.

Farmer's co-ops

These co-ops are where farmers can purchase items they need in bulk to save money. The products are sold at a lesser price because there is no "middle man" present. You do not need to become a member in a co-op to shop at one, but if you are, you enjoy added advantages because shopping here keeps money local and gives back to your community. Here are some ways you can locate a co-op:

- Look in your local yellow pages.

- Check online at Co-Operative Feed Dealers Inc. (***www.co-opfeed. com***). Established in 1935, this site is a distributor for independent farm, garden, or pet supplies in the Northeast.

- Check online at Local Harvest (***www.localharvest.org***). This website allows you to type in your ZIP code or city and state to help you locate farmer's markets, farms, and places to go for sustainable and organic products and food in your area. The site is also a source of information on community-supported agriculture.

Supply stores

These stores are helpful because the staff is usually well educated and ready to help you make your selection. You can go in person to a location or order coops online. If they do not have a product you are looking for, they can often help you find it at another location or order it for you. To locate a supply store near you:

- Check your local yellow pages.

- Check online or at your local Tractor Supply Co. (***www.tractorsupply. com***). This website and store offers farming and agriculture supplies. The site mostly sells products but does offer information on farming.

- Visit Horizon Structures (*www.horizonstructures.com*). This website offers products for farming and agriculture, and it has a variety of coops to choose from.

Online retailers

The benefit of ordering online is it is easy to find what you need. You can peruse a website at any time of day or night, and the product will be delivered to your door. Most websites offer a phone number for a help line, but depending on the time of day you visit the site, service representatives may not be available.

- Egganic Industries (*www.henspa.com*) — This website provides on online store that sells organic chicken feed, coops, and coop accessories.

- Shop the Coop (*www.shopthecoop.com*) — This website provides information on housing for your birds, and you can purchase a coop here.

Farmer's markets and flea markets

These are great places to find bargains and unusual items. If you are purchasing eggs or birds here, ask several questions, especially about the age of the pullet because a hen's laying ability is directly related to her age. Buying a coop here gives you an opportunity to discuss raising chickens with someone who has experience. The downside is there are no refunds or returns on products you buy here.

Once your coop is set up, you are ready to move your chickens in. Do not get your chicks before their home is complete so that you do not need to find a temporary place to keep them. If you are ordering your flock online, you may have to coordinate a pickup or delivery time with your post office. Planning everything ahead of time will make for a smooth transition.

CASE STUDY: A HOME TO NEST

Chanel McDaniel

CLASSIFIED CASE STUDIES
™
directly from the experts

Chanel McDaniel and her father raised sex links chickens for eggs and for showing in both Tennessee and Florida. They had about 25 chickens and kept them in a homemade coop. The coop was approximately 10 feet by 10 feet with an egg laying area on one side and a roosting area on the opposite side. It was made out of 2 x 4s, plywood, and metal they found from a broken down shed. "It was fairly easy to put together," says McDaniel.

For the coop, they made sure there was a way to get to the eggs from the outside to avoid needing to walk through all of the chickens and through the coop itself. They included a panel on hinges that could be opened from the outside so all they had to do was stick their hands inside and take the eggs out of the box.

The pen was approximately 50 feet by 30 feet and was made out of 2 x 4s with the posts at each corner, made out of cedar trees, and wrapped with chicken wire to form an enclosed space. "It should be noted," McDaniel says, "that for 25 chickens this space was WAY too small and was muddied up within days."

In the pen area, McDaniel and her dad placed spikes all around the edge of the area so if predators did get in, they could not get very far. They also included an automatic feeder that they built out of plywood with metal. They designed it so that when the chickens pecked at it, the feeder would not get ruined.

All in all, it took the father daughter pair about a day and a half to build the coop and the pen. They used all recycled materials so it was very inexpensive. After that, it only took about 30 minutes a day to care for the birds. "In that half an hour, you would get the eggs, feed the chickens, clean the water bottles, make sure all the chickens were alive and doing well and that the feeder was full," says McDaniel.

McDaniel's advice to people thinking about getting chickens is this: "Chickens require a lot more room than you think they do. We thought that our pen was big enough, but we probably needed to double the size. If I had chickens again, I would prefer to have free-range chickens. Instead of a non-mobile coop, I would use a tractor coop — one that is on wheels and can move around so the chickens can eat fresh grass."

A Sample Chicken Coop Plan

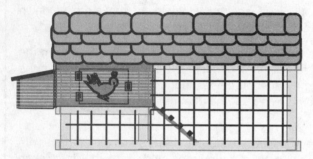

Bill of Material

Item	Qty	Description	Item	Qty	Description
1	6	2x4x3'-0"	16	1	1/2" plywood x 1'-2" x 1'-8"
2	6	2x4x4'-0"	17	4	1/2" plywood x 1'-2" x 1'-2"
3	4	2x4x8'-0"	18	1	1/2" plywood x 1'-0" x 2'-0"
4	2	2x4x2'-9"	19	2	1/2" plywood x 2'-7" x 8'-0"
5	1	2x4x3'-9"	20	4	2" hinges
6	1 box	3" deck screws	21	1	1 latch
7	1	1/2" plywood x 3'-0" x 4'-0"	22	6	1x1x8"
8	1 box	1 5/8" deck screws	23	1	2x4x2'-0"
9	1	1/2" plywood x 2'-11" x 4'-0"	24	2	2x4x4"
10	1	1/2" plywood x 2'-11" x 4'-0"	25	1 bdl	Shingles
11	1	1/2" plywood x 1'-7" x 3'-0"	26	1 box	1" Roofing Nails
12	1	1/2" plywood x 1'-7" x 3'-0"	27	1 roll	Wire Mesh
13	1	1/2" plywood x 1'-2" x 3'-1"	28	1 box	1" heavy duty staples
14	1	1/2" plywood x 1'-0" x 3'-1"	29	1 gallon	primer
15	1	1/2" plywood x 1'-4" x 3'-3"	30	1 gallon	paint

Step 1: Assemble Base Frame:

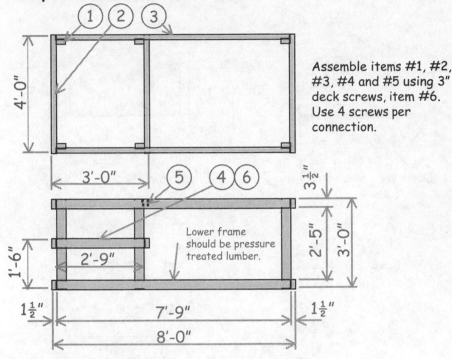

Assemble items #1, #2, #3, #4 and #5 using 3" deck screws, item #6. Use 4 screws per connection.

Lower frame should be pressure treated lumber.

Step 2: Cut Out and Install Coop Floor:

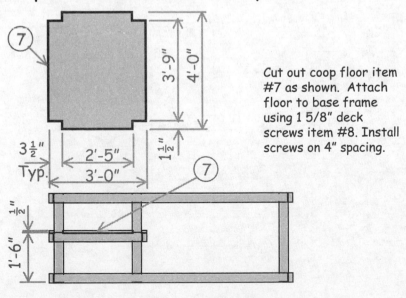

Cut out coop floor item #7 as shown. Attach floor to base frame using 1 5/8" deck screws item #8. Install screws on 4" spacing.

Step 3: Cut out Plywood Components:

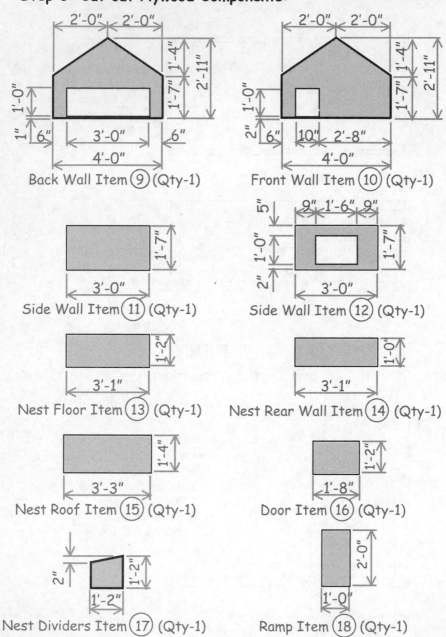

Back Wall Item ⑨ (Qty-1)

Front Wall Item ⑩ (Qty-1)

Side Wall Item ⑪ (Qty-1)

Side Wall Item ⑫ (Qty-1)

Nest Floor Item ⑬ (Qty-1)

Nest Rear Wall Item ⑭ (Qty-1)

Nest Roof Item ⑮ (Qty-1)

Door Item ⑯ (Qty-1)

Nest Dividers Item ⑰ (Qty-1)

Ramp Item ⑱ (Qty-1)

Step 4: Assemble Nest Box:

Assemble nest box items #13, #14, & #17 using 1 5/8" deck screws item #8. Install screws on 4" spacing. Space item #17 dividers equally.

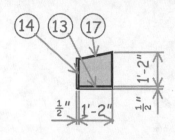

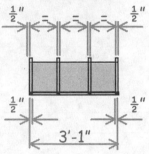

Step 5: Attach Walls and Nest to Base Frame:

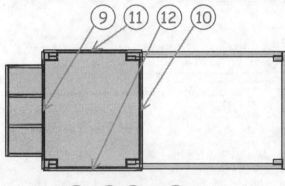

Attach coop walls to base frame using 1 5/8" deck screws item #8. Attach nest box items #13, #14, & #17 to rear wall using 1 5/8" deck screws item #8. Install screws on 4" spacing. NOTE: Nest floor should be 2" lower than coop floor.

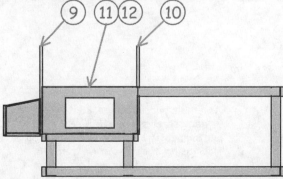

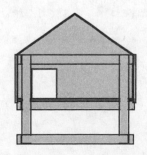

Step 6: Install Roof, Door, Nest Lid, and Ramp:

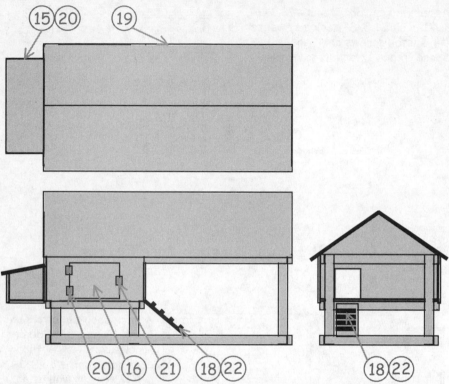

-Attach roof item #19 to walls and base frame using 1 5/8" deck screws item #8.
-Attach nest box lid item #15 to rear wall using 2 hinges item#20.
-Install access door item #16 complete with latch item #21 and hinges item #20.
-Attach ramp item #18 to base frame using 1 5/8" deck screws item #8.
-Attach cleats item #22 to ramp, equally spaced, using 1 5/8" deck screws item #8.

Step 7: Assemble Perch:

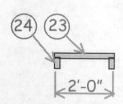

Assemble perch items #23 & #24 using 3" deck screws item #6. Use 4 screws per connection. Attach perch to coop floor using 3" deck screws item #6. Locate 6" from front wall of coop and 3" from side wall, parallel to front wall.

Step 8: Install Roofing Shingles, Wire Mesh, and Paint to suit:

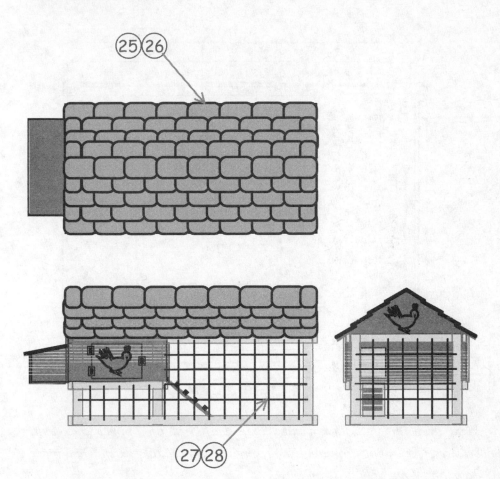

-Install roofing shingles item #25 to plywood roof using roofing nails item #26. Follow manufacturers instructions.
-Attach wire mesh to exterior of base frame using 1" heavy duty staples.
-Prime and paint to suit.

Plan for a 20' x 15' Layer House, 50-80 Hens

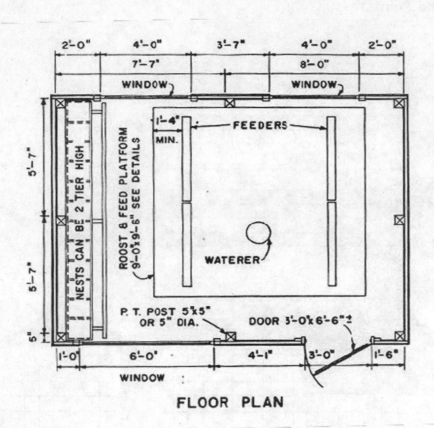

FLOOR PLAN

Plans by Phillip J. Clauer, Poultry Extension Specialist, Animal and Poultry Sciences, Used with permission from Virginia Cooperative Extension, Virginia Tech, and Virginia State University.

Issued in furtherance of Cooperative Extension work, Virginia Polytechnic Institute and State University, Virginia State University, and the U.S. Department of Agriculture cooperating. Alan L. Grant, Dean, College of Agriculture and Life Sciences, and Interim Director, Virginia Cooperative Extension, Virginia Tech, Blacksburg; Wondi Mersie, Interim Administrator,1890 Extension Program, Virginia State, Petersburg.

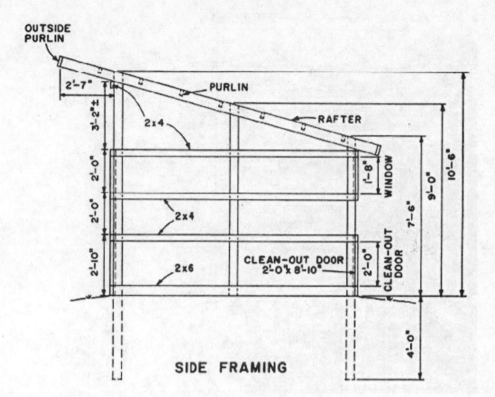

OUTSIDE
PURLIN

2'-7"

3'-2"±

2x4

PURLIN

RAFTER

2'-0"

2x4

1'-8"

WINDOW

2'-0"

2'-10"

2x6

CLEAN-OUT DOOR
2'-0"x 8'-10"

2'-0"

CLEAN-OUT
DOOR

10'-6"

9'-0"

7'-6"

4'-0"

SIDE FRAMING

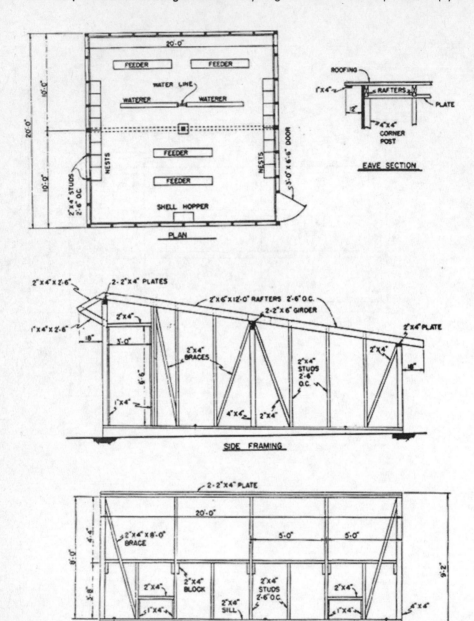

Plan for an 8' x 8' Layer House - 15 to 20 Hens

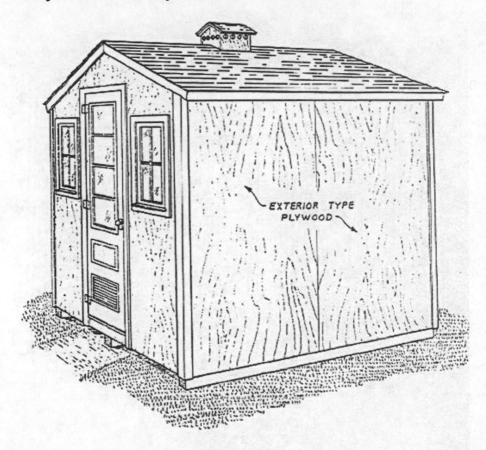

EXTERIOR TYPE
PLYWOOD

PERSPECTIVE

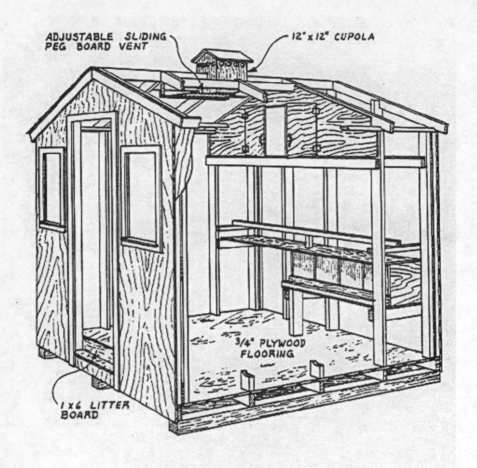

ADJUSTABLE SLIDING
PEG BOARD VENT

12" x 12" CUPOLA

3/4" PLYWOOD
FLOORING

1 x 6 LITTER
BOARD

CUTAWAY   VIEW

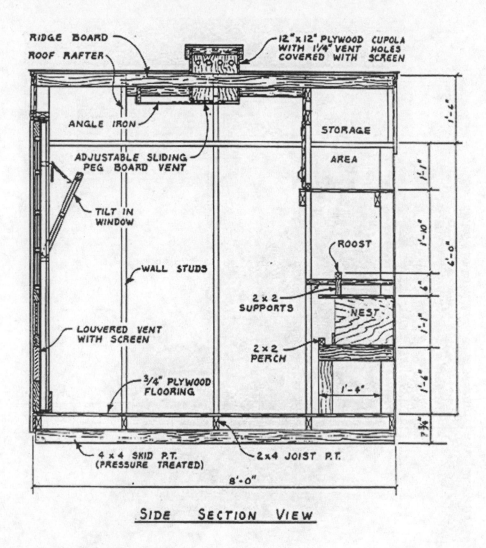

RIDGE BOARD
ROOF RAFTER

12" x 12" PLYWOOD CUPOLA
WITH 1¼" VENT HOLES
COVERED WITH SCREEN

ANGLE IRON

STORAGE

AREA

ADJUSTABLE SLIDING
PEG BOARD VENT

TILT IN
WINDOW

ROOST

WALL STUDS

2 x 2
SUPPORTS

NEST

LOUVERED VENT
WITH SCREEN

2 x 2
PERCH

¾" PLYWOOD
FLOORING

1'- 4"

4 x 4 SKID P.T.
(PRESSURE TREATED)

2x4 JOIST P.T.

8'- 0"

1'- 7"

1'- 1"

1'- 10"

6'- 0"

6"

1'- 1"

1'- 6"

7¾"

SIDE SECTION VIEW

Reviewed by Audrey McElroy, associate professor, Animal and Poultry Sciences

Chapter 6:
Picking up Chicks: *Shopping for Your Flock*

You can own chickens at various stages of their lives: eggs, baby chicks, pullets and cockerels, or hens and roosters; it all depends on what fits best into your lifestyle. Starting out, you may want to keep your flock around the same age to keep things simple because hatching eggs while trying to keep your pullets and cockerels from mating may require more time and attention than you initially expected. Also, bigger, stronger birds will fight the smaller, weaker birds for food. Start small, and remember you can always add to your brood.

Beginning with Eggs

Starting with eggs can be a fun and rewarding experience, especially if you have children. A fertilized egg grows and changes each day in the shell, and after approximately 21 days, it will hatch. You can follow the process inside the egg with a process known as candling. To start your flock with eggs, you will need an incubator, which can be purchased or homemade, to keep the eggs in a constantly heated environment that resembles a mother hen. You will need to turn the eggs every day to avoid deformities. Some incubators are mechanically designed to turn the eggs, which is beneficial because it will turn them all equally at the same time each day.

Not all eggs will hatch. Embryos are delicate and for a variety of reasons may not make it to the last stage of development. If you have children, it might be best not to tell them exactly how many eggs you ordered or what day they are arriving to prevent any disappointments that a cracked egg might cause. A good activity to do with kids is to have them follow the growth of the chick and predict how many eggs will hatch. This prepares them for the possibility that not all the eggs will hatch and helps them focus on the positive side of hatching the eggs. Everyone anticipates the day the baby bird chips its way through the shell and emerges into the world. Soft baby chirps are delightful, and eggs are a fun way to start on your journey of raising chickens.

Proper Handling of Eggs: *From Hen to Consumption 2902-1091*

Phillip J. Clauer
Poultry Extension Specialist
Animal and Poultry Sciences

To insure egg quality in small flocks, egg producers must learn to properly handle the eggs they produce. This article will discuss how you can insure that your eggs will be of the highest quality and safe for consumption.

A. Layer house management

The condition of the egg that you collect is directly related to how well the flock is managed. Feeding a well-balanced ration, supplementing calcium with oyster shell, water, flock age and health all can affect egg quality. However, since these factors are covered in other publications, this fact sheet will place emphasis on egg quality and handling after it is laid.

1. Coop and Nest Management
   - Keep the laying flock in a fenced area so they cannot hide their eggs or nest anywhere they choose. If hens are allowed to nest wherever they choose, you will not know how old eggs are or with what they have been in contact, if you can find them at all.
   - Clean Environment: Keeping the layer's environment clean and dry will help keep your eggs clean. A muddy outside run, dirty or damp litter and dirty nesting material will result in dirty, stained eggs. Clean-out the nest boxes and add deep clean litter at least every two weeks.
   - Clean-out wet litter in coop and make sure the outside run area has good drainage and is not over grazed.
   - Nest Space: Supply a minimum of four nesting boxes for flocks containing 15 hens or less. For larger flocks provide

one (1) nest for every 4 to 5 hens in the flock. This will help limit egg breakage from normal traffic and daily egg laying. Make sure nests have a deep clean layer of litter to prevent breakage and help absorb waste or broken-egg material.

2. Collect Eggs Early And Often

Most flocks will lay a majority of their eggs by 10:00 am. It is best to collect the eggs as soon as possible after they are laid. The longer the egg is allowed to stay in the nest, the more likely the egg will get dirty, broken or will lose interior quality.

Collecting eggs at least twice daily is advisable, especially during extreme weather temperatures.

3. Other Considerations for Layer House Management

- Rotate range areas often or allow enough area for birds in outside runs to prevent large dirt and mud areas from forming by over grazing.
- Prevent eggs from being broken in order to minimize a hen learning to eat an egg and developing egg eating habits.
- Free choice oyster shells will help strengthen the egg shells.
- Keep rats, predators and snakes away from the hen house. They often will eat eggs and contaminate the nesting boxes and other eggs.

B. Proper Egg Cleaning and Handling

1. Collect eggs in an easy to clean container like coated wire baskets or plastic egg flats. This will prevent stains from rusted metal and contamination from other materials which are difficult to clean and disinfect.

2. Do not stack eggs too high. If collecting in baskets do not stack eggs more than 5 layers deep. If using plastic flats do not stack more than 6 flats. If you stack eggs too deep you will increase breakage.

3. Never cool eggs rapidly before they are cleaned. The egg shell will contract and pull any dirt or bacteria on the surface deep into the pores when cooled. Try to keep the temperature relatively constant until they are washed.

4. Wash eggs as soon as you collect them. This helps limit the opportunity of contamination and loss of interior quality.

5. Wash eggs with water 10 degrees warmer than the egg. This will make the egg contents swell and push the dirt away from the pores of the egg. If you have extremely dirty eggs, a mild detergent approved for washing eggs can be used. Never let eggs sit in water. Once the temperature equalizes the egg can absorb contaminants out of the water.

6. Cool and dry eggs quickly after washing. Store eggs, large end up, at 50-55°F and at 75% relative humidity. If eggs sit at room temperature (75°F) they can drop as much as one grade per day. If fertile eggs are kept at a temperature above 85°F for more than a few hours the germinal disc (embryo) can start to develop. If fertile eggs are kept above 85°F over two days the blood vessels of the embryo may become visible.

If eggs are stored properly in their own carton or other stable environment they should hold a quality of Grade A for at least four weeks.

C. Sorting and Grading Eggs

It is best that you sort the eggs before you store, sell, or consume them. The easiest way to sort eggs is to candle them with a bright light. This process can help you eliminate cracked eggs or eggs with foreign matter inside like blood spots.

1. How to Candle Eggs: Hold the egg up to the candling light in a slanting position (see figure 1). You can see the air cell, the yolk, and the white. The air cell is almost always in the large end of the egg. Therefore, put the large end next to the candling light.

Hold the egg between your thumb and first two fingers. Then by turning your wrist quickly, you can cause the inside of the egg to whirl. This will tell you a great deal about the yolk and white. When you are learning to candle, you will find it helpful to break and observe any eggs you are in doubt about.

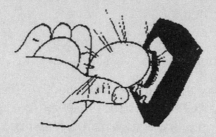

Figure 1.

2. Identifying Cracks: Cracked eggs will appear to have a white line somewhere on the shell. These cracks will open if you apply slight pressure to the shell. Remove cracked eggs and consume them as soon as possible or discard.

3. USDA Grade Standard: Use the specifications given in the table below to determine the grade of an egg by candling. Consider air cell depth, yolk outline, and albumen quality.

Quality Factor			
	Air Cell	**White**	**Yolk**	**Spots (blood or meat)**
AA Quality	1/8 inch or less in depth	Clear, Firm	Outline slightly defined	None
A Quality	3/16 inch or less in depth	Clean, May be reasonably firm	Outline may be fairly well-defined	None
B Quality	More than 3/16 inch	Clean, May be weak and watery	Outline clearly visible	Blood or meat spots aggregating not more than 1/8" in diameter
Inedible	Doesn't apply	Doesn't apply	Doesn't apply	Blood or meat spots aggregating more than 1/8" in diameter

- Air Cell Depth: The depth of the air cell is the distance from its top to its bottom when the egg is held with the air cell up (see figure 2). In a fresh egg, the air cell is small, not more than 1/8 inch deep. As the egg ages, evaporation takes place and the air cell becomes larger and the egg is downgraded.

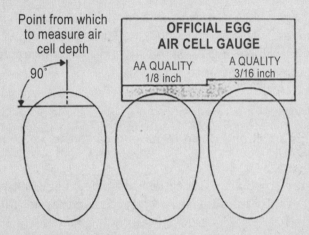

Figure 2. Measuring air cell depth

- Yolk: The yolk of a fresh, high quality egg will be surrounded by a rather dense layer of albumen or white. Therefore, it moves only slightly away from the center of the egg when it is twirled before the candler. Because of this, yolk outline is only slightly defined in the highest quality eggs. As the albumen thins, the yolk tends to move more freely and closer to the shell. A more visible yolk when candled indicates a lower quality egg.

- White or Albumen: The character and condition of the white or albumen is indicated largely by the behavior of the yolk of the egg when the egg is candled. If the yolk retains its position in the center when the egg is twirled, the white is usually firm and thick.

- Eggs with blood or meat spots more than 1/8-inch in diameter are classified as inedible. Eggs with small spots collectively less than 1/-8 inch in diameter should be classified as Grade B. The chalaza is distinguished from a meat spot by a bright area of refracted light that accompanies its darker shadow. Blood spot eggs can be consumed without harm, however, most people find the appearance undesirable.

4. Unusual Eggs: Also remove any eggs with unusual shell shapes, textures, ridges or thin spots on the shell if you plan to sell the eggs. These eggs are edible but break easily and are undesirable to most consumers due to appearance.

D. Storage of Eggs

1. Store eggs small end down in an egg carton to keep the air cell stable.

2. Date carton so you can use or sell the oldest eggs first and rotate your extra eggs. Try to use or sell all eggs before they are three weeks old.

3. Store eggs at 50-55°F and 70-75% relative humidity.

4. Never store eggs with materials that have an odor. Eggs will pick up the odors of apples, fish, onions, potatoes and other food or chemicals with distinct odors.

5. Never hold eggs at or above room temperature or at low humidities more than necessary. Leaving eggs in a warm, dry environment will cause interior quality to drop quickly.

E. Sale of Eggs

There are no laws which prevent the sale of eggs from a home laying flock. However, you should take some basic steps to ensure that the eggs you sale have uniform quality.

1. Follow the suggestions about collection, washing, storage, and sorting above.

2. For marketing it is usually best to size the eggs. Medium, large and extra large eggs sell best. Egg sizes are expressed in ounces per dozen.

Small	Medium	Large	X-Large	Jumbo
18 oz.	21 oz.	24 oz.	27 oz.	30 oz.
Egg scales can be purchased at many farm supply stores.				

3. Never sell eggs in cartons with another egg producer or store name on the carton. It is illegal to do so. Only sell eggs in generic cartons or ask your customers to bring their own carton to carry the eggs home in.

4. Most small flock producers base their prices on the current store prices in the area they live. However, many producers niche market their eggs as a specialty item and receive premium prices. If you have your birds in a fenced outside run and have one male for every 10-15 hens in your flock, you can sell eggs at a premium as fertile, free range eggs. Brown eggs often will bring higher prices as well.

Remember, prices will also be driven by supply and demand. If you do not have a lot of competition and have a good demand you usually can get a higher price for the eggs you sell. It is critical that you pay attention to quality and keep a constant year round supply for your customers. Be prepared to replace any eggs that are not satisfactory to a customer. Learn about and correct the dissatisfaction.

F. What Is the Proper Way to Cook and Handle Eggs Foods?

Consumers should always keep eggs refrigerated until the eggs are used. Also, do not store eggs with other foods containing odors like onions, fish or applies. Eggs should not be eaten raw. Pasteurized eggs should be used in recipes that call for raw eggs which are not going to be cooked (i.e. eggnog, ice cream, etc.) Eggs should not be combined and left to stand at room temperature before cooking for more than 20 minutes. Eggs should be individually cracked and immediately cooked. The USDA recommends that hot food be kept above 140°F and cold foods be kept below 40°F.

Baby Chicks

If you do not have the time to dedicate to hatching, you can purchase chicks one to several days old. The following websites offer them:

- Murray McMurray Hatchery (*www.mcmurrayhatchery.com*) — This site offers baby chicks, other types of birds, equipment, and supplies.

- Estes Farm Hatchery (*www.esteshatchery.com*) — This hatchery website offers different breeds of chicks and pullets available for sale. There is a chick starter kit available for $55 that includes everything you need to begin raising 25 to 50 chicks. It comes with a corrugated boarder, heat lamp, waterer, and vitamins among other items to start your journey.

Before ordering chicks online, do your research. Some online hatcheries require you to purchase a minimum number of chicks; often, the minimum number is around 25 so the chicks have enough body heat to survive the journey. If the minimum purchase is 25 chicks, you need to be prepared to care for that many, or have a plan to share the chicks with others. Hatcheries ship chicks when they are 1 day old because at that point, they consumed enough food to last 72 hours from the hatching process. This gives them sustenance to survive the process.

Chicks are shipped via the United States Postal Service (USPS) with Special Handling. The USPS tells customers to expect two to three days for shipment, and to also ship live animals at the beginning of the week — that way animals are not stuck at a post office during the weekend with no food or water. Take into account current weather conditions as well. Many hatcheries will not ship chicks in extreme conditions, including heat and cold. Your chicks will probably be shipped in a special, vented box, and you will need to schedule a time to pick them up at the post office. Most hatcheries will give you an estimated arrival date and will contact you when your eggs or chicks are scheduled to arrive. At the post office, open your new box of chicks to ensure they are alive. Be sure you understand the online hatchery's policy on chicks that do not survive the journey, and if needed, file a claim with the post office if you think the birds were mishandled. A good seller will have details on their policy regarding transport and what the compensation is in this event.

If you prefer to get your chicks in person, go to your local co-op, farm, farmer's market, or some pet stores to get your birds. Most of these places have chicks available in the springtime, especially around Easter. Be sure to examine the condition of the pen at the store. If the pen, water, and feed are dirty or if there are any dead chicks in the pen, do not purchase your chickens from that store. The chicks' health might already be compromised from a poor start in life. It is important to check the vent of the chicks. If there is any fecal build-up, the chicks might be harboring a disease.

Chicks are cute and fluffy and ready to be a part of your family. Babies need a different blend of food and lots of water. The remnants of the eggs they came from will provide enough nutrients for the chicks for the first few days, but after that they will need a starter mash, which provides extra nutrients as they grow. They also need a heat source such as a heat lamp. Chicks are still adjusting to temperatures outside the egg and the incubator, and they need heat to stay warm to remain healthy.

If you receive your chicks as opposed to hatching them, be sure you have a warming box ready to put them in. Traveling will have created some stress for the birds already, so it is important to make their transition to their new home as comfortable and seamless as possible. Immediately put the chicks in the warming box, which should be 90 degrees. A small, key ring thermometer is easy to attach to the box and will provide a quick reference so you can monitor the temperature throughout the day. If you do not have a box prepared, put the birds in an open box in your oven Keep the oven light on. **Keep the**

temperature at 90 degrees. You do not want to bake your birds. Set up your box, with a heat lamp, bring the temperature up, and promptly transfer the chicks to their new home.

Make sure water is available at all times. Do not use a deep bowl, as chicks can drown. A heavy, shallow bowl that is not easily tipped over can be used. Or, a waterer with a chicken nipple or valve can be used. Some babies have trouble getting started. If you notice one of the chicks not drinking, lead them to the water, and dip their beak gently so they can learn how to drink.

If you do not have starter mash available right away, you can use instant oatmeal or flaked infant cereal. This can be done for the first and second day. After that, the birds should be switched to mash, as they will need the nutrition provided in the starter mash. Be sure to purchase an ample amount or write down the name of the feed so you do not have to change the mixture of the mash. You may want to write down the name of the store you purchased it from right on the bag of feed so you can reference it easily.

Chicks should not be handled too much. They are still delicate babies. You will need to pick them up to check their vent, which is the opening eggs and droppings exit the body, or to move them to a new location. To check the vent, hold the chick by its tummy with one hand and use your other hand to hold the top of the chick firmly, but gently. If you see droppings stuck to the chick's vent, clean them off with a toothpick or a damp cloth; if the vent becomes clogged, the chick will not be able to release droppings and will get sick and die. It will be very tempting to want to cuddle and play with the birds because they are so cute at this age. Try to handle them only when necessary until they are a few days old and are stronger.

Pullets and Cockerels

Pullets or cockerels might be best suited for your needs. These chickens are under 1 year old and are easier to care for at this stage because they are old enough to be on their own. They can be outside without constant supervision because they have feathers to keep them warm and are old enough to fend for themselves. They also will most likely not drown in the water bowl. These birds can also be purchased form online hatcheries.

Pullets begin to lay eggs at 3 to 4 months old. Or, if you are raising them for meat, depending on the breed, you will be able to slaughter them sooner than if you decided to raise the chickens from eggs. If you want to breed your birds, one rooster per ten hens is adequate. Starting with young birds will help start the reproduction cycle of your flock.

Purchasing Your Birds

When you are ready to buy your birds, your home and neighborhood probably will dictate how many you can own. If you are hatching eggs, purchase a dozen because chances are not all of them will hatch. If more hatch than you originally planned for, you can always find homes for your extra chicks. One fun shopping tip about buying eggs is that you can purchase a mixture of bantam eggs, which is usually any mixture the breeder selects, so when the eggs hatch, you will have a surprise variety. You can specify whether you want all male or female. They are sold in groups of as little as three eggs, and for less than $10 you can start your flock. If you are buying chicks or young birds, do not start with any more than four birds. Owning one bird is fine, but it will be lonely, as chickens are social animals.

It is important to be sure you purchase your birds from a reputable source whose top priority is hatching healthy chicks. Mail-order companies and feed stores are fine, provided they can tell you the source of their chicks. Make sure the chicks were hatched in a reputable hatchery, not in a backyard with questionable sanitation standards. You can be sure a hatchery is reputable by researching if they are a part of the National Poultry Improvement Plan (NPIP) and if the breeding flock is yearly tested and certified disease-free. The NPIP is a voluntary program between federal and state governments and the poultry industry to prevent the spread of poultry disease.

Several websites offer eggs and chicks, including:

- Randall Burkey Company (*www.randallburkey.com*) — This website sells chicks as young as one day old, or eggs that are ready to hatch. They offer a variety of chicken eggs and other poultry. Once you place an order, you will discuss a delivery date with the salesperson to be sure you can be there to receive your shipment.

- M&B Farmview Farm (*http://mbfarviewfarm.com*) — M&B Farview Farm sells baby chicks and supplies, in addition to other livestock including pigs and baby Jersey cows. They sell butchered meat and also offer directions to their store in Hamburg, Pennsylvania and their location at a local farmer's market with the hours of operation. They clearly explain what is available for sale online or at their store, as well as pricing.

Another online resource you should try is Craigslist (*www.craigslist.org*) because you may be able to find your poultry for free or for a minimal charge. Always use common sense and take appropriate precautions when buying online. Websites such as Craigslist are not regulated, and occasionally people may try to scam you out of money. Do not give credit card or bank information online unless it is a secure site. Do not be afraid to ask many questions, especially about any guarantees the seller has. Always be sure to inspect the quality of your animals.

If you prefer to go to a local hatchery to pick out your bird, most have day-old chicks available in the springtime. Nothing says spring like the soft chirping of newborn chicks. If you are thinking of buying roosters, check your local ordinances first; some neighborhoods do not allow roosters because of their crowing at sunrise. Roosters are also more aggressive to each other and to people, and they can be harder to handle. Roosters do not lay eggs, but they can provide you with meat. If you consider having both males and females, the roosters are rough when mating. They claw at the chickens' backs and often scratch and peck them.

Having more than one male creates the need for dominance, so be sure you have lots of room for them. A flock of chickens has a pecking order, and if there is one male, he automatically takes the lead. If you have more than one male, the more dominant rooster will be at the top of the hierarchy. You can expect aggressiveness in most roosters, especially if you have several of them. In a flock of all hens, one hen typically will take the leadership role. If you have enough space for the chickens to roam, there is less of a chance of them pecking each other and displaying aggressive behavior.

Buying Your Supplies

Before your chickens arrive, be sure to have everything you need because good planning will help your chickens make a smooth transition. When you are planning for supplies, do not forget chicken feed. You have an array of feeds to choose from, or you may decide to make your own. Remember not to purchase too much feed at once because you should not store it over long periods of time; it can attract rodents, and if it gets moist, it can become moldy.

You can find chicken feed at local feed mills, supply stores, co-ops, and even some grocery stores, depending on where you live. Chickens are natural scavengers, and they will peck and hunt daily for food. But even free-range chickens will need you to supplement their diet with feed unless you have an abundance of land for them to forage. It is estimated that an acre of land can sustain 50 – 400 chickens, but that is probably not accurate in the winter months when greenery is hard to find.

You may be tempted to buy a cheaper feed for your chickens, but be aware that the product is mostly bulked up with fillers such as wheat-milling byproducts. This will fatten your birds up but has little or no nutritional value. It is like junk food for poultry and will affect its flavor. A fat chicken will lay fewer eggs than a healthy chicken.

Chicken feed comes in three forms:

- **Mash** is a mealy or powdered form of chicken feed, usually made of grains.
- **Pellet** is a harder form of chicken food.
- **Crumble** is a mixture of mash and pellet.

Chickens tend to waste more mash because it spills to the ground and dissolves into the dirt. **Chicken scratch** was a popular feed before people realized how important nutrients were to the quality of the chicken and the eggs it produced. The scratch was made up of whole grains and cracked corn. If you use chicken scratch, it should not be their only feed because it does not provide enough nutrients, such as oyster shell, to harden the chickens' eggs.

Chicken feed also comes in different mixtures. Look around the feed store and you will see feed for different chicken ages and purpose: baby chicks, pullets, layers, broilers, and crushed oyster shell, among others. **Oyster shell** helps the development of the eggshell, and if a chicken does not have enough in its diet, the eggs it lays will be brittle or soft. Commercial feed mixtures will be balanced so you do not have to add anything to them.

Making your own feed may save you some money, but it will require more time. You will need:

- Split peas — these have a high protein content
- Lentils — a plant from the legume family producing flattened seeds used as food and a good source of protein
- Oat groats — minimally processed oats
- Hulled barley — these help provide intestinal protection
- Sunflower seeds — benefit the heart
- Sesame seeds — rich in vitamin B and E
- Flax seeds — this provides omega-3
- Winter wheat — higher gluten protein than most wheats
- Whole corn — this provides energy for flock
- Soft white wheat — this is lower in protein and higher in carbohydrates compared to hard wheat
- Quinoa — good source of dietary fiber
- Kelp granules — gives the birds potassium, iron, and fiber
- Oyster shell — provides calcium and helps build hard egg shells
- Granite grit — this helps to aid digestion in birds
- Millet — most nutritious of the grains, providing proteins, carbohydrates, as well as phosphorous and other nutrients
- Kamut — this is known as a high-energy wheat

Mix equal parts of the ingredients, except corn (use two parts), soft white wheat (three parts), and hard red winter wheat (three parts). Mix and store in an airtight bin.

Even though chickens need feed, they love bugs, worms, vegetables, and table scraps. Watermelon rinds are also a delightful treat. Chickens self-regulate their food, meaning they will not overeat, so you can let them have access to their feed all day.

Because chickens do not have teeth, they eat **grit**, which is stored in the crop area of their stomachs. Grit is little stones that break down the food so the chicken can digest it. You can find it at the same places you purchase chicken feed. You can add it to food or give it separately. Grit is not the same as oyster shells; oyster shells dissolve in the chicken's stomach, and grit does not.

After shopping for your birds and purchasing or making their feed, your chickens have all the essentials they need to be welcomed into your home. Enjoy spending time with them. If you opt to hatch eggs, you can look forward to experiencing the birth of new life. New chicks are adorable, and hatching them in your home can provide a wonderful experience for the whole family to enjoy.

CASE STUDY:
STARTING FROM SCRATCH

Jesse Dykes

Jesse Dykes and his wife, Jessica live outside of Nashville, Tennessee on 5 acres of property. The rural location was a prime environment for ticks and spiders. "It was so bad that we would have several ticks on us from the time it took to walk to the house from our car," Says Dykes. They decided to get some chicks to help with insect control. In just a few months, the ticks were almost non-existent. Now their flock is primarily for eggs and meat.

Dykes and his wife started out with eight chickens of mixed breed from Tractor Supply to help learn about them without spending much money. Now nearing a flock of 50 birds, they currently have Rhode Island reds, buff Orpingtons, barred rocks, and they are in the process of getting some Jersey giants.

Dykes recommends starting with day-old chicks, as opposed to hatching your own eggs. He says, "From my experience, it is not economical to buy an incubator, eggs and then hatch them. Most hatcheries charge more for eggs than day old chicks."

He continues, "We initially bought our day old chicks from the Tractor Supply Store … We have since found a local hatchery by the name of Poultry Hollow … My wife and I also source our chicks from mypetchicken.com and mcmurrayhatchery.com. My Pet Chicken is excellent about shipping low number orders. In general, I would suggest new chicken owners buying from their local co-op or Tractor Supply Store for their first batch. The store clerks are very knowledgeable and willing to help customers with questions. In the end, the store route was less stress on us when we first got into raising chickens."

Living on 5 acres of open land has its challenges. Dykes found that hawks were the number one threat to his flock. Keeping them safe was hard. He says, "We lost 5 chickens and 3 ducks in one day to 4 hawks. Identify your predators ahead of time and plan for them."

The coop that they use was made by Dykes himself. "We actually have what most people would call a chicken tractor. I built it from mostly a mixture of scrap wood, cedar mill lumber, and store-bought lumber. The coop section of the tractor is 4' by 4' with two stories. It is about 24 inches from the ground. The run is 12 feet long and includes a section running under the coop. The run is four feet wide and about five feet high. The coop section's roof tops out at about 8 feet or so tall."

Dykes offers some tips on how to build a coop: "First, never use pressure treated wood. The only section of our tractor that has treated wood is the runners. These are the boards that actually come in contact with the ground. We tried to use cedar as much as possible. For wood preservation, there are a few companies that make non-toxic stains. One of them comes in powdered form … Backyardchickens.com has some amazing designs from all over the continent. Their forum is a great resource for design ideas."

Regarding feeders and waterers, Dykes has this advice: "You do not have to buy expensive equipment to feed and water your chickens. Look around on the Internet for lower cost solutions. If you are handy, you can save quite a bit of money with homemade solutions. For example, a 5 gallon waterer usually runs about 40 bucks. A 5-gallon bucket with a few poultry nipples can cost 20 bucks or less. Some people even use food grade plastic barrels that can hold 50 gallons. My feeder is made from a 5 gallon buck and a galvanized feed/ water basin from Tractor Supply Company. It cost me 5 buck to make it. Get creative! I also built an auto feeder that we fill bi-weekly … Initially, we spent a few hundred dollars building a coop, buying the equipment and the chicks. It certainly does not take that much. We intended to get more serious about his adventure, so we were willing to spend more money up front.

Chapter 7:
Hatching Eggs

If you decide you would like to start your flocks from eggs, you can do so naturally or artificially, but you will need fertilized eggs either way. If you choose hatch eggs naturally, you will need a broody hen to sit on them. You can recognize whether a hen is broody because she will sit in her nesting box (or something similar) and not budge. Some breeds of chickens tend to go broody for longer lengths of time than others. This can also happen if you do not collect the eggs daily. A hen can be broody for three to four weeks, which is the time it takes to hatch an egg.

Using Incubators

If you choose to hatch your eggs artificially, you will need an incubator. You can find these at feed and farm-supply stores. Find a location inside your home to keep the incubator, and set it up on a level surface. Follow the directions provided with the equipment, and keep the incubator away from sunlight, as that can affect the inside temperature. Following these steps provides a safe environment secure against predators and the elements.

In general, there are two types of incubators: forced air and still air. Forced air helps spread heat equally throughout the incubator, and a still-air incubator does not promote the movement of heat. The temperature of a forced-air incubator should be at 100 degrees Fahrenheit, while a still-air incubator should be slightly higher at about 102 degrees Fahrenheit.

If you decide to make an incubator yourself, be sure you have a well-designed plan, the right equipment, and the skill level necessary. The website My Pet Chicken (*www.mypetchicken.com*) offers tips and directions on how to make incubators, and it offers incubators for sale in different sizes and shapes. Some are high-tech, and some are basic. You also can purchase egg turners from this site.

Turning Eggs

Eggs must be turned every day, and using an automated egg turner is an easy way to ensure this is taken care of. If you decide not to purchase an egg turner, you can turn the eggs manually. Mark one side of the egg with an X and the other side with an O, and rotate the egg 180 degrees, which is a half-turn, five times a day. Be gentle, keeping in mind you are the egg's parent.

Rotating the eggs an odd number of times per day helps ensure that the same side of the embryo is being rotated. Turn eggs each day until day 18. After that, the chick is preparing to hatch, and should not be moved. Chicks will begin to hatch around day 21, and it should take about 24 hours for all of the eggs to hatch.

Eggs you receive through the mail will need some time to adjust to their new surroundings. Even though the hatchery takes the utmost care in ensuring their safe delivery, eggs can get twisted and need to be set straight. Place eggs, large side up, in a clean egg carton to allow air bubbles to stabilize and move back to their proper place. Leave the eggs stabilized for at least 12 hours, large ends up. Do not wash the eggs, as you may wash away the protective coating, exposing it to disease and infection.

Incubator Settings

Have your incubator set up 24 hours prior to receiving your chicks with the temperature between 99 and 100 degrees Fahrenheit and humidity adjusted correctly. When you put the eggs inside for the first time, the temperature will drop because you will have let some of the warm air out by opening the incubator and because the temperature of the eggs is cooler from transport. The temperature should stabilize and remain constant before you put the eggs in, which could take up to four hours. This is a critical step in caring for your eggs; even a minor adjustment either way could kill your embryos. Humidity should be 58 percent to 60 percent on days one through 18 in the incubator. After that, gradually increase it to 65 percent. As your eggs age, they need more humidity to make the adjustment easier for the birds.

The incubator will have a water pan, or if you are using a homemade model, you can add a water-soaked sponge inside with the eggs. Humidity can vary slightly, as it is difficult to get the perfect setting. Make sure that you monitor the humidity because low humidity will cause the shells to stick to the chicks or may produce small chicks or chicks with rough navels; high humidity will cause an unabsorbed yolk sac that will smear on the baby bird.

High-tech incubators are self-sufficient, which makes the process easier because it does all of the work. If you are using a basic incubator, such as one made of Styrofoam, check on the eggs all day long. These types of incubators work well but require a lot of manual monitoring. Probe thermometers will help determine the temperature.

Make sure your incubator is properly ventilated to keep fresh oxygen in and bad gases out. Vents are important because the buildup of gases can be toxic to the eggs. Vents should be located above, below, or on the side of the incubator. Gradually open them during the incubation period so that by the time the eggs hatch, the vents are fully open. This is also a critical point in the care of the embryos. If you are making your incubator, you must provide a vent. If you are purchasing an incubator, make sure it has vents. The humidity level in an incubator has a strong effect on their development. As long as you keep the humidity level around 58 to 60 percent through the first 18 days, and then increase it to 65 percent after that, your chicks will be healthy and well-formed birds.

Bad odors coming from the incubator mean that one or more of your eggs has gone bad, so remove the affected egg and discard it. If you do not remove it, it may explode because of built-up gases and contaminate the other eggs. Plus, you will surely not want to smell the foul odor for very long. If an egg has not hatched around day 25 or 26, it is safe to assume it will not hatch, so discard it immediately.

After day 18, do not open the incubator except to add water to keep the humidity constant. Close the vents at this time. It will be tempting, as you have been handling your birds for three weeks, but keeping the vents shut will keep the environment stable for your chicks. Newborn chicks should not be touched too much because they are delicate and prone to illness, as their immune system is not strong at this stage. In just a few days, though, they will be bouncing around and you can play with them.

To check the progress of your embryos, you will use a process called **candling**. Candling can be fun for adults as well as children because you get to see the actual development of the chicks. To do this, turn off the lights in the room and remove an egg from the incubator. Take a flashlight (or slide projector or bright light of some kind; you can also buy a candler) and hold it closely behind the egg. You will see a shadow inside. Return the egg to the incubator within 20 to 30 minutes.

The embryo is located at the larger end of the egg with the blood vessels around it. You can start candling at any phase of development, but the chicks are easier to recognize after the eighth day. You will see veins and possibly a beating heart or a kicking chicken. A fertile egg will have a black spot on the embryo, which eventually grows into the chick. An unfertilized egg will appear clear. If you have a dead embryo, you will see a blood ring around the yolk or possibly a dark spot.

The website The Easy Poultry Chicken and Supply (*www.shilala.homestead.com*) offers a homemade candling system:

Materials:

- 60-watt sealed-beam floodlight bulb
- Ceramic light base
- Old lamp cord
- 4 inch by 4 inch utility box
- Clamp connector for nonmetallic cable
- Piece of scrap wood for a mounting base
- Cardboard box with a small hole cut in it
- One roll of black electric tape

Directions:

1. Drill or cut a hole in the side of the utility box and attach the clamp connector on the outside.
2. Take the lamp cord with the bare ends ¾ of an inch and pass through the connector, leaving 6 inches of cord inside of the box.
3. Screw down the 4 by 4 box to your piece of wood that you are using as the base and tighten the connector screws.
4. Attach the lamp cord to the light base. One wire goes on each screw, it does not matter which wire to which screw.
5. Attach your lamp base using the screws that came with it.

Put the light bulb in. Take the cardboard box and cut a small hole in it and start candling. The hole only needs to be large enough to see the egg. Do not leave the candler unattended because the bulb gets hot and could start a fire

Incubator Temperature	Wet Bulb Readings					
100°F	81.3	83.3	85.3	87.3	89.0	90.7
101°F	82.2	84.2	86.2	88.2	90.0	91.7
102°F	83.0	85.0	87.0	89.0	91.0	92.7
Percent Relative Humidity	45%	50%	55%	60%	65%	70%

(From Egg to Chick, Northeast State Cooperative Extension Service)

Prevention of Egg Eating

Phillip J. Clauer
Poultry Extension Specialist
Animal and Poultry Sciences

Egg eating by hens is a habit formed over time which is extremely difficult, if not impossible, to break. It is important you plan and manage your facilities so that the hen never gets the first taste of a broken egg.

Prevention management practices include:

1. **Reducing Traffic in the Nesting Area.** Egg breakage is a major reason why hens start eating eggs. Excessive traffic in the nesting area increases the chance of egg breakage. Some precautions which can be taken include:

a) Provide one 12" x 12" nest for every 4-5 hens in your flock. Never have less than 6 nesting boxes. Always locate the nests at least 2 feet off the ground and at least four feet away from the roosts.

b) Keep 2 inches of clean, dry nesting material in the nests at all times. Many eggs are cracked due to a lack of protective padding in nesting boxes.

c) Remove all broody hens from the nesting area. Broody hens reduce nesting space and cause more traffic in the remaining nests.

2. **Nutrition.** To keep the egg shells strong, feed a complete ration and supplement oyster shells free choice. The oyster shells serve as a calcium supplement to keep the shells strong.

Never feed the hens used egg shells without smashing them to very fine particles. If the hen can associate the shell to the egg; the hens are encouraged to pick at the fresh eggs in the coop.

3. Keep Stress Minimized

a) Don't use bright lights in your coops, especially near the nesting area. Bright light increases nervousness and picking habits.

b) Do not scare the hens out of the nesting boxes. The sudden movement can break eggs in the box and can give the hens a taste of egg and promote egg eating.

4. **Egg Eating Can Be From Outside.** Egg eating can be done by predators such as snakes, skunks, rats, weasels and other predators. If your hens are eating eggs, the hen will usually have dried yolk on their beaks and sides of their heads. Egg eating hens also can be seen scouting the nests for freshly laid eggs to consume.

If you do catch an egg eater, cull her from the flock at once. Egg eating is a bad habit that will multiply the longer you let it continue. If one hen starts eating eggs, other hens will soon follow.

Prevention is the only proven treatment. Collect eggs often and collect eggs early in the day. Most hens will lay before 10:00 am each morning. The longer the eggs are in the barn, the better the chance it will be broken or eaten.

Reviewed by Audrey McElroy, associate professor, Animal and Poultry Sciences

Once They Hatch...

The chicks can stay in the incubator for about four hours after they hatch to dry out and stay warm. Chicks will not need food or water for the first 48 hours after they hatch because their shell will provide enough nutrients for them to survive. Put some food such as starter mash or chick feed and water in their starter box after 48 hours to get them used to it. They also will feel less stress if they eat and drink on their second day. They will not overeat, but they may need you to pick them up and take them to the feeder. Some chicks are more adventurous than others, and timid chicks may not find the food or may get pushed out of the way. Watch your brood to ensure they are getting the nourishment they need.

The **starter box** is the chicks' home after they hatch because they are too fragile and immature to be in the coop at this stage without a mother hen. Your starter box can be a large cardboard box with a heat lamp. The box should be at least 2 feet by 2 feet, and about 1 foot high with a mesh cover. There is enough room in this size box for about ten chicks when they are first born, but they will need more room as they grow. The temperature needs to be kept at 90 to 95 degrees Fahrenheit for the first week, and you should reduce the temperature 5 degrees each week until you reach room temperature. Use a thermometer to gauge the heat inside the box. If you notice the chicks are chirping extra loudly and are standing apart with their mouths wide open, the temperature is probably too high. If the chicks are chirping in a shrill tone, they are most likely too chilly. Content chicks chirp in a soft tone, and close monitoring will help keep the babies comfortable and healthy.

Have 2 inches of bedding in the starter box. Do not use newspaper or any type of slick bedding because it is not good for the development of the chicks' feet and legs. Mesh wire can be convenient for cleaning purposes (if it is removable), but wood chips are the best option because they are soft enough for the chicks' tender toes. Some babies eat the shavings, which can cause blockage in their system and lead to death. Keep a close eye on the babies. Be sure they are not eating things that are not good for them, are not being smothered by the other chicks, or are in the water bowl.

Chicks love water so have plenty available. For a chick's first drink, gently dip its beak into the water, being careful not to wet its feathers. Chicks can catch a chill easily, so keeping them dry is imperative. You also should wash feeders and waterers daily in a mild dish detergent to keep them sanitary.

Chicks poop frequently, so be sure to keep their box and bedding clean so bacteria do not grow. Also, check your chicks' behinds regularly to make sure they are clean. Occasionally, feces will stick to their backsides and block the flow of the poop, so you will need to wash them with a warm, damp washcloth and toothpick. It is not pleasant for you or the bird, but this blockage can kill the chick if not taken care of immediately. If you continue to have trouble, or do not want to handle the bird, take it to your vet. Manure also can build up around the toes, so clean this area in the same manner. If the droppings remain on the feet, other birds may peck at it, and it can cause the chick to walk on the side of its feet, causing crookedness.

Incubation Periods of Other Species

One of the miracles of nature is the transformation of the egg into the chick. In a brief three weeks of incubation, a fully developed chick grows from a single cell and emerges from a seemingly lifeless egg.

Incubation Periods (species and days required to hatch)			
Bobwhite Quail	(23-24)	Guinea	(27-28)
Chicken	(21)	Muscovy Duck	(35)
Chukar Partridge	(23-24)	Pheasants	(24-26)
Coturnix Quail	(16-18)	Ostrich	(42)
Ducks	(28)	Swan	(35)
Geese	(28-33)	Turkey	(28)

Taking Your Chickens Outside

Your chicks can go outside at 4 or 5 weeks old if they are supervised and can go out unsupervised at 8 weeks old. If you have other chickens, the 8-week mark is a good time to introduce your chicks to your adult flock. Some breeds are quicker to mature than others, such as the leghorn, which may require you to adjust their timeline. They should be fully feathered and able to care for themselves before you take them outside. Also take into consideration the weather conditions and the environment they will be in. You will find that roosters and breeds such as Faverolles are active and will not want to be confined for very long.

Chickens have an innate need to scratch and dig at the sand with their claws. They love to roam in gardens and on grass to forage for bugs and worms. Bantams will be lighter and easier on your landscape. Chickens also need dirt. They do not bathe in water, but instead roll around in the dust and consider this a luxury. Their coat of feathers is made up of oils that the dust helps dry out. They also preen themselves, which keeps them clean by getting rid of built-up oil. Chickens love to sunbathe, and the sun provides them with vitamin D and assists in their overall health.

Dealing with Sick Chicks

After several weeks, you may notice that some chicks are weaker or have health problems. Depending on the reasons you are keeping your chickens, you may have to remove sick birds from the brood because their illnesses may be contagious. If you are raising show birds, these chicks will not qualify to participate in exhibitions. Do not breed deformed or weak birds because there is a chance of reproducing that gene. As long as your birds are not sick, deformed, or weak, you can raise them for meat or as pets. Keep them in a separate pen so they do not mate with your show birds.

Vaccinations are an important part of your chickens' health. Any time after they are 8 weeks old, chicks should be inoculated for fowl pox (sorehead) and Newcastle disease (*see Chapter 8 for information on these illnesses*). Fowl pox is a form of canker sores and Newcastle disease is a respiratory disease. Vaccinate for only one disease at a time, leaving approximately three weeks between inoculations. Be sure you vaccinate all birds. Disease can spread rapidly throughout your brood, so prevention is the key.

If you need to give your birds medication that comes in the form of pills, some chickens will peck at it and gobble it up. If this is not the case, and you need to find an alternative method, crush the pill and sprinkle it in a treat for your chicken. To crush a pill, take the back of a spoon, and put the pill on plate and press hard. Mash up any large pieces. You can take this powder and add a little water to it and put it in an eyedropper and dispense into the bird's mouth. If you have an entire flock to dispense medication too, you may want to invest in an inexpensive coffee grinder or small mixer that you can pour the pills into to crush. Then add to treats or add water to the medication and use an eyedropper to give to the chickens individually. Chickens tend to be most hungry first thing in the morning, and last thing at night, even though they can eat throughout the day. Feeding them the medication at these times will help to ensure the birds consume the entire treat with the medicine in it.

Preventing Chicken Stress

Stress is always a part of a chicken's life because these animals are sensitive to their surroundings. When approaching your baby chicks, talk to them in a soothing tone or sing to them because they trust easily and will become attached to you. Most importantly, they also will remain calm. Excess stress in a chicken's life can cause serious illness because it lowers the pH in their system and makes them prone to disease. Causes of stress include climate changes, overcrowding, separation from other chickens, loud children, other animals, noise, and light.

You can take several steps to reduce the stress your chicks might experience:
- Provide a secure coop with adequate lighting.
- Clean their home.
- Provide enough space.
- Keep the coop warm in the winter and cool in the summer.
- Interact with your flock daily to familiarize them with people.
- Teach children to respect your birds.

Blue Partridge Cochin Rooster

Different breeds

Silver Dorking Rooster

Dutch Cap Hen Rooster

Rhode Island Red Chicken

Lemon Pyle Rooster

Silkie Breed Rooster

Black Pekin Birchen Cochin
Bantam Hen

Scots Dumpy Rooster

Crele Bantam Hen

Frizzle Cochin Chicken
(Gallus Gallus)

Cuban Rooster

Brown Hen

Colombian Cochin Rooster
Chicken

Young Buff Orpington

Golden Laced
Wyandotte

Feather of a Chinese Blue
Partridge Brahma Cockerel

Chickens at Little Creek farm in Ocala, FL

Home on the range

"Crackle" the Rooster

"Whitey" the rooster

Little Creek Farm

"Crackle" the rooster in the hen house

Pet hen kept at a home

White hen and rooster

Black Rooster

Two free range chickens

Chicken farm

Black hens

The hen house

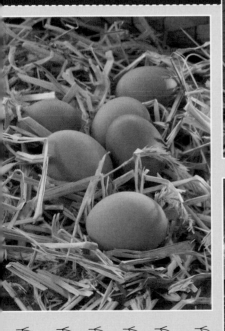

Buff Orpington hen laying on her nest

Chickens ready to roost

Hen in the hen house

Ladder for chickens to roost

Secured hen pen

The house hen pecks food from feeding trough

"Crackle" the rooster feeding free range

Dinner time

Automatic feeding trough

Cracked corn feed

Red chickens

Headless chickens on a butcher block

Off to the market

Roosters in a basket at a market stall

Colorful chicken in an Indonesian market

- Keep other family pets away from your flock if they are aggressive or loud.

- Hold your birds upright and never upside down. It frightens the chickens.

- Have enough food and fresh water available.

- Handle them gently.

- Collect hens' eggs daily so they will continue to produce fresh eggs. Separate the roosters from the hens.

- Provide a roost for the chickens.

- Provide enough grass for your chickens to forage.

- Give your flock adequate attention.

If a chicken is already in a stressful situation, such as laying an egg for the first time, try to avoid adding to the stress. Do not move their home, put them in a different flock, or change their routine. Stress may not just make your bird sick, it could even kill it. Stress hormones will also pass to their eggs or throughout the meat of the bird. Stress makes a chicken's meat less tender, and a stressed hen's eggs may not be as large and flavorful. A good environment will produce a content bird, as well as delicious eggs and meat.

Selling Extra Chicks

Because of your generous care and devotion to your flock, you could end up with an abundance of happy, healthy chicks, perhaps more than you planned on, so you may consider selling your birds. You can set up a booth at a local farmer's market or flea market. Newspaper ads and online sites are also a fast way to get the word out that you have chicks for sale. You may want to contact local farmers who can buy in bulk or ask your neighbors whether they would like to partake in your hobby.

Selling chicks can be a fun way to supplement your income, and you may even decide to raise them strictly for sale. You will need to research how much your breed of chick is selling for in your area. A fancier breed or rare breed will command a higher price. Chicks, pullets, and cockerels most likely will sell faster than older chickens, and although you may be tempted to exaggerate the youthfulness of your bird, be honest about the chicken's age. Because you would not want someone to mislead you if you were the buyer, do not do so to someone else.

You will need a license to sell your chickens' eggs to grocery stores and restaurants, but you can also sell to friends, neighbors, and farmers' and flea markets. To get a license, check with your local county clerk's office. Larger grocery chains most likely will have restrictions on the eggs they can buy and sell, but smaller stores, especially organic stores, will appreciate fresh eggs. Colorful eggs will be in demand because they are rare. Restaurants are another place you can sell your eggs. Farmers' markets, flea markets, and roadside vegetable stands, which popular in coastal states such as Florida, are all outlets to sell your wares. (*Eggs will be discussed more in Chapter 11.*)

Restaurants may be wary of purchasing eggs that are not pasteurized, but organic shell eggs are safe to serve as long as your flock is healthy. Keep records of your chickens' inoculations and documentation from your vet to provide proof that your flock is well taken care of and in good health. Check with your insurance company to see whether you need additional coverage in the event someone gets sick from consuming your eggs or birds. Always make sure you clean the outside of the eggs you bring to your clients.

Besides chicks and eggs, you may want to consider selling your chickens for meat. It is common for old layers to be butchered or sold for meat. Local butchers can cut up your birds if you choose not to do this yourself. If you do not live in an area with a neighborhood butcher, a farmer may be able to do it for you. You also can learn to butcher your own meat; it is not for everyone but is easy enough to do. Just a word of advice: Naming your birds will make it harder to slaughter them in the end. (*Refer to Chapter 12 for more information about butchering*).

After you have your chickens, you will need to care for them and ensure they are healthy through daily maintenance. This begins by knowing a chicken, inside and out, and learning proper terminology. The more you know, the more enjoyment you will get from your chicken-owning experience.

CASE STUDY: INHERITED JOY

Danny Williams

Several years ago, Danny Williams inherited three bantam silkies from a friend who was moving out of state. Named Pickle, Lil Bit, and Elvis, each has their own personality. "I never thought chickens could be so charismatic," Says Williams.

Initially, Williams thought the bantams would be a hassle to care for and maintain. However, he says, "Nothing can be further from the truth. I spend maybe $40 a month on seed and hay. The building supplies cost about $80 to $100. You can sell eggs to cover these costs. Sure, it can be smelly and messy at times but definitely worth it."

The coop Williams and his wife have for their flock was made from left over lumber that Danny used to build an addition on to his house. He also had some shingles for the coop's roof left over from the new roof he put on his own house. Williams explains, "The floor is basic plywood. I stained it with water resistant polymer. This may seem extreme to some, but it is really easy to clean. Just hose it off. That is what I was looking for — something easy. I was afraid the clean up would be a nightmare each week, but it really is not a problem."

Williams does not have trouble with predators, but his old labrador retriever enjoys chasing the birds every now and then. He says, "I do not know if he tries to catch them or is just playing with them. I do not think he would know what to do if he did catch one."

For new chicken owners, Williams has this to say, "It is a joy I never thought I would have. Funny little creatures. I find the clucking noises rather serene and soothing." He adds, tongue in cheek, "Anyone want to buy some eggs?"

Why Have My Hens Stopped Laying?

Phillip J. Clauer
Poultry Extension Specialist
Animal and Poultry Sciences

A common question from small backyard laying flock owners is "Why have my hens stopped laying?" There are many factors which can cause hens to stop laying and in many cases there are multiple causes which add up to few or no eggs.

The most common causes of decreased egg production include: decreasing daylength, improper nutrition, disease, advancing age and stress.

A. Decreasing day length or insufficient day length

Hens require 14 hours of day length to sustain egg production. Once day length drops below 12 hours, production will decrease and frequently stop. This happens naturally from October through February. To prevent this, provide artificial light to maintain a constant day length of at least 14 hours per day. One 40 watt light for each 100 square feet of coop is adequate. The lights should be added in the morning hours so the birds can go to roost as the sun sets. This prevents birds from being stranded in the dark when lights are turned out during dark hours.

Some small flock owners find it easier to leave the lights on continuously. This is not a problem as long as you do not use light bulbs over the 40 watt size. However, the time clock will help lower your electric bill.

B. Improper nutrition

Layers require a completely balanced ration to sustain maximum egg production over time. Improper nutrition can occasionally cause hens to stop laying.

The most common problem is failing to provide a constant source of fresh water. This is especially a problem during the coldest months when the water can freeze. Provide adequate water equipment so the birds always have fresh water.

Inadequate levels of energy, protein or calcium can also cause a production decrease. This is why it is so important to supply your laying hens with a constant supply of nutritionally balanced layer food balanced at 16% - 18% protein.

Feeding whole grains, scratch feeds and table scraps will cause the birds diet to become improperly balanced.

Many times these imbalances can cause other problems like prolapse (egg blow-outs). Prolapse is caused when the bird is too fat and/or egg is too large and the birds reproductive tract is expelled with the egg. Prolapse usually cause permanent damage to the hen and is fatal in many cases.

Feeding oyster shell "free choice" (always available) is also a good idea to help insure strong egg shells.

C. Disease

Disease problems can occur under the best of conditions. Often one of the first signs of disease is a drop in egg production. Other symptoms of disease include dull and listless appearance, watery eyes and nostrils, coughing, molting, lameness and mortality in the flock. Remember some death is normal over the period of a year in any flock. However, if you suspect a disease, contact a skilled veterinarian for help in examining your flock and get an accurately diagnosis and treatment.

Your best protection against disease is to buy healthy stock and keep them isolated from other birds. Buying adult poultry and introducing them to your flock is asking for trouble. If you wish to increase your flock, buy chicks from a reputable hatchery or hatch some of your own eggs. Adult birds can look healthy and carry diseases.

D. Aging Hens

Production hens can lay efficiently for two laying cycles. However, after two or three years, many hens decline in productivity. This varies greatly from bird to bird. Good layers will lay about 50 to 60 weeks per laying cycle. Between these cycles they will be interrupted by a rest period called a molt. Poorer layers and older hens will molt more often and lay less. Removal of non-layers is recommended if economical egg production is your goal.

E. Stress

Any stress such as moving, handling, changes in environmental conditions or fright can contribute to or be the main cause for egg production declines. Common stresses include:

> 1. Chilling. Chickens do not handle damp, drafty conditions well. Prevent excessive exposure to wet, drafty conditions during colder months.

> 2. Handling or moving. Once the laying flock is in place, limit any unnecessary moving or handling. Switching roosters or changing the pens population will also disrupt the pens pecking order and cause some temporary social stress in your flock.

> 3. Parasites. If external or internal parasites are present, get proper diagnosis and treatment.

> 4. Fright. Limit the movement of children, dogs, livestock and vehicles around your flock as well as loud noises to prevent frightening the hens.

> 5. Predators also can stress the birds and create a decrease in production.

F. Other problems to consider when you see a decrease in egg collection:

> 1. Predators and snakes consuming the eggs.

> 2. Egg-eating by hens in the flock.

> 3. Excessive egg breakage.

> 4. Hens hiding the eggs when able to run free.

Reviewed by Audrey McElroy, associate professor, Animal and Poultry Sciences

Chapter 8:
Health and Anatomy of a Chicken

If you are going to own poultry, you need to know the anatomy of a chicken and how to tell whether your bird is healthy. Chickens are not hard to care for, but if they get sick, illness can quickly spread throughout your flock. Knowing how to identify a chicken's parts will help you care for your birds. You also will need to know the proper terminology to discuss your new hobby with fellow bird owners and animal care providers. Terms that you can use when buying chicken parts at a grocery store do not always translate well when discussing your pet to a veterinarian or a fellow bird fancier.

Comb

At the top of the chicken is the fleshy piece of skin called a comb. All chickens have combs, but they can come in different sizes, shapes, and colors. The type of comb can help you identify most breeds. (*The descriptions of the chickens in Chapter 4 can serve as a reference for breeds and their types of combs.*) This appendage serves two purposes. First, because chickens do not have sweat glands, combs are cooling agents. Blood circulates through the head and comb, cooling the warm blood and returning it to the lower part of the body. Secondly, large red combs on males attract the females because female chickens love red.

In cold weather, combs are susceptible to frostbite. This is especially true for chickens with single combs, as the skin is thinner. Single combs also extend from the body, so they are more vulnerable. Cover the comb with petroleum jelly to protect it, but keep in mind this will not prevent frostbite if the bird is continually out in harsh weather. If possible, it is best to keep your flock warm and not expose them to extreme cold temperatures. If this is not an option, continue to coat your bird's comb with petroleum jelly. Although chickens are hardy animals in the winter with the ability to face cold temperatures, if necessary, there are special lamps and heaters available for coops. Shop the Coop (*www.shopthecoop.com*) sells coop warmers.

Here are eight of the most distinctive types of combs on chickens and roosters:

- **Single comb:** This comb is a long, thin, smooth piece of soft-textured flesh. It starts at the beak and runs along the top of the skull, with five or six serrations, depending on the breed. In males, it is larger, thicker, and upright, and in females, it may lop to the side. An example of a single comb can be seen on a leghorn chicken.

- **Rose comb:** The rose comb is solid, low on the chicken's head, close to the beak, and broad. It has no points or serrations on top. Starting at the beak, it tapers to the back of the chicken's head and ends in a spike. Depending on the breed, it may stand straight out or follow the contour of the neckline, as it does in the wyandotte breed. The top of the comb has tiny protuberances with a rough texture.

- **Strawberry comb:** This comb resembles a strawberry in structure and texture. It sits low and forward on the chicken's head and the large end is near the beak. Malay chickens have a strawberry comb.

- **Pea comb:** The pea comb is medium in length and starts at the beak. It is low, with three ridges. The middle ridge is higher than the outer row, and the outer ridges have small, rounded serrations. The Cornish breed chickens have pea combs.

- **Cushion comb:** These combs are solid and low to the chicken's head. The texture is smooth, and the combs have no spikes. Chantecler breeds have cushion combs.

- **Buttercup comb:** From base to beak, the buttercup comb is cup-shaped and sits like a crown on the chicken's skull. The center is a deep cavity, surrounded by a ring of pointed flesh. The Sicilian buttercup is an ornamental breed known mostly for its comb.

- **Walnut comb:** This comb is aptly named because it resembles half of a walnut shell. It can be found on the Yokohama breed of chicken.

- **Silkis comb:** The silkis comb is a rounded, lumpy piece of flesh, greater in width than length. Some are without points; others have points hidden in a bird's crest. Dutch crested fowls have these combs.

Beak

The beak is typically the same on all breeds of chickens. Occasionally a chicken's upper mandible, or top beak, may grow excessively long, which does not hurt the bird but may hinder its ability to eat. If you notice this, take the chicken to a vet to have the beak trimmed. If the beak seems unusually soft, it means the bird is lacking vitamin D in its diet; remedy this by adding it to their food. You can purchase vitamins and supplements at a local pet store or online at websites such as Smith Poultry & Game Bird Supply (*www.poultrysupplies.com*), a site that offers vitamins and minerals for your birds. This site also offers other products for your birds and their coops.

Eyes

A chicken's eyes are red/orange or black and are set on each side of the head. When purchasing or caring for your bird, always make sure its eyes are clear and bright. You should not see the chicken's eyelids when it is awake, and its eyes should not be cloudy or slimy in any way. Conjunctivitis is a common eye disease that is contagious, but it can be cured with medication from a vet. Conjunctivitis is an inflammation of the outermost layer of the eye, commonly referred to as pink eye in humans. Chickens have keen eyesight and can spot the slightest movement of a bug. They tend not to see well at night, though, which is why they retire after dusk.

Earlobes

The earlobes are located on either side of the bird's head, set slightly lower than the eyes. Earlobe color can guide you as to what color the eggs will be. Generally, if a chicken has white earlobes, she will lay white-shelled eggs, and red earlobes tend to yield brown or darker-colored eggs. Araucanas are an exception to the rule, as they lay green and blue-shelled eggs even though their lobes are red.

Wattles

Further down on your bird's face you will see another piece of fleshy skin hanging below its beak that is called a wattle. Like the comb, the wattle helps cool the chicken as blood circulates through it. Unlike the comb, wattles are basically the same rounded shape in all breeds, with both males and females having two. If the wattles appear shrunken or bluish, the chicken is suffering from water dehydration; this is sometimes a sign of an underlying illness or disease. This is also true if the comb appears the same way.

Occasionally, wattles and combs get torn during mating, if frostbitten, or if the bird gets in a fight. It is not uncommon to remove them. You can do this yourself by cleaning the comb or wattle with soap, water, and rubbing alcohol. Trim the skin with a sterile pair of scissors and apply an antibacterial ointment on the area. Bleeding may occur but will heal quickly. If you are uncomfortable or unsure of doing the cutting, take your chicken to a vet. You can attempt to avoid frostbite by putting petroleum jelly on the wattle during cold weather.

Breast and Wings

The breastbone of the bird is located in the chest area. It is actually made up of many bones and covers more than half of the chest cavity. The meat on the breastbone is fleshy and tender and is a popular portion of the chicken for eating. Within the breast is the sternum, which is attached to another bone called the carina. This bone attaches the wings to the body. The chicken has two wings, located on either side of its body. Chickens can fly, but they usually reserve that ability for perching on higher objects or to flee from a predator. Chickens, at their maximum speed, can run about 9 miles an hour, which is their preferred method of motion. They do not fly well.

Tail

The area between the neck and the tail of the chicken, closer to the tail, is the saddle. It is covered with feathers that are longer on some breeds than others. The tail is at the end of the bird. One breed that does not have a tail is the rumpless Araucana. Other breeds, such as the Yokohama, have long, attractive tails. Males' tails tend to angle up, while females' tend to angle down.

Vent

The vent is the opening located under the tail used to pass eggs and feces and is also used for mating. The vent should never be blocked with feces, or have any feces matted around the opening. Check this area daily for your bird's health. It should be free of sores and wounds; otherwise it is an indication something may be wrong with your bird. Trim the feathers around the vent if blockage is a problem. Wash with soap and warm water if the area is caked with excrement.

Legs

Chickens have two legs that can be covered with feathers or be clean and bare. They have four or five toes, with one toe facing backwards. All chickens have a hard, pointy spur on the back of the leg, above the toes. It is small in hens, but roosters use their spurs for fighting. The hock is a joint in the ankle area that gives mobility to the leg.

Chicken legs can have a myriad of problems. Chickens with weak or bow legs are lacking vitamin D. Weak legs are a common problem and can be prevented by keeping young chicks off of slippery surfaces during growth, and by feeding your birds a balanced diet. Also, do not breed deformed birds, as their leg problems may be genetic.

Chickens also can get scaly mites in their legs, and these mites cause infection. Signs of infection are scales that are lifted or separated from the skin and swollenness. You also may see discharge or pus coming from the legs. Birds must be treated for mites immediately, as they will spread to your other birds. Any chickens that have mites should be separated from the flock. Petroleum jelly will help smooth out the scales, and you can get ointment to kill the parasites at your local co-op, pet store, or at your vet's office. Clean the coop and change the bedding for your flock, as the mites can infest the sleeping area. Frequent cleaning will help prevent a mite infestation.

Broken legs are another common injury chickens experience. If a chicken's leg is swollen, crooked, and the chicken is limping or not walking on it, the leg may be broken. Take a bird with a broken leg to the vet to set and wrap the leg or amputate it. Separate the injured bird from the flock because chickens tend to peck at and sometimes attack weak or sick birds. Younger birds will have a better chance of recovery, but an older bird may not survive the break.

Chicken feet should point straight ahead, and the toes should be free of wounds and swelling. They also should be clean and not caked with dirt or manure. It is especially important to check the condition of legs and toes in chicks, as they can become crooked during growth. This can happen if they walk primarily on wire floors. Curled toe paralysis can be identified early in the bird's life if it cannot stand up or if it is walking on its hocks. The best way to do this is to simply look at your chickens every day. Their legs should be straight and not bowed.

Feathers and Skin

Some breeds of chickens have black skin, such as the silkie, but most breeds have white or yellow skin. Diet affects the color of skin. If a bird eats more dark, green, leafy plants, as opposed to corn, it will have a darker pigment. Chicken skin is rather delicate and tears easily. It will heal quickly if the wound is superficial. Putting an antibacterial ointment on scratches or wounds will aid the healing process. Scratches often occur during mating season when a rooster holds on to the chicken with its claws — this is natural.

The outer layer of feathers covering a chicken's body are called contour feathers. Depending on the breed, they come in a variety of styles, markings, and colors. Several different types of patterns are:

- **Laced:** This pattern has a border of a different color on the edges, and a solid color in the center. Barnevelders can be seen with this pattern.

- **Barred:** Horizontal stripes of different colors adorn these feathers. The Plymouth Rock breed is a vivid example.

- **Penciled:** This feather can vary in markings, but the most typical is lines of markings that follow the contours of the edges. Fayoumi chickens have penciled markings.

- **Spangled:** A spangled pattern has different colors and comes to a V marking at the tip. The rare chicken breed Aseel can have spangled feathers.

- **Frizzled:** These feathers curl outward and are seen in the breed named for it, the Frizzle. The feather's texture gives the bird a fuzzy or fluffy appearance.

- **Mottled:** These feathers are black with a white tip. Houdan chickens have mottled feather patterns.

You can identify chicken breeds by the color, texture, and pattern of their contour feathers. Males also have brighter colors than females. Some breeds may have a mixture of patterns and colors, or they could be a possible crossbreed. If you are not able to figure out the type of chicken by looking at its coat, look for other traits that may help, such as the weight, height, and number of toes.

Contour feathers have additional names depending on their location on the body. Saddles are close to the tail; sickles are the tail feathers and are typically longer; and hackles are the feathers on the neck. The contour feathers are composed of keratin, which also makes up human hair and nails. The center of the feather has a hard, bone-like structure called the shaft. The shaft is hollow at the end and attaches to the bird's body with a quill. The light weight of the feather helps birds fly.

Down feathers are the layer of feathers closest to the chicken's body. They do not have shafts or quills. The purpose of these soft, airy feathers is to provide insulation in cold weather. People also use them as insulation in blankets and jackets.

Once a year, usually in the late summer or fall, chickens molt. With each annual molt, a chicken will lose its feathers and then grow them back. During this time, a hen will likely stop laying eggs, but resume once her molt is over. Most chickens experience their first molt around 18 months of age, and the process takes about two to four months.

Characteristics of Healthy Chickens

Even though you may be a novice chicken owner, it will not be hard to determine whether your brood is healthy. Just from their appearance you can tell whether they are in good shape.

- Chickens should have an erect posture and alert mentality.
- Their heads and tails will be held high.
- Healthy chickens have combs and wattles that are bright, full, and waxy-looking.
- Eyes should be bright and shiny.
- Nostrils are clean, and feathers are smooth with a sheen.
- The coat should be full unless the birds are molting or mating, as roosters tend to pull out a chicken's feathers.
- The chicken's breast should be plump, and the abdomen will be firm but not hard.

Appearance is only the first way to inspect your flock. Listening to your birds also can be an indicator. If the chickens are not noisy and it is daytime, they may be ill. Healthy chickens will cackle, crow, peep, or cluck, among other various noises you will come to learn. Chickens squawk if they are scared, and sometimes when they are attracted to another bird. Familiarize yourself with the normal sounds of your flock and you will notice when they are unusually quiet or unusually loud.

When you are close enough to a chicken to hear it breathe, you should not hear wheezing or raspiness, which are indications that the bird may have a respiratory infection. If you are using sawdust as bedding, your wheezing chicken may have particles trapped in its lungs, but bacteria also can also cause an infection. Whistling when you walk into the coop will stop the chickens' noises long enough for you to listen to their breathing. You do not need to be close to the birds to hear their breathing if the flock is completely quiet. If the chicken is in the early stages of infection, increase vitamin E in their diet as it helps their immune system. Purchase vitamin E from a pet store or at one of the online websites and add it to their feed. Keep the bird warm, as the cold will irritate the infection. The chicken will need antibiotics if the infection progresses. To help prevent this, avoid using dusty bedding and make sure the coop has good ventilation.

Smell is another way to help determine illness. Coops will always have a unique odor to them, but be aware of any changes. Visually check chicken droppings on the ground and note any diarrhea or loose stool. Excrement should be firm and gray-brown with white caps.

Taking a bird's temperature after a bird shows signs of sickness also will help confirm an illness. Take a clean thermometer and insert it into the chicken's vent for three minutes or until the timer indicates to remove it. The normal temperature for an adult chicken is 103 degrees Fahrenheit and 106.7 degrees Fahrenheit for a chick.

Common Diseases

Poultry can carry highly contagious diseases. If your flock is diagnosed with certain illnesses, you are required by law to report it to the following office. Failure to do so may result in fines or punishment.

United States Department of Agriculture

Animal and Plant Health Inspection Service

Federal Building

Hyattsville, MD 20782

Reportable diseases include but are not limited to avian flu or bird flu, chronic respiratory disease, and paratyphoid.

Common diseases that affect poultry include:

- **Air-sac disease:** This disease is similar to chronic respiratory disease, except air-sac disease is found in chicks as well as older chickens. Symptoms to look for are nasal discharge, rattled breathing and wheezing, and loss of appetite. Treat with antibiotics.

- **Avian influenza or bird flu:** This spreads quickly through a flock. Symptoms associated with bird flu include sudden death, dark wattles and combs, soft eggshells or no shell, fever, sneezing, coughing, watery eyes, diarrhea, and loss of appetite. The cause is a type A influenza virus. **Bird flu is required to be reported to the U.S. Department of Agriculture.**

- **Breast blister:** This affects the keel or breastbone of the chicken. It is a large blister that becomes a callous and forms when the breast bone leans against a roost with sharp corners, wire flooring, or wet, packed bedding. To treat, open and drain the blister and apply an antibacterial ointment. Prevention includes wrapping sharp corners of the coop in a softer material, keeping the bedding dry and clean, and not using wire flooring for the entire coop.

- **Bumble foot:** This affects the chicken's foot pad, where an abscess will form. The chicken may be resistant to walking. To treat, you may need to take the bird to your vet for antibiotic injections. Keep the foot clean, and keep the chicken on deep, soft, bedding. This is not contagious for other birds, but it may cause impetigo or skin infection in humans.

- **Cage layer fatigue:** Cage layer fatigue is a nutritional disease in chickens and other poultry when their legs becoming bowed or the bones become soft. This is often associated with osteoporosis and is usually observed in egg laying hens. It is caused by a deficiency of calcium, Vitamin D, or phosphorous. Prevention is the key. Providing your flock with nutrient-rich feed will help to keep them healthy.

- **Campylobacteriosis, also known as liver disease:** This disease affects the intestines. It is chronic and spreads slowly. Symptoms include watery diarrhea; scaly, shrunken comb; weight loss; and death of apparently healthy birds. There is no known treatment at this time, so prevention will be key to keeping your flock safe. Keep the coop clean, isolate sick birds from your flock, do not mix birds from different sources, and keep rodents out because they carry disease.

- **Cholera, acute:** This is a curious disease with no known cure. Birds die suddenly, and it spreads rapidly. Symptoms include fever, increased thirst, mucous discharge from the nose and mouth, bluish comb and wattles, and diarrhea. Prevent this disease by avoiding already mature birds that you do not know the health history of, keeping the coop clean, not mixing birds from different sources, and providing good nutrition. This can occur in birds of any age, but if you purchase a mature bird, you do not know if it may be a carrier of the disease. If you identify this disease, you still have time to save the uninfected flock. A chronic form of cholera is rare in chickens.

- **Chronic respiratory disease:** Symptoms to identify this condition are raspy breathing, coughing, sneezing, nasal discharge, and squeaky crow. Antibiotics can be used for treatment, but survivors typically remain carriers. Prevention includes vaccination, keeping the coop clean and well ventilated, and minimizing stress. **This is a disease you will need to report to the USDA.**

- **Colibacillosis:** This disease is also called E. coli infection. Symptoms include fever, swollen joints, lameness, and diarrhea. Treatment includes antibiotics, but they need to be administered in the early stages of the disease to be effective. Prevention includes good sanitation, rodent control, and hatching healthy eggs.

- **Conjunctivitis:** This disease affects the eyes. Signs that your bird has conjunctivitis are if it is rubbing the eyes with its wing, avoiding sunlight, and cloudiness in the eyes. This condition does not spread from bird to bird. It is caused by infection, vitamin A deficiency, and ammonia fumes from excessive accumulation of bird droppings. Prevention entails keeping the coop clean and the bedding dry, and providing good nutrition. Treatment includes increased vitamin A and a visit to your vet if the symptoms persist.

- **Marek's disease:** This disease attacks the organs, nerves, and skin. It is more common in larger breeds than in bantams. Symptoms are enlarged feather follicles or white bumps that scab over, dehydration, rapid weight loss, stilted gait, wing or leg paralysis, and death. There is no known treatment. Remove infected birds from your flock; you will most likely need to kill them. Prevention includes vaccination and good sanitation. Marek's does not affect humans.

- **Newcastle disease:** Newcastle is also called avian distemper and domestic Newcastle. It affects the respiratory system and nervous system. The whole flock can be infected in about a week if the disease is not caught and treated. Symptoms include wheezing, gasping, and coughing followed by drooping wings or dragging legs. Help prevent Newcastle through vaccination, clean coops, and good overall care of your birds through good sanitation and a balanced diet. Treatment includes separating birds from the healthy flock and keeping them warm and well fed. Then watch for the secondary signs as in drooping wings and dragging legs. Take the birds to the vet if symptoms persist. Humans can catch an eye infection from handling sick birds, so use rubber gloves and wash your hands to keep from spreading the virus.

- **Omphalitis:** This disease is present at the time of hatching from an incubator. The cause is typically poor sanitation in the incubator. High humidity during incubation can prevent the chick's navel from healing properly. Also, infection could set in if contaminated dropping are on the hatching eggs or if hatching eggs are cracked. Chicks, up to 4 weeks old, will have a drooping head, mushy or scabby navel, and lack of interest in food and water. There is no cure available; the sick chicks will die or need to be killed. The best way to prevent this is to hatch clean, uncracked eggs in a clean incubator with proper temperatures.

- **Osteopetrosis:** Osteopetrosis affects the bones. It is a retrovirus. Symptoms are thickened leg bones, stilted gait, and stunting. This condition often occurs in combination with lymphoid leukosis, a disease of the blood-forming organs. There is no treatment. Prevention includes purchasing your chicks from a reputable buyer and knowing their background, not reusing chick boxes, not raising chickens on wire, and avoiding flock-wide injections or vaccinations using one needle.

- **Paratyphoid:** This is a common disease that affects the digestive organs and possibly the entire body. It is caused from a salmonella virus in litter and soil. In young chicks, symptoms include dead embryos at the time of hatch, poor growth, increased thirst, huddling in around heat with ruffled feathers, increased chirping, swelling in both eyes, diarrhea, and dehydration. This disease has no treatment, and survivors will be carriers. Prevention is difficult, but keep coops, bedding, and water clean; collect hatching eggs often; and replace nesting litter often. **This is a disease you will need to report to the USDA.**

- **Pasted vent:** Chicks mostly suffer from pasted vent. This occurs when feces clogs the bird's vent, and the chick has blockage when trying to defecate. If the vent seals up, death can occur. Treat this by washing the infected area with warm water and carefully picking at the adhering matter with a toothpick or something similar. Although this is common in chicks, hens are affected as well. Clean droppings that stick to vent feathers as soon as you notice it.

- **Pox (dry):** Pox affects the skin, and can appear in birds of all ages, excluding newly hatched chicks. The virus is identified by wart-like bumps found on the comb and wattles that grow larger and change in color. They start out white, turn yellow, and then proceed to a reddish-brown, gray, or black. Other symptoms include a drop in egg production, weight loss, and scabs on the head and neck. Prevention is difficult, as this virus is carried through mites and mosquitoes. Vaccination is recommended. No treatment is known, so isolate infected birds. There is no harm to humans; chicken pox in humans is a different strain of virus.

- **Staphylococcic arthritis:** This can affect the joints or the entire body. Symptoms include swollen joints, resting on hocks (the part of the leg below the thigh but above the ankle), fever, and hesitancy to move. The cause of staphylococcic arthritis is a common virus strain in the poultry environment. Treatment is obtained through antibiotics. Prevention involves keeping your chickens in uncrowded housing to prevent injuries that allow the virus to enter the body. For humans, consuming infected meat can cause food poisoning.

- **Sudden death syndrome:** This is common in broilers. Although the cause is unknown, it is suspected that giving broilers high-carb feed to induce rapid weight growth affects the heart and lungs, causing a heart attack. Postmortem findings include feed-filled intestines and bloated, bright red lungs. It has no cure, and the best prevention is to eliminate as much stress as possible in your flock's environment.

- **Thrush:** Thrush affects the upper digestive tract. Symptoms include diarrhea, weight loss, and slow growth caused by a Candida yeast-like substance that lives in the chickens' bowels. You can prevent this disease by practicing good nutrition and sanitation. Treatment includes isolating infected birds and cleaning and disinfecting coops, feeders, waterers, and bedding. Clean mouth sores with an antiseptic such as hydrogen peroxide. A home remedy to help cure your bird is to first do a "flush." Add 1 pint of molasses per 5 gallons of water and offer it to your bird for no more than eight hours. Or, give the bird an Epsom salt flush. Use 1 teaspoon of Epsom salt in ½ cup of water and squirt the solution down the bird's throat twice daily for two days or until recovery. You also can try using ½ teaspoon copper sulfate per gallon drinking water every other day. Do not use a metal waterer with this mixture.

- **Twisted leg:** Twisted leg is also known as crooked legs, valgus leg deformity, or long-bone distortion because it affects the long bones of the leg. The chicken may have a pointed protrusion at the hock joint, and affected birds sometimes walk on bruised or swollen hocks. The cause may be nutritional, genetic, or possibly due to the environment they are raised in. There is no treatment. Prevention includes raising birds on litter and not wire. Also, do not feed your birds for rapid growth. This condition will not harm humans.

- **Ulcerative Enteritis:** Ulcerative Enteritis affects poultry including chickens, ducks, turkeys and game birds. It causes inflammation and ulcers in the intestines. This can be fatal, but 90% of the time is not. It appears in both acute and chronic form. It is caused by a bacteria passed on through the feces. If another chicken pecks at feces that are infected with these bacteria, it can contract it. Sometimes, flies that have fed on contaminated feces can carry the bacteria and pass it on to other birds as well. Symptoms include blood in diarrhea, listlessness, and depression. Chickens can be treated for ulcerative enteritis by antibiotics such as streptomyocin or furazolidone added to their feed.

How to humanely euthanize

Sometimes when a chick or chicken is suffering or deformed, it is best for the bird's well being to euthanize it. A vet's price to euthanize can be very steep, but there are a couple methods to humanely do it at home that are quick and painless for the bird. Euthanizing at home also reduces stress at the end of the chicken's life — a trip to the vet will only add stress. One way to humanely kill a chicken is to remove its head with a very sharp axe or hatchet. (*Refer to Chapter 12 on how to humanely remove a chicken's head*).

When it comes to euthanizing, some chicken owners prefer to put the bird to sleep. This method works for grown chickens, as well as for chicks that are too small to have their head removed. To put a bird to sleep, soak a few rags with starter fluid, which contains ether. Place the bird in the bottom of a large container that has a tight-fitting lid, such as a 5-gallon bucket. If you are euthanizing a small chick, you can place them in a tight-sealing sandwich bag. Put the completely saturated rags in the bucket or bag with the bird and tightly seal the container; the bird will fall asleep and pass away quickly. It is very important to make sure you use enough starter fluid — it is better to use too much than too little, so be sure to thoroughly soak the rags.

No chicken owner likes to kill one of their flock, but in some cases if a bird is suffering it is best to let it go.

Parasitic Worms

Worms are a common problem in birds and poultry. The key to success is ridding the source or host of the parasite so you are not continually treating a recurring problem. A host is any living thing that provides an ideal environment for the parasite to survive. Treatment can become costly and frustrating, and parasites can become resistant to medications. Prevention and cleanliness of your bird's environment will be your best defense in this fight. Six common parasitic worms found in chickens are:

- Nemathelminthes, a type of roundworm
- Nematodes, a type of roundworm
- Acanthocephalans, a thorny-headed worm
- Platyhelminthes, a flatworm
- Cestodes, a tapeworm
- Trematodes, a flukeworm that has external suckers so it can attach to the host body

Chickens will develop a resistance to parasites over time. These microbes exist in the poultry world just like germs and common colds exist in the human world. When a chicken is ill or stressed, it is more susceptible to suffering from the consequences of these infestations. Parasites can make your bird lose weight, cause breathing problems, and block the respiratory organs and airway.

Parasites can be passed from chicken to chicken indirectly. An infected chicken can shed a worm's eggs in its excrement. Chickens tend to eat feces, and they may ingest contaminated chicken droppings. New worms will hatch in the chicken's intestines, making that chicken its home and beginning the cycle again.

Sometimes, there is an intermediate host body. For instance, a grasshopper may eat the chicken droppings infested with the parasite's eggs. Then, a chicken may eat that grasshopper, thereby ingesting the parasitic worm and starting a new cycle. This is why it is hard to prevent parasites entirely, and at some point in your ownership of chickens, you will encounter this problem. By keeping your chickens' home and environment clean, including their feed and water, you will be able to keep most illnesses at bay. Like children, chickens will get sick from time to time. By educating yourself and spending time with your chickens, you will be able to catch any signs of sickness in your flock. Early detection will help care for them and potentially save their lives.

Mites and Lice

Parasitic worms live inside a host's body, whereas mites and lice live outside the body. Their damage can cause mild irritation, infection, and possibly death. They carry diseases from bird to bird. If not treated immediately, external parasites spread quickly. Their ability to multiply, compounded with the fact they are microscopic, make it very difficult to maintain control of these parasites.

Mites are more active at night, which is a good time to check your birds. They come in a variety of types:

- **Red mites:** These are more common in litter-raised birds than in caged birds and are predominant in warmer climates or during summer months. One female mite lays as many as 120,000 eggs. Chicks are vulnerable and can die if you have a severe red mite infestation in your flock.

- **Scaly leg mite:** These mites burrow under the unfeathered part of skin on a chicken's legs. Infestation causes the scales on the bird's legs to raise up and away from the skin. Visually check your bird to see that its legs and scales are healthy. In a severe case, these mites will move to wattles and combs. Treat them with petroleum jelly.

- **Feather mites:** These mites live in the bird's plumage and damage the chicken's coat by eating the feathers. They are not common in North America.

- **Fowl mites:** Fowl mites are very common and are found in cooler climates. Symptoms of infestation include large numbers of mites on the skin during the day, scabby skin around the vent, darkened feathers around the vent, and mites crawling on eggs in the nest. Using a pesticide approved for poultry will help control infestation. The appropriate pesticide will list on the bottle that it is approved for poultry. The danger involved with the fowl mite is that it lives its entire life on a chicken, which is about a week. This means a higher rate of reproduction as it goes through its life cycle.

Lice also come in a variety of species. Some lice prefer chickens, and no other type of bird or mammal. Different types of lice have different preferences for the parts of the body they feast on. These parasites feed on the feathers and skin, but some varieties eat through the skin to get to the blood.

- **Head lice:** This is the most common lice infestation. The Polish and Cochin chicken breeds are susceptible to head lice because of the amount of plumage around their faces. Spraying them lightly with poultry-approved pesticide will help prevent lice. Be careful to avoid their eyes.

- **Wing lice:** They like to hide under a chicken's wing and may also infect the vent area and breast.

- **Body lice:** If a chicken is infested with body lice, you will notice scabs on the bird's skin and egg masses at the base of the feathers.

- **Fluff lice:** This is one of the least invasive forms of lice. It is predominantly common in the South. They live on the fluff and cause little irritation because they are not very active.

Again, the best prevention is honing good sanitation practices and keeping chicken bedding clean and dry. Check your birds at least once a month for mite or lice infection. Disinfectant spray is the best defense for controlling these external parasites. Make sure any chemicals you use on your flock or within their environment are safe for you and your birds.

You can find a plethora of products to help prevent or conquer mites and lice at your local pet store, co-op, or online. Poultry Protector is one product that you might choose to use. It is organic and can be used on your birds and in their coop. The average cost for a bottle is between $6 and $12.95. This product can be found on these websites:

- Smith Poultry & Game Bird Supply (*www.poultrysupplies.com*) — This site offers a variety of products for caring for your flock. It includes products for your birds as well as their surroundings.

- American Livestock and Pet Supply, Inc. (*www.americanlivestock.com*) — This website offers products for chickens and other farm animals.

- IPS-CareFree Enzymes, Inc. (*www.carefreeenzymes.com*) — This site offers a variety of organic and chemical-free products for chickens and other farm animals.

- Another product that kills mites and lice is Orange Guard, which is a water-based pest control product found at Orange Guard (*www.orangeguard.com*) and on Amazon (*www.amazon.com*).

You can choose from a variety of shelf products when purchasing insecticides. Shop around and see which work best to fit your needs and your lifestyle. Be sure to keep you, your family, and your birds safe and healthy so you can enjoy a long and satisfying relationship.

Stress

One last key element regarding your birds' welfare is stress. Chickens are deeply affected by stress. Causes of anxiety can include loud noises, bad weather, predators, overcrowding in a coop, excessive bright light, not enough bright light, the lack of a regular routine, and living with other aggressive birds. Some stressors, such as loud noises, are common and affect most birds, but for the most part, anything can trigger a stressed reaction in a chicken. Why is stress so bad? Too much stress produces higher levels of hormones in chickens, which can be stored in their muscles. If these chickens are used for slaughter, you may be consuming unnecessary hormones. The muscles also tend to be tougher in highly stressed birds. This is why cage-free birds often are more tender than commercial birds. But this is not the only reason to limit stress in a chicken's life. Stressed birds are much more likely to contract illnesses because of weakened immune systems, and sick birds can ruin an entire flock.

Stress also has an effect on egg layers and they may reduce the amount of eggs they produce. The quality of the egg may decrease as well because of the excessive hormones produced in the chicken's body and passed down to the egg.

Symptoms of a bird with anxiety are loss of appetite, changes in normal behavior patterns, diarrhea, labored breathing, and sometimes death. To help prevent stressful conditions, make sure your flock has a clean, safe, and dry environment. Provide adequate ventilation and plenty of sunshine. The great part is you do not need to have years of experience to know what constitutes a happy home.

To get the most enjoyment from your birds, strive to keep them as stress free as possible. Certain types of breeds are heartier and able to endure stress and harsher environments more than other breeds. If you decide you want to breed chickens, the next chapter will provide insights on the process.

CASE STUDY: GIRLS' MOVIE NIGHT

Carol Peluso

CLASSIFIED CASE STUDIES

TM

directly from the experts

Carol Peluso has "movie night" at her house, but it is not your typical showing. "It is actually Chicken Movie Night," says Peluso. "We watch any and all chicken programs available on television. I cover the couch in old sheets in preparation for the show. I invite one or more of the girls in to watch television and share grapes with me ... The girls enjoyed the crowing in the background from the chickens on the show." Peluso refers to her hens as "the girls."

Movie night started when Peluso was having her coop built. The chickens had the run of the backyard, and they soon learned that Peluso was "the source of all food." Everyday when she returned home from work, the chickens would be on the back door stoop, just waiting for her. Several were bold enough to come into the house every time the door was open. Thus began movie night.

In Phoenix, Arizona where Peluso lives, heat is a major concern for her pets. Her coop, which was designed by a family member who is an architect, and built by another family member who is an engineer, was constructed to ensure there was adequate ventilation. "It helps to have talented and kind family members," says Peluso. "For us in Arizona, airflow and coolness were priority for their housing. It is critical to keeping the chickens healthy."

Her coop houses six hens, which include: one purebred Barred Rock, one purebred Rhode Island red, two purebred Americauna's, and two mixed breed Easter eggers. The coop is 9' x 10'. It is connected to a large run. The run is about 12' x 20' that also encloses a large tree for shade and some other landscape elements to enhance the chicken's environment. The building has two solid sides and two screened sides to allow for ample airflow. The roof is made of tin. Additional shade is provided in the run with partial overhang areas of shade cloth.

Cool, clean water is provided at all times, both indoors and out. All dry food is fed indoors with treats and table scraps fed outside. Peluso also provides several shallow "wading pans" for the hens. During the summer months, especially, they love to stand in the water and cool their feet. Blue ice packs that people use for picnics and lunch boxes come in handy for the chickens to sit or stand on. It refreshes the hens.

Peluso has advice for new chicken owners: "Advance planning for your chicken's housing is a good idea. Check out what works for others in your area and expand on that. Get your chicks from a local breeder if possible. Proper housing for your climate, good quality food, and fresh water are of course necessary."

Chapter 9:
Breeding Chickens

Whether you already have some chickens or you are a novice chicken owner, breeding chickens can be a great way to enhance your experience. Breeding provides you with an opportunity to create the type of bird you want. These birds are designed for your purposes and to fit into your needs. Whether you are doing it for a hobby, for food, or for money, you will be able to achieve your goals with time, patience, and knowledge. Breeding chickens is not recommended for city dwellers, unless you have enough space to accommodate your birds. If you end up with a large quantity of birds while you are breeding, you may find yourself with a lack of space. However, if you do have room for your coop and run, as well as an area for your incubator and chicks, you can successfully breed chickens in your urban home.

Consider what breeding a flock of chickens entails before you begin your new endeavor. This process has many components, although the rewards are worth it. Once you have the physical materials you need, it is time to get started on your plan of action. You must have a clear idea of the process because you do not want find yourself at any point wondering what you should do next. Live animals will not wait for you. Each day will be an adventure, and if you are not prepared, you might miss out.

In the beginning, it is important to start small. As a new breeder, you will want to gain some experience before you tackle large amounts of birds. Start small by owning and breeding one rooster and two hens. Do not get two roosters because they will fight for male dominance. In the future, you may want to produce more than one type of chicken, and at that point you will need more than one rooster. But in the beginning, keep it simple. It is natural to want to take on more, but be aware that if you are successful from the very beginning and your hens' eggs are fertilized, you could end up with many eggs. Those eggs will hatch baby chicks, and before you know it, your flock is more than you may be able to handle.

Selecting the Right Breed

Part of your plan will be deciding which breed of chicken to raise. Take into consideration the size of the bird and the amount of room you have to offer. Decide upon the reasons you want your birds, and also consider other family members or children who will be affected by the choice to raise chickens.

Breeding egg layers

If you are seeking to breed birds for their egg-laying ability, you can choose the type of eggs you will get by the bird you intend on breeding. It is fine to inbreed for show birds, meaning that you use the same birds from the same family, but it does not work for egg layers. Crossbreeding is a successful method to create hearty egg layers. Crossbreeding entails taking a hen from one family of chickens and breeding it with a rooster of another bloodline. Also, a good egg layer does not necessarily carry that particular gene and those genes are not passed directly from mother to chick.

Breeding for meat

Even if you are not raising your chickens for meat, there will come a time when you will need to cull chickens from the flock, especially if you are breeding. Often you will find a weak or sick chick, even under the best conditions, and instead of trying to nurse it back to health, most of the time the humane choice is to kill the bird. This is not easy for some animal owners, and if you do not feel comfortable taking on this task, have a plan so that when the time arrives, you are not in a panic. If you know other chicken owners, talk with them to see what they do in these circumstances. They may know someone to refer you to for these purposes.

Breeding for show

Breeding for show requires more attention to detail when you purchase the bird. When you choose an ornamental bird, you do not want to reproduce its flaws. This is true when you make your selection for any breed, but a show bird's main purpose is its physical attributes. Do not mistakenly think certain genes will not appear in your future flock, because there are no guarantees. You do not want to set yourself up to be disappointed. Pick a bird that has the most ideal traits for its breed, and you can then improve one trait at a time. Part of the enjoyment of breeding for show is creating the most perfect bird for you.

Once you select your breeds, you will need to find high-quality birds to get started. You can find quality breeders through other chicken owners. It is always better to get a recommendation and purchase a bird from someone you trust. When buying an adult bird, or a pullet or cockerel, it is easy to be misled on the quality of the bird you are getting. Even experienced chicken owners can be duped when buying an older bird because you really do not know its exact age or history. If you do not know anyone who can give you a reference, ask around at your local pet store or co-op. Chicken owners most likely frequent these places, and salespeople are there to help you. They almost always can point you in the right direction. If this is not an option, check local classified ads. You may not know your seller, but do not be hesitant in asking questions. Inspect your bird for any physical deformities or parasite infestation. If the bird looks and sounds healthy, and has the qualities you want to breed, take your bird home.

Selective Breeding and Cross Breeding

Selective breeding entails mating two birds of the same breed that have the desired characteristics you are looking for to produce a new bird that will hopefully have all of the qualities you want. This can help establish a new bloodline for your flock. **Cross breeding** is taking two or more different breeds of birds and mating them together to achieve a new breed that has the most promising characteristics you want. These are known as hybrid chicken breeds. Creating the perfect bird is not always successful as some genes may not be passed down to the new chick on the first try or ever. However, if you keep breeding your chickens, you should be able to get the outcome you desire.

Types of hybrid chickens:

1. Golden comet = crossing a leghorn and Rhode Island red
2. Isa brown = crossing Rhode Island reds and Rhode Island whites
3. Daisy belles = crossing Rhode Island reds Sussex
4. Black sex link chickens = crossing Rhode Island reds or New Hampshires and barred rock hens
5. Cream legbar = crossing a brown leghorn with a barred rock and Aracauna

You can create your own breed. Just like dogs and other domestic animals that are crossbred, chickens can have many types of breeds in their bloodline if they are not a purebred. These breed mixtures can provide beautiful and distinct birds.

Here is an example if you want to breed blue laced red wyandottes:

If you mate:

- Blue with blue you will get: 50% blue, 25% black, and 25% splash
- Blue with a splash you will get 50% blue, 50% splash
- Blue with black you will get 50% blue, 50% black
- Splash with black you will get 100% blue
- Black with black you will get 100% black
- Splash with splash you will get 100% splash

Roosters

Roosters, or cocks, are male chickens. Young roosters are called cockerels, and castrated roosters are called capons. You will need to have one rooster to fertilize your hen's eggs. Roosters can have an aggressive nature, especially if you own more than one. The chicken's innate need to fulfill the pecking order can cause them to fight, even to the death, for dominance. If you plan on having more than one rooster, you may need to separate them from each other, but keep them with several hens. Chickens are social creatures that need to interact with other birds or people for their overall well-being.

Roosters are known for their crowing. Typically, roosters crow at the crack of dawn, but they can crow at any hour, even in the middle of the night. They do not usually do this; often it is triggered by a noise that startles the bird.

Roosters are also the more colorful gender. Their markings are brighter and more intense than most of their female counterparts' markings. They also care for their hens and chicks. If a rooster finds food, he will call out to the rest of the flock and indicate by the tone in his voice that food is available. A rooster also may pick a favorite among the flock to mate with. He will save the best food for her and is more gentle with her during mating. Roosters are known to guide their little chicks when walking around the yard, and they will fight to the death to protect their flock from predators. They are loyal to their families.

Taming a mean rooster

Mean roosters have turned many people off from raising chickens. With their well-developed spurs, rooters can inflict serious wounds when they see you as a threat to their flock dominance. Each time you enter the coop, you will have to remind your rooster that you are the top dog of the flock by following the steps given in this section.

An alpha rooster usually dominates the pecking order of a flock by getting first dibs at food, water, and hens. The hens also have an alpha hen that is the boss. Unlike the roosters, hen social order is harder to see, but it is there. The alpha rooster asserts his dominance constantly. If another chicken attempts to eat first or another rooster tries to mate a hen, the alpha male will rush over and administer a good peck or even pummel the out-of-bounds interloper with beak, claws, and wings.

Your job is to make sure you are not the victim of such an attack. Starting when the chickens are small, take a few minutes each day to observe their behavior. When the chicks start to fight (or spar), break them apart by gently pushing them back with your fingers. Each fight you see, do the same thing. This will let the flock know that you are in charge. As they get older, you will still have to reinforce your dominance. It is fine to pick up a rooster and pet him. But a rooster should not be eager to approach you. If he does, he will think that he is the top chicken not you. It will not hurt to take an occasional swat at him if he seems too comfortable with you.

Do not let the rooster eat before the hens. Doing so will give him the cue that he is dominant in the flock when in reality you should be the dominant member (in his mind) of the flock. In essence, you are top rooster and need to allow the hens to eat before him, the less-dominant rooster. If he tries to come to the feeder first, push him away so the hens eat first. After the hens are eating, it is fine if the rooster begins to eat. If a rooster tries to breed a hen in your presence, push him off and chase him away. It is the same concept as eating; he has to wait until you leave to be able to breed the hens.

The main thing when it comes to roosters is that you have to be on guard at all times. If these techniques do not work, or if you are unable to be consistent in asserting your dominance, it might be safer for the rooster to be destined for the soup bowl.

Broody Hens

An egg-laying hen will produce eggs every one to two days. The average egg-laying cycle takes about 25 to 26 hours to complete. Right before a hen lays an egg, her hormone levels rise. This gives the hen her "homemaking" initiative, and she seeks out a nest and lays her egg. Most of the time, the hormone level drops, and the hen leaves her nest and will return when she is ready to lay her next egg. Sometimes, though, the hormone level does not drop as quickly. This happens more frequently in winter when not as much daylight is available and makes the hen want to sit on her eggs. As each day progresses, the hen leaves the nest less and less, instead collecting her eggs and sitting on them. This is known as going broody. Hens then like to wait until they have laid about 10 eggs, which can take about ten days if they lay one egg a day. Hens do this because they think they are going to hatch the eggs, and instinctively, they want their chicks to hatch at the same time, which is 21 days later.

When a hen is broody, she becomes very territorial. She may make low, growling noises if she is approached or if she feels her eggs are in danger. Mother hen may even peck at you. She will leave her nest only for food and drink, and some hens do not even do that, which may be dangerous to their health. They may defecate on the eggs, which you will need to clean if you intend on hatching them.

Certain breeds of chickens tend to go broody more than others. Examples of broody chicken breeds are australorp, brahma, buckeye, and chantecler. Other breeds have been bred to remove the broody gene. Examples of non-broody birds are Rhode Island reds, leghorns, Minorcas, and barred rock.

Collecting the eggs each day will help prevent a chicken from going broody. If the broodiness is a big problem, you may want to remove the nesting boxes. A hen's broodiness is a problem if your bird is no longer producing additional eggs, or if she is aggressive and preventing other hens from laying eggs. A hen will find anything that resembles a nest to lay her eggs in, such as a planter or crate. Once she is on there, it will be hard to remove her because she will be feisty because her hormones kicked in.

If you want your hen to become broody, for instance if she is producing more eggs than you need, leave several golf balls or plastic eggs in her nest to induce the process. Chickens can be tricked into thinking they are hatching their own eggs. They will not know the difference. You can even do this to help move her cycle along. She will be broody for an average of 21 days if she sits on her eggs, and when they do not hatch she will lose interest and go back to her normal daily routine.

Mating

There are several different mating techniques you can try to mate chickens depending on your skill level and the number of birds you have. One type of mating is flock mating, which is not recommended for the novice breeder and chicken owner because it can produce a large quantity of birds, and as a novice you may not be ready to handle so many birds immediately. With flock mating, flocks are made up of approximately 14 hens and one rooster, and the rooster can mate freely with the hens. This is a good method if you want to produce many chicks. The main negative aspect is that you cannot keep an accurate record of which hens the rooster is mating with and how many eggs they are producing. Also, you have less control over the quality of the birds you are creating. This may be a method to choose once you have more experience and plan on having a large flock of chickens.

The other method of mating is in pairs or trios. One or two hens grouped with one rooster will help control the quality of the chickens you hatch. This is especially important for breeders who will be showing their birds. You can do this by putting the birds in pens or cages together. Their natural instincts will take over.

Some roosters will court their hens first. If a rooster has many hens to choose from, the courting appears to be less frequent. To court, the rooster may circle the hen, and she will bend over in front of him. He will then jump on the hen's back, holding on to her with his beak and claws. They will mate for several seconds, and the process will be over.

Some roosters are more aggressive than others when mating. Often a chicken will have feathers missing and scratches on her back from a rooster. Although most chickens are compliant when a rooster is ready to mate, some hens run away. The rooster may accept this but also may chase the chicken and forcibly mate with her. The mating ritual is initiated by chemical changes in the birds, and this usually makes the birds compatible for reproducing.

Using only two or three birds allows you to keep excellent records. You will want to do this so you know which birds produced a particular offspring. Write down the dates, the traits, and the birds that you used to create your breed. You may want to change the traits or reproduce them, and your memory may not always be accurate.

Nesting Boxes

Nesting boxes, where broody hens sit on their eggs, are an essential part of the mating and breeding process. You can make them out of wood or plastic, or you can purchase pre-made ones. You should have one box for every two to four hens you own. Some breeds will not want to share their nesting box, like a Cornish chicken, while breeds such as silkies would prefer to climb into one nesting box and hatch their eggs together. If you are unsure of whether your birds will like sharing their nest, plan on getting more boxes.

Nesting boxes are typically placed in the coop and can be on one level, or stacked on top of each other. If you stack them, make sure they are not higher than the roosts in your coop. Otherwise, the birds will want to sleep in them, and you may run out of room for your broody chickens. The nests should be about 12 inches wide by 12 inches long by 12 inches deep. You can customize boxes to fit your needs, but that size should work fine for your flock.

Wood shavings or straw makes a comfortable bed. Sawdust is popular because it is inexpensive, and it absorbs any droppings, but it can cause the birds to develop breathing problems. Commercial chicken bedding can be purchased from a farm and feed supply store. Some of the recycled wood bedding that is offered works well because it has less moisture content than fresh wood shavings. Drier wood means less chance for mold and mites, thereby keeping your chicken healthy and happy. If you prefer not to purchase commercial bedding, you can always use straw or hay. The main objective is to find a filler that works for both you and your flock.

Always keep the bedding clean and dry and use 2 to 4 inches of bedding. After all of your hard work in selecting a breed and mating your birds, you do not want to have your fertilized eggs ruined because they sat in a dirty bed. Cleaning the box once a week or more frequently as needed should be sufficient.

Purchasing Fertile Eggs

If you do not want to go through the process of finding the perfect hen and rooster to start your flock, you can purchase fertile eggs to hatch at home. This will save you the time of searching for a suitable pair of birds to mate, and waiting for them to produce fertile eggs.

You can find a hatchery locally or online. Many websites will let you shop for the breed of chick you want, like Murray McMurray Hatchery *(www. mcmurrayhatchery.com)*, and they will ship your eggs to you to start your cycle of breeding.

You will not be able to select the gender of your bird using this method. Instead, you must wait until the chick is old enough to determine its sex. You also will want to purchase more eggs than you actually need to increase your chances of getting both sexes in your batch. And, not all eggs will endure the shipping process so it will be beneficial to order extra so you are not disappointed in the amount of chicks you hatch.

Artificial Insemination

Although mentioned here, artificial insemination should be reserved for a more experienced flock owner. This is a simple procedure, but it takes time to learn how to handle your birds and perform a successful insemination. It is also a good idea to have an assistant help you. You can find the necessary equipment at drug stores or in the pharmacy section of another store. You will need:

- **Glass eye cup**
- **Medicine eye dropper**
- **1 cc plastic syringe**
- **Glass rod**
- **Rooster:** Mature, healthy, without physical deformities
- **Two hens:** Need to be in production and should not have eggs already in the lower part of their oviducts

Here are the steps you will need to take to inseminate your birds:

1. First, pick up the rooster and hold him with his head facing you. He should be young and vital, meaning he is alert and active. He will constantly be watching the flock and his surroundings, and walking around his property. A vital rooster will not be sulking or sleeping during the day.

2. Take the right leg between the first and second fingers of your left hand. Be gentle and do not use loud noises, as these will scare the bird. Then, hold the left leg with the second and third fingers of your left hand. This will keep your right hand free. The rooster probably will fight you this entire time. Wearing rubber gloves and a rubber apron will help to protect you. Remain calm and firm. Your assistant should be nearby to help hold onto or calm the bird if it is flighty.

3. Using your right hand, stroke the back of the rooster from the midpoint of its back to the tail. While you are holding him with your left hand, use your fingers to massage his abdomen. Your assistant may need to help you to hold the bird and keep him calm.

4. After several strokes, move your right hand to a position where it can apply pressure on both sides of the vent. Keep massaging and applying pressure with your left hand.

5. At this point, the copulary organ should extend. A slight milking action may be required to increase semen flow. Your assistant should collect the semen in the eyecup. The volume of discharge varies. Some birds pass feces as well as semen, but be careful to only collect semen; otherwise the sample will be contaminated. You must use the semen within the first two hours of collection, as the fertility decreases with passing time. You can collect semen every two to four days from the rooster.

6. Next you will gather your hens and hold them the same way you held the rooster. Be gentle with them, as they are more delicate than the males. Stimulation in the female is similar to stimulation in the male. Stroke her back from the midpoint of the back to the tail. As you apply the pressure and the massage, the chicken's vent will exert itself, and an orifice will appear on the left side.

7. The assistant should then fill the medical dropper or the syringe with semen and inserts it into the chicken's orifice, about ¼ to 1 inch deep. Once all of the semen is used, relax the pressure on the female's body so the oviduct can return to the normal state, which will naturally push the insemination forward.

Once some of your eggs are fertilized, you can continue the insemination process once a week to maintain a satisfactory level of chicks. This can be a great experience for you as a chicken owner, but you need to be sure you have a clear understanding of what you are doing. If you are unsure of the proper insemination practices, you could hurt your birds or yourself. You may want to see if a nearby vet or chicken fancier practices artificial insemination and ask whether you can watch a demonstration.

After insemination, hens can store semen in their body for two weeks. If you decided to let your chickens mate naturally, isolate your hen for the first three weeks to be sure her eggs are from your rooster. If you are not concerned about fertilization from another bird, it is all right to allow the birds to be together.

Chicken Sexing

In new and young chicks, it is very difficult — if not impossible — to determine their sex until they mature. Some breeds have markings or distinctive colors that help identify gender much earlier than with other birds. There will be some chicks that are hard to identify and you may not be able to identify the chicken's sex at all. Even experienced chicken owners have difficulty at times determining the sex. Do not get frustrated, and understand that this is a hard process. If you really must know the sex of your chick, and you are not able to do it on your own, consider taking it to a local hatchery or farm and ask for assistance.

When you ordered your fertile eggs, you may have specifically requested hens or roosters. Keep in mind that one rooster is all you need for a flock. If you ordered a mixture of eggs and are unsure of the sex of the chicks, you can use a process called **sexing** to tell whether your bird is a hen or rooster. The first way is called **vent sexing;** the other is called **feather sexing.** Either method can be done as early as 1 day old, but it is not an easy process because a chick's sexual organs are inside its body, and sexing should not be done by someone with little or no experience.

Vent sexing

Vent sexing is difficult for the novice chicken owner but can be learned. The best way to start out is to purchase already-sexed chicks and practice on them. Always remember that these are delicate babies that you need to handle with care. To vent sex a chick, it must be between 12 and 36 hours old. The vent is harder to open after the first 36 hours of life, and the process could hurt the chick. Use clean hands with short fingernails. Have bright lighting so you will be able to see the tiny opening.

Hold the chick in your left hand on its back with the rump away from you. The legs should be between the first and second fingers of your left hand. Place one thumb on either side of the vent and apply light pressure. You will need to roll the skin away on each side of the vent. Warning: This may cause the chick to poop. Just clean up and try again.

After you apply light pressure, inspect your chick's vent. If the chick is a male, you will see a bump about the size of a match head or smaller. This is the intermittent organ and should be in the center of the vent. The organ is usually dark, but in light pigmented birds, it will be pinkish. For female chicks, you should not see any bumps once you open the vent. A bump, no matter how small, always indicates the chick is a male. Female birds may have a dark spot inside the vent, which may look like a bump but is actually just color. You may need a magnifying glass to help see.

Do not make the process longer than it needs to be to reduce the chance of harming your bird. If you are having trouble determining the sex, put the chick back under its heating lamp and try again later. If you apply too much pressure on the chick's vent, you may expose some of its internal organs. If this happens, release pressure and make sure the bird's vent is closed with the organs back inside. Wipe the chick clean and put it back under its heat source. Do not sex this chicken further. The chick should heal properly, as its body is still developing, and the organs will move back into place. Do not sex bantam chicks because their size and body parts are very small, and even the most delicate of handlers may harm them because of their fragile nature.

Novice chicken owners or owners who are new to sexing chicks often make mistakes in determining gender. Do not feel discouraged if the rooster you thought you had begins to lay eggs or the hen you have been doting on starts to crow. Even experienced owners make mistakes because the process is very challenging.

If you decide you do not want to try vent sexing your chick, you can try feather sexing.

Feather sexing

Feather sexing, or sexing by appearance, is the second method for determining gender. Physical characteristics that appear as the chicks grow can indicate whether the bird is male or female. Feathers are the first indicator. Certain breeds of chickens such as the black sex link and the red sex link show differences between males and females through genetic traits. The black sex link female is born completely black. A black sex link male hatches black with one white spot atop its heads. The red sex link female is colored buff or red as a chick, and the red sex link males hatches white. While most breeds do not have this distinction, you can still use a chicken's feathers to determine its sex. Patterns and markings are usually different for the hen than for the rooster. As the chicks feather out, you can get a better view of the patterns. The colors of the feathers are another indication. Males are more colorful and their coats are made up of more vibrant colors. The hackle feathers around the neck are pointed on a male and rounded on a female. These secondary characteristics should give you the clues you need to identify the gender.

If you still cannot tell from the feathers, look at other physical traits. Combs and wattles tend to grow faster in males. In most cases they are larger as well. The legs and feet of roosters are typically bigger and grow more quickly, too. Lastly, if the feathers and body parts do not give away the bird's gender, its behavior can lead you to the answer. Males will have a more dominant personality and may even scuttle with other males.

Once you determine the sexes of your flock, you will want to separate them as they mature into pullets and cockerels. Males and females grow at a different rate, and separating the birds keeps them on an even keel. The cockerels frequently chase the pullets to mate with them, and separation will help control breeding. If you fail to separate your chicks, your flock can grow quickly before you are ready.

You now have all of the resources as an educated chicken owner to breed or purchase your flock. After you purchase and set up everything, you can focus on caring for and raising your birds. Enjoy them. Do not worry if you make mistakes because everyone does, especially when trying something new. Chickens are resilient animals and can endure a surprising amount. The added tenderness you provide when caring for them will enhance your experience and add to the quality of the birds. They will provide you with much happiness and food for you and your family.

CASE STUDY: A FARM FULL OF CHICKENS

Annette and Kathleen Fernholz

The Fernholz sisters decided to raise chickens as their mother had a real devotion to caring for her birds. They keep around 150 Bovan Goldline hens and follow organic standards to produce a high-quality egg, rich in omega-3 fatty acid. Their chickens run free around the homestead and eat organically raised feeds, such as buckwheat, barley, and flax that help boost the omega-3 in the eggs. They also have four acres of garden to provide the local community with fair cost of production produce through a Community Supported Agriculture (CSA) program. The rest of the 240-acre farm is farmed organically by three of their brothers.

They caution beginning farmers to keep meticulous records in order to track costs of production versus the price of eggs. Feed costs can quickly exceed the price of eggs. The Fernholz's also suggest that a chicken producer should make certain they enjoy working with chickens, as there will most likely be some years where the egg enterprise may not break even with cost of production. Starting with a small number of birds will go a long way to helping understand the bird and to help a beginning farmer develop a market. One way to help with markets is to join with other egg producers in the area to set a minimum price for the eggs so no one person can undercut the other.

Earthrise Farm is a busy place with chickens scratching around the grounds and workers busy with the chicken chores. The most time-consuming chores on Earthrise Farm are: collecting, cleaning, candling, and packaging the eggs, cleaning the hen houses, and distribution of eggs to CSA members and local grocery stores. They recommend a beginning organic-egg farmer have an insulated barn that is heated to 55°F in the winter to ensure egg production stays steady. Securing an affordable and nearby source of organic grain is also a necessity to the organic egg producer.

At Earthrise Farm, the Fernholz sisters are accomplishing their mission of providing the local community with nutritious, fairly priced food along with community education.

Chapter 10:
Training and Showing Your Chickens

Besides raising chickens for meat, eggs, or sale, many chicken owners raise their chickens to train and show. Training and showing chickens can be a rewarding hobby for children and adults alike. The key to a successful show bird is good training and familiarity with human contact.

Training Your Birds

When training your flock, the most important thing to remember is that chickens are easily startled. Do not scare, trap, or chase your birds — the result of these actions is a flock that is not trained, but rather scared of you. Remember that not all chickens like to be held, and they should not be forced into being held. Chickens are quick, so their lessons need to be quick as well; forcing a chicken to work on a trick for too long will result in a bird that does not like being around humans.

Chickens have four basic response patterns: tugging or pulling, raking, pecking or grabbing, and picking up objects, and each of these actions can be used in different tricks. Work on one trick at a time that focuses on one of the response patterns. For instance, a good starting point is to train your chickens to come when you call. This will also serve a productive purpose because at the end of the night, when you want to put your flock to bed, they can be trained to come at the sound of a bell. Other tricks are teaching your chicken to pick up something specific, like a toy, or pull on a string, or have he or she ring their own bell. Reinforced behavior is the key through treats and sound. It is important to reinforce positive behavior while the bird is doing the action or immediately thereafter. This will help instill the behavior.

When teaching a trick, first plan your course of action. You will not have much time to work with your birds if you do not have a plan because the chickens may be frightened or run away if you delay too long. Also, they may remember a bad experience, and it will be harder to train them after that. Keep training short and pertinent. Training your bird around a mealtime will serve as motivation for your bird — food can serve as positive reinforcement for your bird as they associate training with receiving food afterwards.

Next, have your treat ready. You can use virtually any food for a treat, but it is probably smart to use a food that is small and easily given by hand such as cereal, beans, or popcorn. Making a noise in conjunction with giving your birds a treat will help in training. For instance, if you ring a soft bell each time you give them a special treat, soon you will only have to ring your bell, and your birds will associate the noise with good feelings. They will perform the act you are trying to instill in them. Never ring the bell, or the trigger, in a teasing manner without the conditioned response. It will confuse your birds.

Training your chickens to come when called is very simple and practical. First, decide how you want to call them. You could have a short phrase you say each time, such as "Come chickens!" Other options include having a clucking noise or a bell that you ring. When it is time to feed, simply use your call, and give them food directly after you give the call. Soon, the chickens will come running whenever they hear their call.

A bird that is familiar with humans and does not mind being touched and held is important when it comes to showing chickens. That is why it is important to instill in your birds a positive association with humans through the use of treats and noise. However, there is much more to showing chickens than familiarity with humans.

Showing Your Chickens

After deciding on what breed of chicken you would like to show, it is important start preparing your bird for show very early in its life. Remember that a bird's health and disposition reflect the quality of care and training it receives from its owner — it will be obvious to a judge the exhibitor's knowledge of care, skill, and training. Prize-winning birds come from knowledgeable owners who understand that a judge is looking for a chicken that is strong in all categories.

Choosing the best show birds from your flock

The most important factor in choosing which birds to show is health. Only healthy birds receive prizes in shows. Also, a sick bird could spread disease to other flocks of birds. You should check your birds for illness or external parasites two weeks before a show.

At shows, there are two categories of classes: production or purebred. The production category focuses on commercial birds and their body conformation and sexual maturity. Research the qualities of good health and conformation for your breed, especially in terms of the bird's head, body, feathers, feet, and toes. A hen in this category should be producing eggs, and the bird should be at sexual maturity, which is apparent through a fully developed comb, wattle, and earlobe. The purebred category is more about exhibition and mirroring your breed's standards, as described in the American Poultry Association's Standards of Perfection (*www.amerpoultryassn.com*). A winning bird conforms to its breed's standards of weight, body shape, plumage color, skin and shank color, earlobe color, and comb shape or type.

A judge of chickens will know the qualities of your breed, so it is important to do your homework before a show. There is much literature available on good chicken conformation and health. Refer to the American Poultry Association Standards of Perfection, and also consult your local extension office for showing standards and information.

Training and preparing your bird for show

After you choose the birds you will show, it is important to ensure they are docile and ready to show. A large part of training for show is making sure your birds can handle being confined in a cage and be handled by humans. In preparation for a show, you should place your birds in cages similar to the ones they use at shows and handle your birds. Practice taking your bird in and out of its cage, as you will have to do this at the show. The following is the proper way to remove a chicken from a cage, as described by the University of Florida Institute of Food and Agricultural Sciences (IFAS):

1. Approach cage slowly, open the door quietly, and prepare to remove the chicken, head first. Move the bird in the cage so its head is either to your right or left, depending on what feels more comfortable for you. Reach into the cage with your dominant hand and firmly grasp the most distant wing at the shoulder, being gentle and keeping the wing folded at the bird's body.

2. Situate the bird so its head is pointing towards the cage door and you.

3. Slide your other hand, palm facing up, underneath the bird's breast. At the same time, grasp the chicken's right leg with your index and middle fingers. Bring the bird out of the cage.

While you have your chicken out of the cage, practice handling it like a judge would. Hold it, lift its wings, and examine its body parts. A judge will determine a bird's balance by dropping a heavy bird 6 inches to the cage floor — a quick recovery means a bird with a good "set of legs." Practice handling your chickens often, and always return the chicken to the cage head first. A judge will know a bird is not trained if it shows signs of nervousness, which include standing in a crouched position, abnormal stool, struggling against being handled, and holding its tail to one side. Get your chickens accustomed to being handled so when the judges come to the cage to inspect them, they are not excitable and start cackling and flapping around. Blue-ribbon birds are docile, yet interactive, healthy, shiny, and meaty.

You will also need to wash your bird for a show. It is advisable to practice washing your bird so it goes smoothly come show time. Winning birds are clean with unspoiled plumage, and it is especially important to wash light-colored birds, as dirt will show up on their plumage. Wash your birds in a draft-free room using a bathtub or sink, depending on the bird's size. Water used to clean chickens should be 80 to 90 degrees Fahrenheit. Have a clean cage with new straw or shavings ready to place the bird in after it is clean. You can use detergent to wash your bird, but beware that some kinds will dry out your bird's feathers. The University of Florida IFAS recommends Lux flakes, Ivory, Cheer, or Casteel soap. With the bird standing at the bottom of the tub, hold the bird's wings, and use your free hand to work into its feathers soapy water with a brush, sponge, or your hand. Use a toothbrush to remove any stubborn dirt from the bird's legs. Rinsing the bird of the soapy water is easy with clean water that contains a small amount of vinegar. After the vinegar water, rinse the bird one more time with plain water.

Birds with white plumage might need special treatment. Stained feathers can be cleaned with a tub of water that contains a bluing agent, such as Boraten, which helps whiten and polish feathers. Do not use too much bluing, otherwise you could accidentally dye the feathers blue. After cleaned with bluing, the bird should be rinsed in a tub of clean water. Some bird owners set up four tubs to make this process easy and seamless; theses tubs include: the tub of water and detergent, the tub of water and vinegar, the tub of water and bluing, and the tub of plain, clean water. Chickens with dark plumage will not need the third tub of bluing, and can simply go from the vinegar tub to the tub of clean water. Do not wash a bird too often, as it can dry out their feathers.

It could take your clean chicken 12 to 18 hours to dry, so be sure to wash it early enough that it is dry before show time. To dry, the chicken should be in a drying cage that is placed in a warm room. You should refer to your breed's showing standards to learn about specific drying and grooming techniques because some birds, like silkies with their loose feathers, need special attention.

A clean bird should be examined for remaining dirt that can be removed with a toothpick, its toenails should be trimmed with a dog nail trimmer, its nostrils should be cleaned with a toothpick, and a light dusting of corn starch will help keep a white bird clean. Their legs should be moist, not dry and cracked. Put petroleum jelly on their feet to make them more pliable and less scaly and on their **combs,** the fleshy part of skin on top of the head that is typically red or purple; this can also be done in the winter to keep this area moist and protect it from frostbite in cold weather.

Show day

On show day, use a shipping cage to transport your bird. The bottom of the cage should have dry and clean shavings or straw. While traveling, do not have a bowl of water that could tip over and soil your clean bird. If needed, make a stop along the way to give your bird water. Make sure you bring plenty of water and feed for your chickens, or find out if it will be provided at the show. It is also good to be prepared with grooming supplies for last minute cleaning.

You should attend and watch several shows before submitting your chickens into one yourself. While some classes at shows focus solely on the bird's appearance, conformation, health, and other factors, there are classes that require the exhibitor to know showmanship techniques and answer questions from the judge. Study up on what is expected in terms of showmanship and attend shows so you can watch how experienced exhibitors handle their birds and answer judges' questions. If you have a child who is interested in showing chickens, consider having them join the 4-H (*www.4-H.org*). Chances are, your local 4-H extension will have chicken clubs that can teach your child an abundance of information about chicken health, care, and showing. The 4-H also provides opportunities to show chickens at county fairs. Visit the 4-H website to find your local Extension Office.

CASE STUDY: BLUE RIBBON BIRDS

Angie Maher

Angie Maher, a 4-H Poultry Leader for her son's 4-H group, has over 70 chickens at her private home in Tuscon, Arizona. She owns her chickens for show, for eggs, and as pets. She says, "We started out with five chickens for my son for 4-H. We decided that since we already had a place for the chickens, we wanted to get some layers. And here we are with about 75 … We love owning chickens because they all have different personalities. Some are friendly. Some are not. Some will fly and sit on our shoulders, heads or arms. It is fun watching them interact with each other. It is the pecking order."

Maher and her family show their chickens in poultry shows and at the Pima County Fair. Their Rhode Island red bantam hen got Best of Breed and Reserve Champion Bantam. Several of their old English games and Dutch received Best of Breed, Reserve Breed, and 1st Place Blue Ribbon.

Among her flock, Maher has Rhode Island reds, both bantams and standards, Dutch, buckeyes, buff Orpingtons, barred rocks, and old English game bantams. She says, "If you want to use your chickens for show, such as 4-H or poultry shows, it is best to get your eggs or chicks from a breeder. If you want your chickens for layers, order from a hatchery or a local person who is raising production chickens."

The coop that Maher and her husband use is an enclosed stable that is 13' x15' and a screen room that is 8' x 10'. "Since we live in the desert," says Maher, "We wanted a predator-proof enclosure. If you are building or designing one for a new chicken owner, be sure it will be easy to clean. The chickens are terrible housekeepers! Have lots of ventilation, shade, Maher advises new poultry owners to research your town ordinance laws to see how many chickens you can have and if roosters are allowed. She also recommends checking with your neighbors to see if there are any objections and find out how they feel about you owning chickens. "They can be your worst enemy. But most of all, enjoy your birds!"

Chapter 11:
Glorious Eggs

This would not be a complete chicken book without offering information on a big part of a chicken's life: the egg. Eggs come in all sizes and have many components. They have a myriad of uses and are enjoyed universally. Let us start with the anatomy of an egg and its properties. Identifying the parts of an egg is equally as important as knowing the anatomy of a chicken.

As points of reference, the top of the egg is the pointy, thinner portion, and the bottom of the egg is the wider, rounder part. The following is the anatomy of an egg, starting from the outside and going in:

- The entire egg is covered with a hard coating called the eggshell. It is made of calcium carbonate and has approximately 17,000 pores to allow moisture and air to circulate. A light coat or membrane around the egg keeps out bacteria.

- The outer shell and inner shell membranes are next inside the shell. They surround the albumen, or the egg white. They also help keep bacteria out.

- The **chalazae** are located at the top and bottom of the egg. They are long, twisted cords that attach to the shell and hold the yolk in place. A fresher egg will show more prominent chalazae.

- The **exterior albumen** is the narrow fluid layer next to the shell membrane.

- The **middle albumen** is the thick, white layer of dense matter known as the egg white.

- The **vitelline membrane** is the clear coating enclosing the egg yolk. If you hear the term *mottled* in reference to the egg, it means the membrane is covered with blotches or pale spots.

- The **Nucleus of Pander** is a plug of whitish yolk located inside the yolk that is purely for nutritional value.

- The **germinal disk**, or **blastoderm**, is a small circular spot on the surface of the yolk. This is the point where the sperm enters the egg. It will gradually send out blood vessels into the yolk once it is fertilized for nutrition as it develops.

- The **yellow yolk** is at the center of the egg and can range in color from yellow to orange, depending on the hen. The yolk makes up about 33 percent of the egg and is comprised of valuable nutrients, such as protein, calcium, iron, and vitamin B12. The older the egg gets, the larger the yolk becomes because it absorbs water and nutrients from the albumen.

- The **air cell** is located at the bottom part of the egg. When the egg is first laid, it is warm. When it cools, it contracts. The inner shell membrane pulls away from the outer shell membrane and forms an air pocket.

Hens can start laying eggs as early as 4 months old, so you can expect to have farm-fresh eggs relatively soon if you started your brood from chicks. The color of the hen's first egg will be the same color as all of the eggs she will lay throughout her life. You can identify the egg color from the earlobes of a chicken, as discussed in Chapter 8. For an easy reference, here are breeds and the color of the eggs they lay:

White eggs:

- Leghorn
- Houdan
- Polish
- Sultan
- Cornish (although some of their eggs are a creamy, white color)

Brown eggs:

- Rhode Island Red
- Wyandotte
- New Hampshire
- Orpington
- Welsummer (these are a chocolate brown egg)

Blue, green, green-blue, pinkish-brown and cream-colored:

- Ameraucana produces more colorful eggs than any other breed.
- Silkies mostly produce tinted or cream-colored eggs.
- Plymouth produce light pink to medium brown eggs.

Egg Oddities

Most eggs have only one yolk, but occasionally you will find a double yolk or even a triple yolk egg. This usually happens when the chicken is new to laying eggs and her cycle is adjusting. When ovulation starts too rapidly, an additional yolk is produced but has nowhere to go. It connects to the next yolk and ends up inside one egg. Double yolks and triple yolks are safe to eat.

Occasionally, an egg is passed through a chicken that does not have any yolk at all. These eggs are referred to as "wind" eggs or "dwarf" eggs. This also occurs more frequently in pullets rather than older hens. As the hen's cycle is just beginning, it may take a few times to get in sync with the bird's body.

Even more rare than finding extra yolks or no yolks is an egg within an egg. Sometimes you will crack an egg open only to find another egg inside. The cause is not quite clear, but it is possible the egg developed and then while it was in the duct, it either reversed direction or got stuck when the next cycle began. It is rare, but it has happens.

Once in a while, an egg is dropped from a hen and does not have an outside shell, but just the yolk and white part of the egg covered in a membrane sac. This is an accident of a hen's reproductive system. You do not need to be concerned about the chicken's health if these oddities occur. If they happen regularly, take your bird to the vet or investigate its eating habits. The bird is most likely lacking nutrients.

Sizes

Eggs come in different sizes: small, medium, large, extra large, and jumbo. Small eggs weigh about 18 ounces, medium eggs weigh 21 ounces, large eggs weigh 24 ounces, extra large eggs weigh 27 ounces, and jumbo eggs weigh 30 ounces. They come in a variety of colors and can be enjoyed in limitless ways. The largest chicken egg in the Guinness Book of World Records weighs 201 grams.

Candling Eggs

To candle, all you need is a very bright light, such as a flashlight, and a dark room. Hold the egg up to the flashlight's light, and you should be able to see the yolk or at least the outline of a dense mass within the shell. If you are candling a fertilized egg, you should see something by the third day of incubation. Do not keep your egg out for more than 30 minutes at a time because the temperature drops in the egg. Otherwise, you can candle your eggs every day to see the chick grow inside.

Bad eggs sometimes are hard for a beginner to spot, but generally if you see rings inside the egg, they are bacteria rings that have infected the bird and you will need to discard the egg. If you are unsure, you can always wait 21 days for the eggs to hatch. If any eggs that you suspect are bad have not hatched, discard them immediately. If they break, they will smell, so dispose of them properly.

Candling will also tell you whether the eggs you have stored in your refrigerator are old. Hold one up to the light and find the air sac at the bottom of the egg. The smaller the air sac, the fresher the egg will be.

Collecting and Storing Eggs

The fun part is when you can reap the rewards for all of your hard work. Each day you need to go to the chicken coop and retrieve any eggs you do not plan on hatching. If you leave eggs in the nest for too many days, the chickens may peck at it, or you may initiate broodiness in one of your hens. Also, if you plan on consuming the egg, you will want to wash it off and refrigerate it.

Go to your hen house and take a basket or bowl with you to carry your eggs. The hen most likely will be out of the coop by now and about her daily business. Pick up the eggs and gently place them in your basket or bowl. If you find broken eggs or dirty nesting boxes, clean them out so they do not create a bigger mess or health problems later.

When you return from the coop, you will need to clean your eggs. Submerging them in cold water will actually push bacteria through to the egg, so it is better to dry clean your egg. To do this, sanitize a sponge or washcloth and blot and rub the outside of the egg to remove dirt and feces. If the egg is just too messy to clean in this manner, you will need to use water, preferably running water. Use warm water and rinse the egg well using your sponge or washcloth and sanitizer. Set the eggs out to dry in a wire or mesh basket, or dry them with a paper towel.

Next, put the eggs in a carton or crate (or whatever you choose to keep them in) and label with a date. Put them in your refrigerator to maintain freshness. Eggs are good for about a month when stored in the fridge, as they are chemical-free and do not have hormones or preservatives to extend their shelf life.

Selling

You may find you have more eggs than you know what to do with, even after eating them at every meal. Selling your extra eggs may be an option. First, check with your local county extension office to see whether any laws regulate the sale of eggs in your area. Find your office by searching the National Institute of Food and Agriculture (*www.nifa.usda.gov*). This website has information on the laws and regulations concerning agriculture in your community. The Local Extension Office page has a map. Just click on your state to find the branch nearest you.

You can sell your eggs at a local farmer's market or flea market. If your city allows, you also could set up a table in front of your house with a large sign promoting homegrown eggs. For an inexpensive way to advertise your eggs, put an ad in your newspaper's classified section. Craigslist (*www.craigslist.org*) is another great way to advertise for free. Selling eggs from home is an easy and fun way to make some extra cash. You can even put them in decorative cartons or baskets.

Always make sure the eggs are clean and free of any chicken droppings or feces. Also, make sure the eggs are whole and not cracked. Do not sell old or questionable eggs because people can get very sick from contaminated eggs. If you are unsure of the quality of an egg, throw it out.

Spring and summertime offer more opportunities to sell eggs outside the perimeters of your home. When the weather is warm, lots of communities get together and have multiple family yard sales. This is a great place to catch a flow of people in a shopping mood. Most people who attend yard sales are looking for a bargain, so price your eggs cheaper than a grocery store would.

The warm weather also indicates the start of fair season. County fairs and festivals provide a delightful environment to sell your eggs. Food tables are typically set up close to one another, and you can network with other people in your community and connect with more potential customers. As families browse the food tables, you can strike up conversations about your flock and the eggs they just produced.

Local restaurants and caterers may be looking for wholesome food opportunities year-round, especially if they are customizing their menus to maximize the sustainable food in their region. This is a good time to have organic food to sell. Look up restaurants in your community and target your sales to smaller food outlets. Obviously, you would not try to sell your wares to major chains, as they have their own approved purveyors to supply food, but smaller, independently owned restaurants, grocery stores, and caterers have the freedom to purchase from whomever they wish.

Once you do find some clients, they may want to order eggs from you on a regular basis. Be sure you will be able to deliver on any promises that you make with your customers. If you are inconsistent in your sales, they may not utilize your services. Discuss the options with your clients when you start your sales calls. Find out what their expectations are before you sell to them. Be sure you can meet their needs. Let them know what the turn-around time is between placing an order and delivery. Also decide upon a time to deliver the eggs. Communication with your customers will build your relationships. Keep records of all orders and sales so if there are any questions or concerns you will always have documentation to rely on.

Gifts

Fresh eggs make wonderful gifts for neighbors, co-workers, friends, and family. Buy or make little baskets or decorative cartons. Craft stores have inexpensive markers and stickers you can use to personalize egg cartons for your friend or neighbor. Include recipe cards with your basket so your friends can enjoy their eggs in different ways, too. They will be delighted at your thoughtfulness, and your excess eggs will not go to waste.

Eggs are a benefit of owning chickens. They are wholesome and are a staple in most people's diets. Regardless of whether you have a rooster, your hen will continue to produce eggs until she is too old to do so. In the meantime, you can harvest your cache and share your wealth. If you do not want to keep a hen past her egg-laying years, which is about five years, you can give her away as a pet, donate her to a farm, or butcher her for her meat. If roosters are butchered, they are usually butchered as cockerels for the young meat. Compared to roosters, hens have better meat for eating. If you decide you will butcher your birds, the next chapter will show you how to do so.

CASE STUDY: PEPPER FOR PRODUCTIVITY?

Jeri Burks

In Sparta, Tennessee, Jeri Burks keeps 75 to 100 chicks and chickens on her spacious, private property. She has Ameraucans, Turkens, and standard size Cochins. "I keep them as pets and for fresh eggs," says Burks. She bought most of her starter chicks from Stromberg's Catalog.

The coop that houses her flock is 10 ½ feet by 14 feet and is homemade. Big nesting boxes kept at a slant help to prevent the chickens from roosting on top of each other. One tip that Burks learned to keep mites away is to take burnt motor oil and paint it on top of the roosts. Another tip for the coop if you have feather footed birds, use sand on the floor of the coop to keep their feathers pretty.

Burks states, "New chicken owners should start small until you know what you are doing. Keep to one breed. Ask lots of questions. Find someone who has raised chickens and ask for advice." She continues, "Start up costs vary. Be sure to factor in that plus the day to day expenses. And when it comes to feed, we found that adding ground up cayenne pepper to the mix helped the hens to lay more frequently and it helped to make the roosters more active."

Shell Eggs from Farm to Table

Eggs are among the most nutritious foods on earth and can be part of a healthy diet. However, they are perishable just like raw meat, poultry, and fish. Unbroken, clean, fresh shell eggs may contain Salmonella Enteritidis (SE) bacteria that can cause foodborne illness. While the number of eggs affected is quite small, there have been cases of foodborne illness in the last few years. To be safe, eggs must be safely handled, refrigerated, and cooked.

What is the History of the Egg?

"Eggs existed long before chickens," according to *On Food and Cooking: The Science and Lore of the Kitchen* by Harold McGee. "The first eggs were released, fertilized, and hatched in the ocean. Around 250 million years ago, the earliest fully land-dwelling animals, the reptiles, developed a self-contained egg with a tough, leathery skin that prevented fatal water loss. The eggs of birds, animals that arose some 100 million years later, are a refined version of this reproductive adaptation to life on land. Eggs, then, are millions of years older than birds. Gallus domesticus, the chicken more or less as we know it, is only a scant 4 or 5 thousand years old."

How Often Does a Hen Lay an Egg?

The entire time from ovulation to laying is about 25 hours. Then about 30 minutes later, the hen will begin to make another one.

How Does *Salmonella* Infect Eggs?

Bacteria can be on the outside of a shell egg. That's because the egg exits the hen's body through the same passageway as feces is excreted. That's why eggs are washed and sanitized at the processing plant. Bacteria can be inside an uncracked, whole egg. Contamination of eggs may be due to bacteria within the hen's ovary or oviduct before the shell forms around the yolk and white. SE doesn't make the hen sick. It is also possible for eggs to become infected by *Salmonella* Enteritidis fecal contamination through the pores of the shells after they're laid.

What Part Carries Bacteria?

Researchers say that, if present, the SE is usually in the yolk or "yellow." However, they can't rule out the bacteria being in egg whites. So everyone is advised against eating raw or undercooked egg yolks and whites or products containing raw or undercooked eggs.

What Safe Handling Instructions are on Egg Cartons?

All packages of raw, shell eggs not treated to destroy *Salmonella* must carry the following safe handling statement:

SAFE HANDLING INSTRUCTIONS: To prevent illness from bacteria: Keep eggs refrigerated, cook eggs until yolks are firm, and cook foods containing eggs thoroughly.

Who is "At Risk" for Eating Raw or Undercooked Eggs?

Infants, young children, older adults, pregnant women, and people with weakened immune systems are particularly vulnerable to SE infections. A chronic illness weakens the immune system, making the person vulnerable to foodborne illnesses.

No one should eat foods containing raw eggs. This includes "health food" milk shakes made with raw eggs, Caesar salad, Hollandaise sauce, and any other foods like homemade mayonnaise, ice cream, or eggnog made from recipes in which the egg ingredients are not cooked. However, in-shell pasteurized eggs may be used safely without cooking.

Who is Working on Eliminating the *Salmonella* in Eggs?

Federal and state governments, the egg industry, and the scientific community are working together to solve the problem. Involved government agencies include: USDA's Food Safety and Inspection Service (FSIS), Agricultural Research Service (ARS), and the Animal and Plant Health Inspection Service (APHIS); the U.S. Food and Drug Administration (FDA); and State departments of agriculture.

Government agencies have implemented an Egg Safety Action Plan to eliminate *Salmonella* Enteritidis illnesses due to eggs. The Action Plan identifies the systems and practices that must be carried out in order to meet the goal of eliminating SE illnesses associated with the consumption of eggs by 2010.

What Government Agencies are Responsible for the Safety of Shell Eggs?

Many government agencies cooperate to ensure the safety of shell eggs from farm to table.

USDA Agencies

Agricultural Marketing Service (AMS)

- AMS administers a voluntary egg-quality grading program for shell eggs paid for by processing plants.
- AMS also is responsible for the Shell Egg Surveillance Program to assure that eggs in the marketplace are as good as or better than U.S. Consumer Grade B quality standards. AMS conducts inspection of handlers and hatcheries four times each year to ensure conformance with these requirements. Eggs exceeding the tolerance for checks or loss must be diverted from the marketplace for further segregation or processing.
- The USDA grade mark on egg cartons means the plant processed the eggs following USDA's sanitation and good manufacturing processes.
- Effective June 19, 2006, AMS announced final rulemaking prohibiting the repackaging of eggs previously shipped for retail sale that were packed under its voluntary grading program.

Animal and Plant Health Inspection Service (APHIS)

- APHIS conducts activities to reduce the risk of disease in flocks of laying hens.

- APHIS administers the voluntary National Poultry Improvement Plan (NPIP), which certifies that poultry breeding stock and hatcheries are free from certain diseases. Participation is necessary for producers that ship interstate or internationally.

- APHIS' National Animal Health Monitoring System is currently conducting a nationwide survey of the egg industry whose purpose is to estimate the national prevalence of SE layer flocks.

Food Safety and Inspection Service (FSIS)

- FSIS is responsible for the import of eggs destined for further processing and for assuring that imported shell eggs destined for the retail market are transported under refrigerated conditions.

- FSIS verifies shell eggs packed for the consumer are labeled "Keep Refrigerated" and transported under refrigeration and ambient temperature of no greater than 45 °F.

- USDA also educates consumers about the safe handling of eggs. FSIS has developed numerous publications on egg safety and uses a variety of networks (such as the USDA Meat and Poultry Hotline, "Ask Karen," and USDA cooperative extension agents) to get this information to consumers.

Agricultural Research Service (ARS)

- USDA also carries out food safety research through ARS and through a program administered by USDA's Cooperative State Research, Education & Extension Service (CSREES). Subjects include studying how *Salmonella* adheres to chicken cells, and developing an oral vaccine against SE.

- In 2005, ARS established the Egg Safety and Research Unit at the Russell Research Center in Athens, GA, to expand egg safety and egg processing research.

National Agricultural Statistics Service (NASS)

- USDA collects processing and distribution information for the economic analysis of the egg products industry through NASS.

Other Government Agencies

FSIS/FDA Cooperation

- FSIS and the FDA share authority for egg safety and are working together toward solving the problem of SE in eggs.
- FSIS and FDA are working to strengthen the Food Code and to encourage its adoption by States and local jurisdictions.

State Agriculture Departments

- State agriculture departments monitor for compliance of the official U.S. standards, grades, and weight classes by egg packers who do not use the USDA/AMS shell egg grading service.

State and Local Health Departments

- State and local health departments monitor retail food and foodservice establishments for compliance with state and local health department requirements.

What is Candling?

Candling is the process of using light to help determine the quality of an egg. Automated mass-scanning equipment is used by most egg packers to detect eggs with cracked shells and interior defects. During candling, eggs travel along a conveyor belt and pass over a light source where the defects become visible. Defective eggs are removed. Hand candling—holding a shell egg directly in front of a light source—is done to spot check and determine accuracy in grading. Advanced technology, utilizing computerized integrated cameras and sound wave technology, is also being applied for the segregation of eggs.

How Are Eggs Transported Safely to Stores?

The U.S. Department of Commerce's 1990 Sanitary Food Transportation Act requires that vehicles be dedicated to transporting food only. On August 27, 1999, FSIS made effective a new rule requiring:

- Shell eggs packed for consumers be stored and transported under refrigeration at an ambient (surrounding) air temperature not to exceed 45 °F.
- All packed shell eggs be labeled with a statement that refrigeration is required.
- Any shell eggs imported into the United States, packed for consumer use, include a certification that they have been stored and transported at an ambient temperature of no greater than 45 °F.

What Is Included Under the Egg Products Inspection Act?

The term "egg products" refers to eggs that have been removed from their shells for processing at facilities called "breaker plants." The safety of these products is the responsibility of FSIS. Basic egg products include whole eggs, whites, yolks, and various blends—with or without non-egg ingredients—that are processed and pasteurized. They may be available in liquid, frozen, and dried forms. Most are not available in supermarkets, but are used in restaurants, hospitals, and other foodservice establishments as well as by bakers, noodle makers, and other food manufacturers.

Egg products are pasteurized. The 1970 Egg Products Inspection Act (EPIA) requires that all egg products distributed for consumption be pasteurized. They are rapidly heated and held at a minimum required temperature for a specified time. This destroys *Salmonella*, but it does not cook the eggs or affect their color, flavor, nutritional value, or use. Dried eggs are pasteurized by heating in the dried form.

While inspected pasteurized egg products are used to make freeze-dried egg products, imitation egg products, and egg substitutes, these products are not covered under the EPIA and are under FDA jurisdiction. No-cholesterol egg substitutes consist of egg whites, artificial color, and other non-egg additives. Direct questions about egg substitutes to the manufacturer or to the FDA. For more information about egg products, read "Egg Products and Food Safety" (*www.fsis. usda.gov/Fact_Sheets/Egg_Products_and_Food_Safety/index.asp*).

Can Shell Eggs Be Pasteurized?

Shell eggs can be pasteurized by a processor if FDA approves the process. Pasteurized shell eggs are now available at some grocery stores. Like all eggs, they must be kept refrigerated. The equipment to pasteurize shell eggs isn't available for home use, and it is not possible to pasteurize shell eggs at home without cooking the contents of the egg.

Are Powdered Egg Whites Pasteurized?

Yes. Egg white powder is dried egg white (pure albumen). It can be reconstituted by mixing the powder with water. The reconstituted powder whips like fresh egg white and, because it is pasteurized, can be used safely without cooking or baking it. The product is usually sold along with supplies for cake baking and decorating.

What Points Should You Consider When Buying Eggs?

Always purchase eggs from a refrigerated case. Choose eggs with clean, uncracked shells. Don't buy out-of-date eggs. Look for the USDA grade shield or mark. Graded eggs must meet standards for quality and size. Choose the size most useful and economical for you.

Is Grading of Eggs Mandatory?

USDA's grading service is voluntary; egg packers who request it, pay for it. The USDA grade shield on the carton means that the eggs were graded for quality and checked for weight (size) under the supervision of a trained USDA grader. Compliance with quality standards, grades, and weights is monitored by USDA. State agencies monitor compliance for egg packers who do not use the USDA grading service. These cartons will bear a term such as "Grade A" on their cartons without the USDA shield.

What Are Egg Grades?

There are three consumer grades for eggs: U.S. Grade AA, A, and B. The grade is determined by the interior quality of the egg and the appearance and condition of the egg shell. Eggs of any quality grade may differ in weight (size).

- *U.S. Grade AA* eggs have whites that are thick and firm; yolks that are high, round, and practically free from defects; and clean, unbroken shells. Grade AA and Grade A eggs are best for frying and poaching where appearance is important.

- *U.S. Grade A eggs* have characteristics of Grade AA eggs except that the whites are "reasonably" firm. This is the quality most often sold in stores.

- *U.S. Grade B* eggs have whites that may be thinner and yolks that may be wider and flatter than eggs of higher grades. The shells must be unbroken, but may show slight stains. This quality is seldom found in retail stores because they are usually used to make liquid, frozen, and dried egg products.

Sizing of Eggs

Size tells you the minimum required net weight per dozen eggs. It does not refer to the dimensions of an egg or how big it looks. While some eggs in the carton may look slightly larger or smaller than the rest, it is the total weight of the dozen eggs that puts them in one of the following classes:

Size or Weight Class

Minimum net weight per dozen

Jumbo	Extra Large	Large	Medium	Small	Peewee
30 ounces	27 ounces	24 ounces	21 ounces	18 ounces	15 ounces

Dating of Cartons

Many eggs reach stores only a few days after the hen lays them. Egg cartons with the USDA grade shield on them must display the "Pack date" (the day that the eggs were washed, graded, and placed in the carton). The number is a three-digit code that represents the consecutive day of the year (the "Julian Date") starting with January 1 as 001 and ending with December 31 as 365. When a "sell-by" date appears on a carton bearing the USDA grade shield, the code date may not exceed 45 days from the date of pack.

Use of either a "Sell-by" or "Expiration" (EXP) date is not federally required, but may be State required, defined by the egg laws in the State where the eggs are marketed. Some State egg laws do not allow the use of a "Sell-by" date. Always purchase eggs before the "Sell-by" or "EXP" date on the carton.

After the eggs reach home, they may be refrigerated 3 to 5 weeks from the day they are placed in the refrigerator. The "sell-by" date will usually expire during that length of time, but the eggs are perfectly safe to use.

Why Should Eggs Be Refrigerated?

Temperature fluctuation is critical to safety. With the concern about *Salmonella*, eggs gathered from laying hens should be refrigerated as soon as possible. After eggs are refrigerated, they need to stay that way. A cold egg left out at room temperature can sweat, facilitating the growth of bacteria. Refrigerated eggs should not be left out more than 2 hours.

Should You Wash Eggs?

No. It's not necessary for consumers to wash eggs. When the chicken lays the egg, a protective coating is put on the outside by the hen. At the plant, government regulations require that USDA-graded eggs be carefully washed and sanitized using special detergent.

Why Do Hard-Cooked Eggs Spoil Faster than Fresh Eggs?

When shell eggs are hard cooked, the protective coating is washed away, leaving bare the pores in the shell for bacteria to enter and contaminate it. Hard-cooked eggs should be refrigerated within 2 hours of cooking and used within a week.

Safe Storage in Stores

At the store, choose Grade A or AA eggs with clean, uncracked shells. Make sure they've been refrigerated in the store. Any bacteria present in an egg can multiply quickly at room temperature. When purchasing egg products or substitutes, look for containers that are tightly sealed.

Bringing Eggs Home from the Store

Take eggs straight home and store them immediately in the refrigerator set at 40 °F or below. Keep them in their carton and place them in the coldest part of the refrigerator, not in the door.

Is It Safe to Use Eggs That Have Cracks?

Bacteria can enter eggs through cracks in the shell. Never purchase cracked eggs. However, if eggs crack on the way home from the store, break them into a clean container, cover it tightly, keep refrigerated, and use within 2 days. If eggs crack during hard cooking, they are safe.

How Are Eggs Handled Safely?

Proper refrigeration, cooking, and handling should prevent most egg-safety problems. Persons can enjoy eggs and dishes containing eggs if these safe handling guidelines are followed:

- Wash utensils, equipment, and work areas with hot, soapy water before and after contact with eggs.
- Don't keep eggs out of the refrigerator more than 2 hours.
- Raw eggs and other ingredients, combined according to recipe directions, should be cooked immediately or refrigerated and cooked within 24 hours.
- Serve cooked eggs and dishes containing eggs immediately after cooking, or place in shallow containers for quick cooling and refrigerate at once for later use. Use within 3 to 4 days.

Are Easter Eggs Safe?

Sometimes eggs are decorated, used as decorations, and hunted at Easter. Here are some safety tips for Easter eggs.

- *Dyeing eggs:* After hard cooking eggs, dye them and return them to the refrigerator within 2 hours. If eggs are to be eaten, use a food-safe coloring. As with all foods, persons dyeing the eggs should wash their hands before handling the eggs.
- *Decorations:* One Easter bread recipe is decorated with dyed, cooked eggs in the braided bread. After baking, serve within 2 hours or refrigerate and use within 3 to 4 days.
- *Blowing out eggshells:* Because some raw eggs may contain *Salmonella,* you must use caution when blowing out the contents to hollow out the shell for decorating, such as for Ukrainian Easter eggs. Use only eggs that have been kept refrigerated and are uncracked. To destroy bacteria that may be present on the surface of the egg, wash the egg in hot water and then rinse in a solution of 1 teaspoon liquid chlorine bleach per half cup of water. After blowing out the egg, refrigerate the contents and use within 2 to 4 days.
- *Hunting Eggs:* Hard-cooked eggs for an egg hunt must be prepared with care to prevent cracking the shells. If the shells crack, bacteria could contaminate the inside. Eggs should be hidden in places that are protected from dirt, pets, and other sources of bacteria. The total time for hiding and hunting eggs should not exceed 2 hours. The "found" eggs must be re-refrigerated and eaten within 7 days of cooking.

Does the Color of the Shell Affect the Egg's Nutrients?

No. The breed of the hen determines the color of her eggs.

Araucuna chickens in South America lay eggs that range in color from medium blue to medium green. Nutrition claims that araucuna eggs contain less cholesterol than other eggs haven't been proven.

Are Fertilized Eggs More Nutritious?

No. There is no benefit in eating fertilized eggs. There is no nutritional difference in fertilized eggs and infertile eggs. Most eggs sold today are infertile; roosters are not housed with the laying hens. If the eggs are fertile and cell development is detected during the candling process, they are removed from commerce.

Per Capita Consumption

Egg consumption in America was on a 40-year downward slide until the 1990's. Then eggs became increasingly popular. The following figures are from USDA's Economic Research Service.

Year	2008	1990	1950
Eggs per Person	247	236	389

Is the Appearance of Eggs Related to Food Safety?

Sometimes, but not usually. Variation in egg color is due to many factors.

- *Blood spots* are caused by a rupture of one or more small blood vessels in the yolk at the time of ovulation. It does not indicate the egg is unsafe.

- A *cloudy white* (albumen) is a sign the egg is very fresh. A clear egg white is an indication the egg is aging.

- *Pink or iridescent egg white* (albumen) indicates spoilage due to *Pseudomonas* bacteria. Some of these microorganisms—which produce a greenish, fluorescent, water-soluble pigment—are harmful to humans.

- The *color of yolk* varies in shades of yellow depending upon the diet of the hen. If she eats plenty of yellow-orange plant pigments, such as from marigold petals and yellow corn, the yolk will be a darker yellow than if she eats a colorless diet such as white cornmeal. Artificial color additives are not permitted in eggs.

- A *green* ring on a hard-cooked yolk is a result of overcooking, and is caused by sulfur and iron compounds in the egg reacting on the yolk's surface. The green color can also be caused by a high amount of iron in the cooking water. Scrambled eggs cooked at too high a temperature or held on a steam table too long can also develop a greenish cast. The green color is safe to consume.

How Do Time and Refrigeration Affect Egg Quality?

The egg, as laid at 105 °F, normally has no air cell. As the egg cools, an air cell forms usually in the large end of the egg and develops between the two shell membranes. The air cell is formed as a result of the different rates of contraction between the shell and its contents.

Over time, the white and yolk of an egg lose quality. The yolk absorbs water from the white. Moisture and carbon dioxide in the white evaporate through the pores, allowing more air to penetrate the shell, and the air cell becomes larger. If broken open, the egg's contents would cover a wider area. The white would be thinner, losing some of its thickening and leavening powers. The yolk would be flatter, larger and more easily broken. The chalazae (kah-LAY-zuh), the twisted cord-like strands of egg white that anchor the yolk in the center of the white, would be less prominent and weaker, allowing the yolk to move off center. Refrigeration slows the loss of quality over time.

What Does It Mean When an Egg Floats in Water?

An egg can float in water when its air cell has enlarged sufficiently to keep it buoyant. This means the egg is old, but it may be perfectly safe to use. Crack the egg into a bowl and examine it for an off-odor or unusual appearance before deciding to use or discard it. A spoiled egg will have an unpleasant odor when you break open the shell, either when raw or cooked.

Safe Cooking Methods

Many cooking methods can be used to cook eggs safely including poaching, hard cooking, scrambling, frying and baking. However, eggs must be cooked thoroughly until yolks are firm. Scrambled eggs should not be runny. Casseroles and other dishes containing eggs should be cooked to a safe minimum internal temperature of 160 °F. Use a food thermometer to be sure.

Use Safe Egg Recipes

Egg mixtures are safe if they reach 160 °F, so homemade ice cream and eggnog can be made safely from a cooked egg-milk mixture. Heat it gently and use a food thermometer.

- Dry meringue shells are safe. So are divinity candy and 7-minute frosting, made by combining hot sugar syrup with beaten egg whites. Avoid icing recipes using uncooked eggs or egg whites.

- Meringue-topped pies should be safe if baked at 350 °F for about 15 minutes. Chiffon pies and fruit whips made with raw, beaten egg whites cannot be guaranteed to be safe. Instead, substitute pasteurized dried egg whites, whipped cream, or a whipped topping.

- To make a recipe safe that specifies using eggs that aren't cooked, heat the eggs in a liquid from the recipe over low heat, stirring constantly, until the mixture reaches 160 °F. Then combine it with the other ingredients and complete the recipe.

- To determine doneness in egg dishes such as quiche and casseroles, the center of the mixture should reach 160 °F when measured with a food thermometer.

- Use pasteurized eggs or egg products when preparing recipes that call for using eggs raw or undercooked.

What Makes Hard-Cooked Eggs Hard to Peel?

The fresher the egg, the more difficult it is to peel after hard cooking. That's because the air cell, found at the large end of the shell between the shell membranes, increases in size the longer the raw egg is stored. As the contents of the egg contracts and the air cell enlarges, the shell becomes easier to peel. For this reason, older eggs make better candidates for hard cooking.

What Are Thousand-Year-Old Eggs?

These Chinese eggs are not really 1,000 years old, but are somewhere between a month and several years old. The egg is not retained in its original state, but rather converted into an entirely different food, probably by bacterial action. They are exempt from inspection and grading. The following are several types of thousand-year-old Chinese eggs.

- "Hulidan" results when eggs are individually coated with a mixture of salt and wet clay or ashes for a month. This process darkens and partially solidifies the yolks, and gives the eggs a salty taste.
- "Dsaudan" eggs are packed in cooked rice and salt for at least 6 months. During this time, the shell softens, the membranes thicken, and the egg contents coagulate. The flavor is wine-like.
- "Pidan," a great delicacy, is made by covering eggs with lime, salt, wood ashes, and a tea infusion for 5 months or more. The egg yolks become greenish gray and the albumen turns into a coffee-brown jelly. Pidan smell ammonia-like and taste like lime.

Do Pickled Eggs Keep a Long Time?

Pickled eggs are hard-cooked eggs marinated in vinegar and pickling spices, spicy cider, or juice from pickles or pickled beets. Studies done at the American Egg Board substantiate that unopened containers of commercially pickled eggs keep for several months on the shelf. After opening, keep refrigerated and use within 7 days. Home-prepared pickled eggs must be kept refrigerated and used within 7 days. Home canning of pickled eggs is not recommended.

Egg Storage Chart

Product	Refrigerator	Freezer
Raw eggs in shell	3 to 5 weeks	Do not freeze.
Raw egg whites	2 to 4 days	12 months
Raw egg yolks	2 to 4 days	Yolks do not freeze well.
Raw egg accidentally frozen in shell	Use immediately after thawing.	Keep frozen; then refrigerate to thaw.
Hard-cooked eggs	1 week	Do not freeze.
Egg substitutes, liquid Unopened	10 days	Do not freeze.
Egg substitutes, liquid Opened	3 days	Do not freeze.
Egg substitutes, frozen Unopened	After thawing, 7 days, or refer to "Use-By" date on carton.	12 months
Egg substitutes, frozen Opened	After thawing, 3 days, or refer to "Use-By" date on carton.	Do not freeze.
Casseroles made with eggs	3 to 4 days	After baking, 2 to 3 months.
Eggnog, commercial	3 to 5 days	6 months
Eggnog, homemade	2 to 4 days	Do not freeze.
Pies, pumpkin or pecan	3 to 4 days	After baking, 1 to 2 months.
Pies, custard and chiffon	3 to 4 days	Do not freeze.
Quiche with any kind of filling	3 to 4 days	After baking, 1 to 2 months.

Chapter 12:
The End of the Road

The cycle of life means that you will need to decide what to do with your birds as they stop producing eggs or they are too old to be a part of your flock. If you are raising your birds for meat, then you already know the fate of your chickens. If your bird is a pet, and you choose to let it die a natural death, you do not need to have a plan for butchering it. Butchering a chicken can be a daunting task for some, but if you are well prepared, then the process can be quick and you will provide fresh meat for your family.

Many chicken owners raise their flock for meat. Chickens grow relatively quickly, and once your flock is in production, you can have plenty of meat about 12 weeks from the time you hatch your chicks. Broiler birds such as the Cornish hen were bred to plump up quickly and to contain adequate amounts of meat on their bones to be provided as food.

Meat birds are not as economical as you may think. The cost of raising and butchering them may be more expensive than purchasing chicken at a grocery store, but the benefit to owning your bird is that you control what it is fed and the environment it lives in. If you have not eaten organic or free-range chicken, be aware that the flavor is different than commercially produced broilers. It has more of a natural, gamey flavor. This taste may take some time to get used to, but it is healthier for you because it provides more nutrients and goes through less processing.

You can butcher a chicken at any stage of its life, but if you wait until the bird is too old, it may have health problems. If you do it too young, you may not get as much meat on the bones. A bird's meat yields about 2 pounds less than the live weight of the bird. For example, an 8-pound chicken will yield about 6 pounds of meat. You may want to butcher your birds all at once, or on an as-needed basis. If you butcher them all at once, make sure you have ample freezer space to store the meat.

Getting Ready

The first thing you should do during the butchering process is to find a location to butcher your birds. If you have children or other family members in your home who would prefer not to witness the process, select a location outside your home. Ideally, a separate shed or building with ample lighting would work well. For an indoor space, you also will need a table, water access, and some type of drainage for waste. If you opt to butcher outdoors, you may want a temporary screen or fence for discretion, but the choice is yours.

The following is a checklist of items you will need prior to butchering your birds.

Checklist: Items you will need

- Ax, meat cleaver, or large sharp knife. The Country Horizons (*http://countryhorizons.net*) offers these for sale in addition to other poultry and farming products.

- Table with cutting-board top. Butcher Block Co. (*http://butcherblockco.com*) and AWP Butcher Block, Inc. (*http://awpbutcherblock.com*) offer these. The size of the table depends your preference. A small butcher block table is about 28 inches wide by 24 inches deep and 33 inches tall. The AWP Butcher Block, Inc. offers this size and the next size larger, which is 48 inches wide by 24 inches deep and 36 inches tall. Find the size that meets your needs, and be sure it is treated to prevent microorganisms and germs from inhabiting the block of wood.

- Rubber gloves. You can find these at most grocery stores and department stores or online through Rubbermaid (*www.rubbermaid.com*). This website provides a place to shop for durable household items that can be easily cleaned and stored.

- Rubber apron. You can find these at a sporting goods store or in the garden department of larger department stores. Amazon (*www.amazon.com*) offers useful products such as a butcher's apron made of cloth that is 34 inches long and will protect your clothes from blood and dirt.

- Large pot to boil water. This pot should be large enough to fit your largest bird.

- Stove or propane burner large enough to fit the pot.

- Kill cone or hooks or large nails. Find kill cones at feed stores and hardware stores. The website Sure Hatch (*http://surehatch.com*) has kill cones in different sizes.

- Trash receptacle. These can be found at any home store or department store such as Walmart, Target, or Bed Bath and Beyond.

- Plastic tubs to ice down the birds after butchering. These tubs can be found at a local department store, party supply stores, or online at Target (*www.target.com*). Just type "plastic tub" in the search engine and you'll find a variety of sizes and shapes. An 18-gallon tub is deep enough to submerge the birds in plenty of ice.

- Sink or hose with running water.

- A knife sharpener to sharpen blades can be purchased from Country Horizons (*www.countryhorizons.net*).

- Boning knife or butcher knife. These are sold at sporting goods stores, kitchen supply stores, and larger department stores. Online, a variety of boning knives can be found from Cutlery and More (*www. cutleryandmore.com*). This site has different blades and handles to suit your needs.

- Rags or paper towels. These can be purchased at our local grocery store or you can use old cloth towels that you do not plan on discarding after you use them for butchering.

- Cleaning spray, soap, or disinfectant. These can be found at your local grocery store or department store.

- Freezer bags. The size will depend on the size of the bird you want to freeze. These can be found at your local grocery store.

- Freezer space to store your birds. The size of the freezer you need will depend on how many birds you want to store. You make kill and use your birds immediately. You may want to kill your flock and store them for future use. Have a plan of action and that will help you determine how much freezer space you need.

- Work table to debone and carve the carcass. Butcher Block Co. (*www. butcherblockco.com*) has a selection of worktables to choose from if you do not have one already.

Before you butcher your chicken, you will need to put on a rubber apron, gloves, and protective eyewear. This will keep you clean and safe from cuts and scratches. Next you will need your equipment. Some people kill chickens with their hands; others prefer to use a sharp knife or ax. Always make sure the blade is sharp. The table you use will be on the receiving end of the blade, so it should have a chopping-block top or be made of wood. Use a tree stump if you are outdoors.

A piece of cone-shaped metal or plastic, known as a killing cone, can be purchased from sporting goods stores or online. The cone slides over the chicken's head and is inverted either to kill the chicken or let the blood drain from a dead chicken. If you do not have a cone, you can hang the carcass upside down from a nail or hook for the same effect. Hang them at least 3 feet off the ground over a bucket to collect the blood. You will need a trash receptacle for the waste.

Butchering is best done before daylight. The chickens will be sleeping in their hen house, and it will be easier to pick them up and bring them to the slaughter area. The dark helps keep the birds stay calm, and the quietness of the morning hours will keep them from being excessively stressed. Birds that are less stressed will taste better because they have fewer hormones running through their body. Also, they bleed cleaner, making the butchering less messy.

Do not feed the birds the night before, and provide little if any water. The birds will be easier to clean if their digestive tracts are empty. Also, keep their coop dark. When entering the coop in the morning, be quiet and calm as you collect your birds. Ideally, you want to have the slaughter part finished before sunrise so the bird can drain and be butchered for dinnertime.

Methods of Killing your Chickens

When it is time to kill a chicken, it is important to keep the process as humane and stress free for the bird as possible. Also be sure to make the process as sanitary as possible, as you and your family will be eating the chicken's meat. If you have the opportunity, watch a friend or butcher kill and process a chicken before you attempt it on your own. If you do not have this option, the following steps will ensure a quick and painless end to the bird's life.

Without a knife or ax

One way to kill a chicken is to wring its neck. Pick up the chicken and hold it upside down with one hand. Slide your free hand down the chicken's neck to just below the bird's head and take hold. Grasp the neck firmly and jerk it down and back up again with a twist to break the chicken's neck. Pull hard, but be aware that if you pull too hard, you may yank its head off.

Another way to kill a chicken without a knife is to kill it with a stick. Lift one end of a long stick, such as a broom handle, and slide the chicken's neck under the stick. Put one foot on one end of the stick, keeping it on the ground, and pull back on the other end of the stick, letting go of it quickly. It should snap back and break the bird's neck. You will need to hold on to the chicken's feet the entire time so it does not escape.

After killing the chicken, you will need to cut off its head and turn it upside down in a kill cone or hang it on a nail or hook to let the blood drain. Dispose of the blood by pouring it down the sink or drainage system and flush with lots of water. Clean and disinfect the entire area.

With a knife or ax

To kill your chicken with a knife or ax, first put on your rubber apron and make sure your knife or ax is sharp. Dull blades will only cause the animal to suffer and will not get the job done. Get your knife professionally sharpened or use a knife sharpener, found at any department store in the house ware section.

If you are using an ax, you will need a tree stump or table with a top that can handle the blade slicing into it. The surface you choose should be low and give you enough room to swing your ax up and then bring it down on the bird's neck. Also, you will need to hammer two nails into the stump or run a wire across the area. The chicken's neck will slide between the nails or under the wire to hold it in place. The nails only need to be as far apart as a chicken's neck, and the wire only has to be loose enough to slide the chicken's head underneath it.

Hold the chicken upside down, with your ax in one hand and the bird in the other. Slide the chicken's head between the nails or under the wire. Do this quickly. Pull back on the bird's legs slightly so the neck is stretched out. In one swift move, strike the ax down on the chicken's neck, making a clean, quick cut. Hold on to the feet because you do not want to let the bird go, as it will move. The body will still run off in those first few moments after the kill because of residual nervous energy. Letting the bird run will be a bloody mess and can be a traumatic sight for some people.

Kill cones make slaughtering a bird with a knife easier. Hang the cones in your slaughterhouse or somewhere you plan to do the killing. Put your bird in the cone, with the small opening on the bottom and the large opening on the top. Your bird will be upside down with its head through the small hole at the bottom. Pull to stretch its neck and make a quick cut right below its jaw. If you do not have a kill cone, tie the birds together and hang them from a nail or hook that is at least 3 feet from the ground. Kill the bird within seconds of putting it in the cone or hanging it from the nail. It is not humane to let it just hang there; plus, it may escape.

Once the bird is hanging, stretch its neck a little and then slit the throat with a sharp knife. You can either perform one clean, quick cut to remove the chicken's head, or you can make a slit to only drain the blood — if taking this approach, be sure to only cut the jugular and not the windpipe. Cutting the windpipe will cause the bird anguish. If you do not immediately take the head off, the bird may feel some distress for a few moments until it bleeds out. Once the blood is drained, then you can cut the head off. Have buckets beneath the cones to catch the blood. Let the chickens hang until all of the blood runs out of their bodies.

Whichever method you chose to use, your priority should be to provide a fast, painless death for the chicken. The first time you butcher an animal, it may be difficult for you. This is natural, especially if you raise the chickens and become attached to them. A humane death is an honorable ending for any bird. Aside from the emotions, butchering is a messy task. This is why some owners prefer to do a group slaughter, which entails killing more than one bird in your flock at the same time. The process is still the same; however, you need more kill cones to hang the birds upside down. Gather your birds one at a time. After you slit the throat or remove the head, hang your bird in the kill cone then get another bird and do the same. After you have your desired amount of birds slaughtered, proceed with the butchering.

Processing the Carcass

The next step is to pluck the chickens. To do this, put on your rubber gloves if you have not already. Have a large pot with scalding hot water ready to soak the chickens to kill germs and clean them. The water should be about 140 degrees Fahrenheit, which you can test with a candy thermometer or deep-fryer thermometer. Hold the chicken carcass by the feet and dip it into the pot for about ten to 15 seconds. Pull the bird out and try pulling one of the feathers. If it comes out easily, the chicken is ready to be plucked. If the feathers do not come out easily, dip the chicken again. Keeping the bird in the water for too long or having the temperature too high will cook the skin, so monitor the process. If the chicken is partially cooked, cool it immediately or discard it so bacteria do not grow in the meat. Warm temperatures are the perfect breeding ground for bacteria.

At this point, when the feathers are ready to come out, dip the bird into an ice bath using the plastic tubs to help prevent tears in the skin. This is not necessary, but it may make plucking easier. Now, pull out the feathers in the direction they grew. This may seem time-consuming, but it is faster than some of the automated plucking machines available commercially. Once you get the hang of it, the process will move quicker.

Featherman Plucker (*www.featherman.net*) and Schweiss Welding (*www.schweisswelding.com*) are two companies that sell automated chicken pluckers. Pluckers are also available online at Fleming Outdoors (*www.flemingoutdoors.com*). Fleming Outdoors has an expanded inventory of items that you may need for your journey owning chickens. They have incubators, feeders, waterers, poultry laying nests, wooden coops and hutches, electric poultry fences and poultry catchers, along with poultry scalders and pluckers. Schweiss Welding sells several pieces of equipment. Their products are more streamlined; they offer a chicken plucker that promises to pluck your chicken in 30 seconds, including pinfeathers. It sells for $495.00 and arrives already assembled. The Featherman Plucker retails for $975.00, and it holds four or five birds and plucks them in less than 20 seconds.

If automated pluckers are out of your price range, then you may want to build your own. The book *Anyone Can Build a Tub-Style Mechanical Chicken Plucker*, written by Herrick Kimball from Cumberland Books, is a guidebook on building a machine that plucks feathers. The cost of the book is $15 to $20 and is available on the websites Cornerstone Farm Ventures (*www.cornerstone-farm.com*), Amazon, and Egg Cartons (*www.eggcartons. com*). The book details how to build the Whizbang plucker, and testimonials claim that the machine can pluck your chicken in 15 seconds or less, including pinfeathers. Building your own plucker is a fraction of the cost of purchasing a new, commercial plucker and scalder. The book contains plans on how to build your own plucker.

After plucking, examine your bird. Make sure the flesh does not have any sign of diseases. If you have a small flock, you should have been monitoring your birds all along. But if you own many birds, it may be hard to keep track of each one, especially if they have hidden lesions or bumps on their bodies. If you come across a chicken with abscesses or lumps filled with pus, do not eat the bird.

Other problems to look for are sores or open wounds and tumors. If you find them on a chicken, discard the carcass. These sores and wounds can be signs of something toxic for you if consumed. When in doubt, throw it out. Throw out the carcasses if the butchered birds were left for more than an hour at temperatures over 40 degrees. Do not eat birds that were found dead.

Inedible and Removable parts

- Neck
- Oil gland
- Crop, esophagus, and trachea tubes
- Tail
- Spine
- Organs
- Feet

Now that you inspected your plucked bird, take the carcass to the worktable and get your knife out. Remove the chicken's head if you have not done so already. If you want to save the neck, carefully remove the esophagus and trachea tubes. If you do not want to save the neck, slice it off near the body and discard it.

Cut the feet off, slicing through the cartilage above the foot at the first joint. This is easier to cut through than the bone. Lift and then slam down a meat cleaver or sharp knife to make a clean cut. Discard the feet unless you like to cook with them. If you do want to keep them, put them in a storage container and refrigerate. They can be deep-fried or made into a soup.

At the bottom of the spine, you will see a yellow spot or yellow bump near the tail. It is the oil gland. Lay the bird breast-side down. Lop off the tail at the spine and throw it away. Or, if you prefer to leave the tail on, take your knife and slice under the oil gland, down and past the tail, to cut out the gland and bypass the tail. Some people leave the oil gland in, but it gives the chicken a bitter taste if you do.

Flip the bird over onto its back, and cut into it above the vent. Your objective is to make a small hole in the carcass to remove the organs. Do not cut too wide or too deep, but the hole should be wide enough to fit your hand into. Stick your fingers in and pull apart the skin. If you find bird feces, wash them out. Take the carcass to the sink or to a running hose and, while holding your bird, flush out the feces. The water should run down the vent side, not across the whole body, so it does not get contaminated. You may even want to use a mild dish detergent to wash off any affected areas. Rinse completely.

Once the bird is clean, wash any contaminated areas on your table. If you plan on cutting the bird into pieces, use kitchen shears to slice through its back and remove all of the organs. Otherwise, you will need to insert your hand inside the bird. Place your hand inside the carcass and move your arm up until you reach the bird's neck. Spread out your fingers, as much as you can, and rake your hands down the inside of the carcass to pull the organs out. Do this gently. Do not grab, as you may break open some of the organs inside the bird. Once you pull the organs down to the vent, scoop them out and toss them into the trash.

At this point, check the chicken's liver, which should be reddish-brown. If it is pale or discolored, it is probably diseased, and you should discard the chicken. If you want to save the heart, liver, and gizzards, sort through the internal mass that you just removed and separate the organs you want to save. Once you do that, double-check to make sure the cavity is clear of debris. Take the chicken back to the sink or water source and rinse it inside and out. Refrigerate your bird as soon as possible.

Spray down the cutting area with disinfectant or bleach cleaner, and use rags or paper towels to dry the area well. Spray down the area a second time and repeat the process. Be thorough in your cleaning, as some diseases can live on countertops and surface areas. Clean the kill cones by soaking them in warm bleach water to disinfect, then rinse them well. Wash your rubber gloves and aprons by spraying them with bleach and rinsing. Clean your hands every time you come into contact with the carcass or pieces of the bird. Good sanitation is important for you and your family's safety.

Cutting your chicken

After your bird is plucked, clean, and processed, it is ready to cut. You may not have the skills of a professional butcher, but you can cut your chicken similar to the way you would find it packaged. The simplest way to cut your chicken is to begin with cutting the chicken in half lengthwise, which means down the breast, and then cutting the parts away width wise. You will need a very sharp chef's knife and a pair of very sharp kitchen shears. In just a few simple steps, you can have your chicken completely cut up.

- Step one — With your kitchen shears, cut the chicken in half along the breastbone. You need to make sure that your kitchen shears are very sharp in order to accomplish this.

- Step two — Flip the chicken over and cut along both sides of the bone to remove it from the breasts. You can either discard the bone or save it, storing it in the freezer so you can use it to make your own stock.

- Step three — Now you should be staring at two halves of the chicken. The next thing to do is flip one of the halves over so that it is laying skin side up. Then, using your sharp chef's knife, cut halfway between the wing and the leg. If you are having difficulty cutting it, then you can place the knife in the spot that you want to cut it and push down on it with your other hand. Repeat this same process with the other half of the chicken. If you want to, you can cut the remaining pieces in half a second time.

The Poultry Label Says "Fresh"

"I am shopping for a fresh chicken because I do not want the hassle of defrosting a frozen one. When should I buy it and how do I know if it is fresh? What does 'fresh' on the label really mean?"

Prior to 1997, poultry could be sold as "fresh" even if it was frozen "as solid as a block of ice". However, consumer concerns about "rock" frozen poultry being sold as "fresh" led USDA to reconsider the term "fresh" as it applies to raw whole poultry and cuts of poultry. Furthermore, national press coverage and testimonies at public hearings indicated strong interest in the term "fresh" being re-defined.

After lengthy hearings, surveys and reviews of science-based information, USDA published a "fresh" labeling rule that went into effect in December 1997. Today the definition of "fresh" is intended to meet the expectations of consumers buying poultry. Below are questions and answers about the "fresh" labeling rule and the terms "fresh" and "frozen."

Why is 26 °F the lowest temperature at which poultry remains fresh?

Below 26 °F, raw poultry products become firm to the touch because much of the free water is changing to ice. At 26 °F, the product surface is still pliable and yields to the thumb when pressed. Most consumers consider a product to be fresh, as opposed to frozen, when it is pliable or when it is not hard to the touch.

What are the labeling requirements for frozen, raw poultry?

Raw poultry held at a temperature of 0 °F or below must be labeled with a "keep frozen" handling statement.

What does the "fresh" rule mean to consumers?

For consumers, "fresh" means whole poultry and cuts have never been below 26 °F. This is consistent with consumer expectations of "fresh" poultry, i.e., not hard to the touch or frozen solid. Fresh poultry should always bear a "keep refrigerated" statement.

Is there an increased microbiological safety risk associated with raw poultry that is maintained at 26 °F?

No. The National Advisory Committee on the Microbiological Criteria for Foods, as well as several scientific organizations, agreed that there is no increased microbiological risk associated with raw product maintained at 40 °F or below.

How should consumers handle fresh or frozen raw poultry products?

Fresh or frozen raw poultry will remain safe with proper handling and storage.

Fresh, raw poultry is kept cold during distribution to retail stores to prevent the growth of harmful bacteria and to increase its shelf life. It should be selected from a refrigerated cooler which maintains a temperature of below 40 °F and above 26 °F. Select fresh poultry just before checking out at the store register. Put packages in disposable plastic bags (if available) to contain any leakage that could cross-contaminate cooked foods or fresh produce.

At home, immediately place fresh raw poultry in a refrigerator that maintains 40 °F or below and use it within 1 to 2 days, or freeze the poultry at 0 °F or below. Frozen poultry will be safe indefinitely. For best quality, use frozen, raw whole poultry within 1 year, poultry parts within 9 months, and giblets within 4 months.

Poultry may be frozen in its original packaging or repackaged. If you are freezing poultry longer than 2 months, you should wrap the porous store plastic packages with airtight heavy-duty foil, freezer plastic wrap or freezer bags, or freezer paper. Use freezer packaging materials or airtight freezer containers to repackage family-sized packages into smaller units.

Proper wrapping prevents "freezer burn" (drying of the surface that appears as grayish brown leathery spots on the surface of the poultry). It is caused by air reaching the surface of the food. You may cut freezer-burned portions away either before or after cooking the poultry. Heavily freezer-burned products may have to be discarded because they might be too dry or tasteless.

What is the difference in quality between fresh and frozen poultry?

Both fresh and frozen poultry are inspected by USDA's Food Safety and Inspection Service. The quality is the same. It is personal preference that determines whether you purchase fresh or frozen poultry.

What does the date on the package mean?

"Open Dating" (use of a calendar date as opposed to a code) on a food product is a date stamped on the package of a product to help the store management determine how long to display the product for sale. It is a quality date, not a safety date. "Open Dating" is found primarily on perishable foods such as meat, poultry, eggs, and dairy products. If a calendar date is used, it must express both the month and day of the month (and the year, in the case of shelf-stable and frozen products). If a calendar date is shown, immediately adjacent to the date must be a phrase explaining the meaning of that date such as "sell by" or "use before." A "sell-by" date tells the store how long to display the product for sale. You should buy the product before the date expires. A "use-by" date is the last date recommended for the use of the product while at peak quality. In both cases, the date has been determined by the food processor.

There is no uniform or universally accepted system used for "Open Dating" of food in the United States. Although dating of some foods is required by more than 20 states, there are areas of the country where much of the food supply has almost no dating.

What should you do if you find poultry that is frozen, but labeled "fresh"?

You can call the USDA Meat and Poultry Hotline and file a complaint.

Professional Butchering

You may know right from the start that you do not want to butcher your birds. If no one in your household wants to slaughter your birds, you will need to find someone to do it for you, such as a friend or fellow chicken owner. You could also have a professional butcher handle the slaughter for you.

In the early 1900s, butcher shops were common on city streets. There was an art to butchering. In cities such as New York and Los Angeles, butchers may still have storefronts. Today, though, most grocery chains have their own meat departments inside the stores, and machines now take the place of professional butchers. So where can you find a butcher?

The website Local.com (*www.local.com*) can help you find any type of service anywhere in the United States. Type "butcher" in the search engine and your ZIP code in the "area" box. You also can type in the radius you want your search area to cover. The names, addresses, and phone numbers of all of the butchers in that area will appear on your screen. Then, just start contacting them to see who can get the job done for you. AT&T (*www.yellowpages. com*) provides a similar service. Type "butcher" and your ZIP code into the search fields, and information will pop up on all relevant businesses listed with the yellow pages.

If you still cannot find a butcher, try advertising in the local classifieds under the "wanted" section. Or go to your local grocer and ask someone who works in the meat department whether he or she can do it for you or can recommend someone who can.

A knowledgeable butcher will know how to cut any type of meat. Chicken is a very common meat, and any butcher should be able to cut it up for you. Butchers should know a healthy bird or carcass when they see it. They should not be willing to cut up poultry that is sickly or tainted. A good butcher will know how to make clean cuts, and will be able to distinguish prime cuts of meat from lesser cuts. Most butchers have been an apprentice or have on-the-job training. Your butcher should be able to discuss the parts of the bird with you in detail and have a clean environment in which your bird is prepared.

Meat Chicken handling tips

No matter if you process and cut your chicken yourself or find a butcher to do it, the result is the same — you have fresh meat for you and your family. Storing and handling raw chicken is very important when is comes to the health of your family as knowing the proper food handling methods will keep your family from getting salmonella poising. Here are some tips to follow to ensure you keep your family and kitchen supplies safe:

- Always use a solid plastic cutting board when you are working with raw chicken. Immediately after each use and before you use it for anything else, you must scrub the board with hot, soapy water. If you are having a moment of doubt in your ability to properly clean the cutting board, run it through the dishwasher. It is alright to use a wooden cutting board, but make sure to scrub it in water that is hotter than you can handle. Make sure to use a pair of rubber gloves so that you do not burn your hands.

- You must scrub any knife or utensil that comes in contact with the raw chicken in hot, soapy water immediately after it is used.

- Never defrost a chicken on your kitchen counter; this just breeds bacteria onto your surface top. To properly defrost a chicken, you should place it in the refrigerator in its original packaging and in a bowl of very cold water that needs to be changed every 45 minutes. You can also defrost your chicken in the microwave.

- It is utterly important that you discard any type of marinade that you used to coat the chicken in during its storage time. Do not ever baste a chicken with the cold marinade it was stored in.

- Do not ever serve your family "rare" chicken, because there is no such thing. A chicken has to be fully cooked, which entails that its juices run clear and, more importantly, that the internal temperature reads 165 degrees Fahrenheit when a meat thermometer is inserted into the meat.

- Sometimes, you will find a recipe that calls for you to pat dry a chicken before you cook it. Do this using a piece of paper towel; never use a dish towel to pat the chicken dry.

- If you are going to handle the chicken with your bare hands, always remember to vigorously wash your hands in hot, soapy water before you touch anything else. Touching the raw chicken and then touching a different substance, such as butter, vegetables, or utensils, can spread the chicken's bacteria to other things without you knowing it, which will in turn cause the next person who uses or eats it to be sick. Whenever possible, use gloves to handle the raw chicken, then take them off immediately after you finish handling the chicken.

New Homes for Chicks and Chickens

Even though your adventure with chickens is new and exciting, at some point you may decide that keeping birds is not for you. What should you do? One option is giving your birds to a local farmer. Experienced farmers might be happy to take your birds from you, providing they are healthy and in good condition.

In case you find yourself in a predicament where you need to get rid of your birds, keep any health records and visits to the vet on record to give to the new owner. This way, the owner can continue to care for the birds properly. Having this information will help you place your birds more quickly.

You also can try to sell your birds. Be honest about their ages and health histories. List your birds for sale in the local classified ads and on online websites:

- CC.CC (*www.cc.cc*) allows you to set up your own domain for free.

- Plaza.Net (*www.ec.plaza.net*) allows you to post your chicken eggs for sale.

- Backpage.com (*www.backpage.com*) lets you post items for sale for free. First, locate your city on the homepage, then find the appropriate post to sell your birds. There is a farm and garden section and a pet section.

- Freeadforum.com (*www.freeadforum.com*) is a website that will allow you to post and sell your chicks and eggs for free.

Some neighborhoods have exchange programs where you can offer your birds and supplies to someone who has something to barter with you. The social networking website Facebook (*www.facebook.com*) also has exchange programs that may help you find a new place for your flock and get something for yourself as well.

Even if you no longer want your birds, do not neglect them. It may take a little time, but you will find a solution. Problems will just compound if you do not care for your poultry and they get sick or die off. Disease can create havoc. If time is of the essence, contact your local animal shelter or animal control officer and explain your situation. They should be able to assist you or at least put you in contact with someone who can help.

Natural life span of chickens

The life span of chickens is between 5 and 7 years, although some breeds can live longer. There is always the rare situation where an animal may live much longer than their life expectancy due to a healthy and safe environment and probably good genetics as well. Chickens can provide many substantial years of companionship and providing food for you. Their life with you can be rewarding and fulfilling for both you and your birds.

The life cycle of the chicken starts with a fertilized egg. The hen sits on her eggs to hatch them. Twenty-one days later, baby chicks emerge from the eggs. The chick's body is covered with soft down feathers. Chicks can walk right away. Within the first 4 weeks of their life, chicks will grow more feathers and be able to eat bugs, worms, and seeds.

Chicks are full grown at 6 months of age, and most hens begin laying eggs at 4 or 5 months of age. Different breeds may vary on their maturity level, and some hens may not produce at all due to health problems or other outside factors. The cycle of life begins again with each new fertilized egg. Chickens constantly give back to their owners and you will be pleased with your return whether it is their companionship, their eggs, their meat or their reproduction of baby chicks. You will have a more bountiful, sustainable existence thanks to your new flock of feathered friends.

CASE STUDY: HUMANE TREATMENT BEGINNING TO END

Paula Naughton

"It all started one day after my husband said 'no chickens,'" tells Paula Naughton, "My granddaughter and I went to the feed store. I had her call Grandpa at work to ask if she could have a baby chick. He couldn't say no to *her*. We had to get at least two. 'But what if one dies, it can't live alone,' I thought. So we got six, just to be sure." That first year, Naughton's granddaughter won first place at the Berrien County Fair with her market birds. Naughton now raises Cornish Cross Broilers and various egg layers.

In the beginning, she brought her birds to a local butcher with no intent to slaughter her own chickens. The flock grew, and Naughton went from bringing 25 chickens to 50 chickens to be butchered. Then, one year, intense heat was killing her birds. Confident that she could butcher her own birds before the heat could get to them, she gathered as many as she could and started with the biggest birds. One by one, she humanely killed her chickens for food.

Naughton realized that she could save even more money by doing her own butchering. She invested in some equipment and honed her skills. On butchering Naughton says, "Now it takes me about ten minutes to process a bird by myself. Many books talk about equipment, methods, care, among other things. One thing they do not mention is how to stage equipment and arrange your day to make it easier. Processing is physically demanding and time consuming. Plan everything. Plan your steps, your counter height, making sure to keep things out of your way, and learn how to entertain your brain during physical mindlessness to make it 'nicer.'

Take care of your feet with your shoe and clothing selection. Think about disposal of unwanted parts." Naughton continues, "The key to making the job easier is a good scald. The feathers come out much easier. It is a struggle every step of the way if the scald is not good. Dawn dish soap also helps. If I could have one piece of equipment, it would be a scalder."

As far as the actual butchering is concerned, Naughton says, "I want to humanely kill the bird by holding it on a slightly downward angle on my lap and make a small cut just behind its jaw. I have cut myself many times so I know how it feels. The knife is as sharp as a scalpel. It is a knife that was made for the job. The bird bleeds out and basically looks like it falls asleep. The meat does not contain any blood, leaving it cleaner and healthier." She adds, "I have heard stories and seen examples of how people process birds with pruning shears or beat it to death or make a half hearted attempt with an ax. I cringe. I have also seen many people feed whole corn to their birds that they cannot even digest … One sensitivity that I have developed is humane treatment of the animals that we eat. Humane treatment is key in my approach from beginning to end."

After raising chickens for the past 10 years, Paula notes, "The eggs are better. The yolks are darker. The whites are clearer. In comparison the eggs in the store look anemic. I can not imagine those chickens living in small cages as their eggs are collected day after day for the rest of their miserable life."

Focus On: Chicken By The USDA

What's for dinner tonight? There's a good chance it's chicken -- now the number one species consumed by Americans. Interest in the safe handling and cooking of chicken is reflected in thousands of calls to the USDA Meat and Poultry Hotline, second only to turkey in number of specific inquiries. The following information answers many of the questions these callers have asked about chicken.

History & Definitions

The chicken is a descendant of the Southeast Asian red jungle fowl first domesticated in India around 2000 B.C. Most of the birds raised for meat in America today are from the Cornish (a British breed) and the White Rock (a breed developed in New England). Broiler-fryers, roasters, stewing/baking hens, capons and Rock Cornish hens are all chickens. The following are definitions for these:

- *Broiler-fryer* a young, tender chicken about 7 weeks old which weighs 2 1/2 to 4 1/2 pounds when eviscerated. Cook by any method.
- *Rock Cornish Game Hen* - a small broiler-fryer weighing between 1 and 2 pounds. Usually stuffed and roasted whole.
- *Roaster* - an older chicken about 3 to 5 months old which weighs 5 to 7 pounds. It yields more meat per pound than a broiler-fryer. Usually roasted whole.
- *Capon* - Male chickens about 16 weeks to 8 months old which are surgically unsexed. They weigh about 4 to 7 pounds and have generous quantities of tender, light meat. Usually roasted.
- *Stewing/Baking Hen* - a mature laying hen 10 months to 1 1/2 years old. Since the meat is less tender than young chickens, it's best used in moist cooking such as stewing.
- *Cock or rooster* - a mature male chicken with coarse skin and tough, dark meat. Requires long, moist cooking.

Chicken Inspection

All chickens found in retail stores are either inspected by USDA or by state systems which have standards equivalent to the Federal government. Each chicken and its internal organs are inspected for signs of disease. The "Inspected for wholesomeness by the U.S. Department of Agriculture" seal insures the chicken is free from visible signs of disease.

Chicken Grading

Inspection is mandatory but grading is voluntary. Chickens are graded according to USDA Agricultural Marketing Service regulations and standards for meatiness, appearance and freedom from defects. Grade A chickens have plump, meaty bodies and clean skin, free of bruises, broken bones, feathers, cuts and discoloration.

Fresh or Frozen

The term *fresh* on a poultry label refers to any raw poultry product that has never been below 26 °F. Raw poultry held at 0 °F or below must be labeled *frozen* or *previously frozen*. No specific labeling is required on raw poultry stored at temperatures between 0-25 °F.

Dating of Chicken Products

Product dating is not required by Federal regulations, but many stores and processors voluntarily date packages of chicken or chicken products. If a calendar date is shown, immediately adjacent to the date there must be a phrase explaining the meaning of that date such as *sell by* or *use before*.

The use-by date is for quality assurance; after the date, peak quality begins to lessen but the product may still be used. It's always best to buy a product before the date expires. If a use-by date expires while the chicken is frozen, the food can still be used.

Hormones & Antibiotics

No hormones are used in the raising of chickens.

Antibiotics may be given to prevent disease and increase feed efficiency. A "withdrawal" period is required from the time antibiotics are administered before the bird can be slaughtered. This ensures that no residues are present in the bird's system. FSIS randomly samples poultry at slaughter and tests for residues. Data from this monitoring program have shown a very low percentage of residue violations.

Additives

Additives are not allowed on fresh chicken. If chicken is processed, however, additives such as MSG, salt, or sodium erythorbate may be added but must be listed on the label.

Foodborne Organisms Associated with Chicken

As on any perishable meat, fish or poultry, bacteria can be found on raw or undercooked chicken. They multiply rapidly at temperatures between 40 °F and 140 °F (out of refrigeration and before thorough cooking occurs). Freezing doesn't kill bacteria but they are destroyed by thorough cooking.

USDA's Food Safety and Inspection Service has a zero tolerance for bacteria in cooked and ready-to-eat products such as chicken franks or lunch meat that can be eaten without further cooking.

Most foodborne illness outbreaks are a result of contamination from food handlers. Sanitary food handling and proper cooking and refrigeration should prevent foodborne illnesses.

Bacteria must be consumed on food to cause illness. They cannot enter the body through a skin cut. However, raw poultry must be handled carefully to prevent cross-contamination. This can occur if raw poultry or its juices contact cooked food or foods that will be eaten raw such as salad. An example of this is chopping tomatoes on an unwashed cutting board just after cutting raw chicken on it.

Following are some bacteria associated with chicken:

- *Salmonella* Enteritidis may be found in the intestinal tracts of livestock, poultry, dogs, cats and other warm-blooded animals. This strain is only one of about 2,000 kinds of *Salmonella* bacteria; it is often associated with poultry and shell eggs.

- *Staphylococcus aureus* can be carried on human hands, in nasal passages, or in throats. The bacteria are found in foods made by hand and improperly refrigerated, such as chicken salad.

- *Campylobacter jejuni* is one of the most common causes of diarrheal illness in humans. Preventing cross- contamination and using proper cooking methods reduces infection by this bacterium.

- *Listeria monocytogenes* was recognized as causing human foodborne illness in 1981. It is destroyed by cooking, but a cooked product can be contaminated by poor personal hygiene. Observe "keep refrigerated" and "use-by" dates on labels.

Rinsing or Soaking Chicken

It is not necessary to wash raw chicken. Any bacteria which might be present are destroyed by cooking.

Liquid in Package

Many people think the pink liquid in packaged fresh chicken is blood, but it is mostly water which was absorbed by the chicken during the chilling process. Blood is removed from poultry during slaughter and only a small amount remains in the muscle tissue. An improperly bled chicken would have cherry red skin and is condemned at the plant.

How to Handle Chicken Safely

- **Fresh Chicken:** Chicken is kept cold during distribution to retail stores to prevent the growth of bacteria and to increase its shelf life. Chicken should feel cold to the touch when purchased. Select fresh chicken just before checking out at the register. Put packages of chicken in disposable plastic bags (if available) to contain any leakage which could cross-contaminate cooked foods or produce. Make the grocery your last stop before going home.

- At home, immediately place chicken in a refrigerator that maintains 40 °F, and use within 1 or 2 days, or freeze at 0 °F. If kept frozen continuously, it will be safe indefinitely.

- Chicken may be frozen in its original packaging or repackaged. If freezing longer than two months, over wrap the porous store plastic packages with airtight heavy-duty foil, plastic wrap or freezer paper, or place the package inside a freezer bag. Use these materials or airtight freezer containers to repackage family packs into smaller amounts or freeze the chicken from opened packages.

- Proper wrapping prevents "freezer burn," which appears as grayish-brown leathery spots and is caused by air reaching the surface of food. Cut freezer-burned portions away either before or after cooking the chicken. Heavily freezer-burned products may have to be discarded because they might be too dry or tasteless.

- **Ready-Prepared Chicken:** When purchasing fully cooked rotisserie or fast food chicken, be sure it is hot at time of purchase. Use it within two hours or cut it into several pieces and refrigerate in shallow, covered containers. Eat within 3 to 4 days, either cold or reheated to 165 °F (hot and steaming). It is safe to freeze ready-prepared chicken. For best quality, flavor and texture, use within 4 months.

Safe Defrosting

FSIS recommends three ways to defrost chicken: in the refrigerator, in cold water and in the microwave. Never defrost chicken on the counter or in other locations. It's best to plan ahead for slow, safe thawing in the refrigerator. Boneless chicken breasts will usually defrost overnight. Bone-in parts and whole chickens may take 1 to

2 days or longer. Once the raw chicken defrosts, it can be kept in the refrigerator an additional day or two before cooking. During this time, if chicken defrosted in the refrigerator is not used, it can safely be refrozen without cooking first.

Chicken may be defrosted in cold water in its airtight packaging or in a leak proof bag. Submerge the bird or cut-up parts in cold water, changing the water every 30 minutes to be sure it stays cold. A whole (3 to 4-pound) broiler fryer or package of parts should defrost in 2 to 3 hours. A 1-pound package of boneless breasts will defrost in an hour or less.

Chicken defrosted in the microwave should be cooked immediately after thawing because some areas of the food may become warm and begin to cook during microwaving. Holding partially cooked food is not recommended because any bacteria present wouldn't have been destroyed. Foods defrosted in the microwave or by the cold water method should be cooked before refreezing.

Do not cook frozen chicken in the microwave or in a slow cooker. However, chicken can be cooked from the frozen state in the oven or on the stove. The cooking time may be about 50% longer.

Stuffed Chicken

The Hotline does not recommend buying retail-stuffed fresh whole chicken because of the highly perishable nature of a previously stuffed item. Consumers should not pre-stuff whole chicken to cook at a later time. Chicken can be stuffed immediately before cooking. Some USDA-inspected frozen stuffed whole poultry MUST be cooked from the frozen state to ensure a safely cooked product. Follow preparation directions on the label.

Marinating

Chicken may be marinated in the refrigerator up to 2 days. Boil used marinade before brushing on cooked chicken. Discard any uncooked leftover marinade.

Safe Cooking

FSIS recommends cooking whole chicken to a safe minimum internal temperature of 165 °F as measured using a food thermometer. Check the internal temperature in the innermost part of the thigh and wing and the thickest part of the breast. For reasons of personal preference, consumers may choose to cook poultry to higher temperatures.

For approximate cooking times to use in meal planning, see the following chart compiled from various resources.

Approximate Chicken Cooking Times

Type of Chicken	Weight	Roasting 350 °F	Simmering	Grilling
Whole broiler fryer+	3 to 4 lbs.	1¼ - 1½ hrs.	60 to 75 min.	60 to 75 min*
Whole roasting hen+	5 to 7 lbs.	2 to 2¼ hrs.	1¾ to 2 hrs.	18-25 min/ lb*
Whole capon+	4 to 8 lbs.	2 to 3 hrs	Not suitable	15-20 min/ lb*
Whole Cornish hens+	18-24 oz.	50 to 60 min.	35 to 40 min.	45 to 55 min*
Breast halves, bone-in	6 to 8 oz.	30 to 40 min.	35 to 45 min.	10 - 15 min/ side
Breast half, boneless	4 ounces	20 to 30 min.	25 to 30 min.	6 to 8 min/ side
Legs or thighs	8 or 4 oz.	40 to 50 min.	40 to 50 min.	10 - 15 min/ side
Drumsticks	4 ounces	35 to 45 min.	40 to 50 min.	8 to 12 min/ side
Wings or wingettes	2 to 3 oz.	30 to 40 min.	35 to 45 min.	8 to 12 min/ side

+ Unstuffed. If stuffed, add 15 to 30 minutes additional time.
* Indirect method using drip pan.

Microwave Directions:

- Microwave on medium-high (70 percent power): whole chicken, 9 to 10 minutes per pound; bone-in parts and Cornish hens, 8 to 9 minutes per pound; boneless breasts halves, 6 to 8 minutes per pound.

- When microwaving parts, arrange in dish or on rack so thick parts are toward the outside of dish and thin or bony parts are in the center.

- Place whole chicken in an oven cooking bag or in a covered pot.

- For boneless breast halves, place in a dish with 1/4 cup water; cover with plastic wrap.

- Allow 10 minutes standing time for bone-in chicken; 5 minutes for boneless breast.

- The USDA recommends cooking whole poultry to a safe minimum internal temperature of 165 °F as measured using a food thermometer. Check the internal temperature in the innermost part of the thigh and wing and the thickest part of the breast. When cooking pieces, the breast, drumsticks, thighs, and wings should be cooked until they reach a safe minimum internal temperature of 165 °F. For reasons of personal preference, consumers may choose to cook poultry to higher temperatures.

Partial Cooking

Never brown or partially cook chicken to refrigerate and finish cooking later because any bacteria present wouldn't have been destroyed. It is safe to partially pre-cook or microwave chicken immediately before transferring it to the hot grill to finish cooking.

Color of Skin

Chicken skin color varies from cream-colored to yellow. Skin color is a result of the type of feed eaten by the chicken, not a measure of nutritional value, flavor, tenderness or fat content. Color preferences vary in different sections of the country, so growers use the type of feed which produces the desired color.

Dark Bones

Darkening around bones occurs primarily in young broiler-fryers. Since their bones have not calcified completely, pigment from the bone marrow can seep through the porous bones. Freezing can also contribute to this seepage. When the chicken is cooked, the pigment turns dark. It's perfectly safe to eat chicken meat that turns dark during cooking.

Pink Meat

The color of cooked chicken is not a sign of its safety. Only by using a food thermometer can one accurately determine that chicken has reached a safe minimum internal temperature of 165 °F throughout. The pink color in safely cooked chicken may be due to the hemoglobin in tissues which can form a heat-stable color. Smoking or grilling may also cause this reaction, which occurs more in young birds.

Color of Giblets

Giblet color can vary, especially in the liver, from mahogany to yellow. The type of feed, the chicken's metabolism and its breed can account for the variation in color. If the liver is green, do not eat it. This is due to bile retention. However, the chicken meat should be safe to eat.

Fatty Deposits

Chickens may seem to have more fatty deposits or contain a larger "fat pad" than in the past. This is because broiler fryer chickens have been bred to grow very rapidly to supply the demand for more chicken. Feed that is not converted into muscle tissue (meat) is metabolized into fat. However, the fat is not "marbled" into the meat as is beef or other red meat, and can be easily removed. Geneticists are researching ways to eliminate the excess fat.

Trisodium Phosphate

Food-grade trisodium phosphate (TSP) has been approved by FSIS for use in poultry slaughter as an antimicrobial agent. When immersed in and/or sprayed in a dilute solution on chickens, it can significantly reduce bacteria levels. TSP is "generally recognized as safe" (GRAS) by the FDA, and has been safely used for years, particularly in processed cheese.

Irradiation of Poultry

In 1992, the USDA approved a rule to permit irradiation of raw, fresh or frozen packaged poultry to control certain common bacteria on raw poultry that can cause illness when poultry is undercooked or otherwise mishandled. Irradiation at 1.5 to 3.0 kilo Gray, the smallest, most practical "dose," would eliminate more than 99 percent of Salmonellae organisms on the treated poultry.

Packages of irradiated chicken are easily recognizable at the store because they must carry the international radura symbol along with the statement, "treated with irradiation" or "treated by irradiation."

Storage Times

Since product dates aren't a guide for safe use of a product, how long can the consumer store the food and still use it at top quality? Follow these tips:

- Purchase the product before the date expires.
- Follow handling recommendations on product.
- Keep chicken in its package until using.
- Freeze chicken in its original packaging, overwrap or re-wrap it according to directions in the above section, "How to Handle Chicken Safely".

Refrigerator Home Storage (at 40° F or below) of Chicken Products

Product	Refrigerator Storage Times
Fresh Chicken, Giblets or Ground Chicken	1 to 2 days
Cooked Chicken, Leftover	3 to 4 days
Chicken Broth or Gravy	1 to 2 days
Cooked Chicken Casseroles, Dishes or Soup	3 to 4 days
Cooked Chicken Pieces, covered with broth or gravy	1 to 2 days
Cooked Chicken Nuggets, Patties	1 to 2 days
Fried Chicken	3 to 4 days
Take-Out Convenience Chicken (Rotisserie, Fried, etc.)	3 to 4 days
Restaurant Chicken Leftovers, brought immediately home in a "Doggy Bag"	3 to 4 days
Store-cooked Chicken Dinner including gravy	1 to 2 days
Chicken Salad	3 to 5 days
Deli-sliced Chicken Luncheon Meat	3 to 5 days
Chicken Luncheon Meat, sealed in package	2 weeks (but no longer than 1 week after a "sell-by" date)
Chicken Luncheon Meat, after opening	3 to 5 days
Vacuum-packed Dinners, Commercial brand with USDA seal	Unopened 2 weeks / Opened 3 to 4 days
Chicken Hotdogs, unopened	2 weeks (but no longer than 1 week after a "sell-by" date)
Chicken Hotdogs, after opening	7 days
Canned Chicken Products	2 to 5 years in pantry

Last Modified: July 2014

Chic-tion-ary
A Glossary of Terms

Air cell — The pocket of air located at the end of an egg.

Alektorophobia — Fear of chickens.

American Poultry Association — An organization the continues the publication of the American Standard of Perfection with the breed and variety descriptions for all the purebred fowl. Their mission is to promote and protect the standard-bred poultry industry in all its phases.

Avian — Pertaining to birds.

Avian influenza — Also known as Bird flu, this is a serious illness in birds that is highly contagious and must be reported to the state or local government if it breaks out among your flock.

Band — Markings on a bird's coat. Often black, it runs across a feather.

Bantam — Most chicken breeds have a miniature version of their breed known as a bantam. True bantam breeds have no large counterpart.

Banty — Slang for bantam.

Barring — Markings on a chicken's coat. Barring is alternating horizontal stripes on a chicken's coat.

BLRW — Abbreviation for the breed of chicken known as blue laced red wyandotte.

BO — Abbreviation for the breed of chicken known as buff Orpington.

Booted — Feather feet on a chicken, giving the illusion of "boots" on their feet.

BR — Abbreviation for the breed of chicken known as barred rock.

Broiler — A chicken bred specifically for meat consumption. Typically a smaller bird, and the most common found in the grocery market.

Brood — Another term for flock.

Broody hen — A hen that has stopped laying eggs but continues to sit on her eggs or another hen's eggs in order to hatch them.

BSL — Abbreviation for the breed of chicken known as black sex link. You can distinguish the chicks of this breed by the color of their markings.

Bumblefoot — The swelling of the foot on a chicken.

Butcher — n. A person whose job it is to kill and dress an animal for its meat. v. To kill or dress animals for meat.

Candle or candling — Taking an egg and holding it in front of a bright light in a dark room to see the development of the embryo inside the egg.

Cape — The area of feathers between the shoulders and neck on a chicken.

Capon — A castrated rooster.

Chalazae — The two coils that hold the yolk in place inside of an egg.

Chicks — Baby chickens that are hatched from fertilized eggs.

Chook — An Australian slang term meaning chicken.

Clutch — A group of eggs laid by a broody hen.

Coccidiosis — A protozoal infestation causing disease and sometimes death.

Cock — A male chicken after his first molt.

Cockerel — A male chicken under 12 months of age.

Comb — The fleshy piece of skin on top of a chicken's head. It helps to identify the breed. It comes in a variety of shapes including single, pea, v-shaped, and rose.

Coop — Housing for chickens. Can be made of different material and customized to fit the needs of your flock.

Crest — The feathers on top of a chicken's head.

Crop — Located inside the base of a chicken's neck, right before the gizzard. Food passes through the crop where it is softened and then moves on to the gizzard.

Crumbles — Food for birds, often broken up pellets, into medium size shapes for the birds to eat.

Cull — Killing sick or unwanted birds in a humane fashion.

Debeak — Removing the tip of the beak from a bird. This is considered inhumane and not necessary. Often it is done to birds raised in close quarters in order to prevent them from pecking at each other.

Down — The new, soft feathers on a baby chick before it grows its feathers. It is also the fluffy layer of feathers underneath the main feathers on an adult bird.

Dual-purpose breed — A breed raised to provide both meat and eggs.

Dust bath — Birds "bathe" or roll around in fine dirt or sand to help remove external parasites from their bodies.

Earlobes — Skin below a chicken's ears that can vary in color and shape depending on the breed.

EE — Abbreviation for a breed of chicken known as Easter egger. They lay eggs in different colors including shades of blue and green.

Egg tooth — The very tip of the chick's beak which pierces the egg when the chick is ready to hatch. It falls off within the first week of hatching, after it is no longer needed.

Exterior albument — The narrow fluid layer next to the shell membrane in an egg.

Fertilized egg — An egg that contains an embryo that will produce a baby chick.

Flighty — Unstable behavior.

Flock — A group of chickens.

Free-range — Chickens that are not caged.

Frizzled — Feathers that curl on a bird, and give the appearance of a fuzzy, fluffy look.

Fryer — A chicken, typically smaller in size, bred for meat. Another name for broiler, This is the type of chicken found mostly in grocery stores.

Germinal disk or Blastoderm — This is the small circular spot on the surface of the yolk. It is the point where sperm enters the egg.

Gizzard — The part of the chicken's digestive system that contains the grit that is used to breakdown the food.

GLW — Abbreviation for a breed of chicken known as gold laced wyandotte.

GSL — Abbreviation for a breed of chicken known as gold sex link. These chicks are able to distinguish their gender by the markings on their coat.

Hackles — The feathers located on a chicken's back between the shoulder and neck.

Heavy breed — A breed in which the female weighs more than 5 ½ pounds.

Hen —A female chicken after her first molt.

Hock — The joint between the thigh and shank on a chicken.

Hybrid — A crossbreed.

Incubation — The stage of a chicken's life cycle when the fertilized egg is in an artificial incubator or under a hen as it matures 21 days to hatch.

Keel — The blade of a chicken's breastbone.

Kill cone — A cone-shaped cylinder tube, typically made out of plastic or steel, to place chickens in upside down for slaughter and to drain the blood from their bodies after they have been killed.

Lacing — The markings on a chicken's feathers. This can sometimes help identify the breed. It is a contrasting color on the edge of a feather.

Layer   A hen that is proficient in laying eggs.

LB — Abbreviation for the breed of chicken known as light Brahma.

LBC — Abbreviation for the breed of chicken known as little brown chicken.

Mandibles — The upper and lower part of a beak.

Marek's disease — A highly contagious viral neoplastic disease in chickens.

Mash — Finely ground food usually used to feed baby chicks.

Newcastle's disease — Avian distemper, affecting the respiratory system.

NN — Abbreviation for a breed of chicken known as naked beck.

MG — Abbreviation for a breed of chicken known as modern game.

MGB — Abbreviation for a breed of chicken known as modern game bantam.

Middle albumen — This is the thick, white layer of dense matter known as the egg white inside of an egg.

Molt — The shedding of feathers on a bird. It usually takes 3 months to complete the process and it occurs once a year. Hens do not lay eggs during this time.

Mottled — Markings on a chicken's coat. The feather's tips or spots on the feather have a contrasting color, typically black with a white tip.

Nest boxes — An area in the coop that hens can lay eggs and sit on them until they hatch if they are fertilized.

Nest egg — A fake egg or egg replacement to fool a hen into thinking she has laid an egg to induce egg laying in the bird.

Nucleus of pander — The plug of whitish yolk inside the yellow yolk that is purely for nutritional value.

OEG — Abbreviation for a breed of chicken known as old English game.

OEGB — Abbreviation for a breed of chicken known as old English game bantam.

Ovum — A hen's egg cell.

Pasted vent — A condition in which a chick or chicken's vent is clogged with feces. More common in baby chicks than chickens.

Pecking order — The social hierarchy in a flock of chickens.

Pencil — Markings on a chicken's coat.

Pellet — Food for birds, compressed into a long, cylinder shape.

Pinfeather — Sometimes called a "blood feather." It is a developing feather on a bird. It can be a new feather during infancy, or a replacement feather during molting.

Pluck — To pull off or out.

Plucker — Can be commercial and automated or homemade. It is a piece of equipment that removes feathers from a dead chicken, turkey, duck, or other poultry.

Pox — A virus in which wart-like bumps appear on the wattles and combs of chickens.

Pullet — A female chicken under 12 months of age.

Purebred — A breed of chicken whose parents are the same breed.

RIR — Abbreviation for a breed of chicken known as Rhode Island red.

RIW — Abbreviation for a breed of chicken known as Rhode Island white.

RSL — Abbreviation for a breed of chicken known as red sex link. These chicks are able to distinguish their gender by the markings of their coat.

Run — An area of space for chickens to run, forage, and roam.

Rooster — An adult, male, chicken.

Scald — To burn or injure with hot water or steam.

Scalder — A piece of equipment that submerges an animal, typically a bird or fowl, with the intent to burn the feathers off the carcass.

Sexing — The process of determining the gender of a baby chick.

Sex-linked — This breed of bird can have its sex determined as a chick due to the markings and colors of its coat.

SF — Abbreviation for a breed of chicken known as salmon faverolles.

SLW — Abbreviation for a breed of chicken known as silver laced wyandotte.

Spangled — A "V" marking at the tip of a feather on a chicken's coat.

Splash — A term used to describe the colors and markings on chick's and chicken's coats.

Spur — A stiff, sharp spine on the leg rear of a chicken's leg.

SS — Abbreviation for a breed of chicken known as speckled Sussex.

Stress — To a chicken, stress can be triggered by a number of things, including loud noises, overcrowding, children, other animals and bright light. Stress is harmful for chickens because they are very sensitive birds. Too much stress can cause illness, decreased egg production, and even death in some cases.

Thrush — A condition in a chicken that affects the upper digestive tracts.

Twisted legs — This is a leg deformity in birds.

Wattle — The fleshy pieces of skin that hang down on either side of a chicken's beak. This can be used in identifying a breed of chicken. They are typically larger on males than females.

WCBP — Abbreviation for a breed of chicken known as white crested black Polish.

Wheaton — The color of a chicken's coat, referring to an array of browns and tans.

Vent — The opening in the rear of a chicken where eggs and bodily excretions pass through.

Yolk — The yellow mass of materials found in an egg that surrounds and provides nutrients to the developing embryo and consists of protein, lecithin, and cholesterol.

Appendices

Appendix A: *State Zoning Laws Regarding Owning Chickens*

Alabama: All owners or custodians of animals which die or are killed in their possession or custody, other than such as are slaughtered for food, within 24 hours shall cause the bodies of such animals to be burned or buried at least two feet below the surface of the ground. (*animalhumanefederation.org*)

Alaska: Fairbanks, Chickens are allowed. No permit required. (*www.backyardchickens.com*)

Arizona: Mesa, Ten chickens for each half acre until 2 ½ acres after which there is no limit. Coops must be 75 feet from neighboring buildings and must be sanitary. (*www.mesaaz.gov*)

Arkansas: Little Rock, No limit on the maximum number of chickens. Coops must have 3 square feet of space per bird over 4 months of age. (*www.backyardchickens.com*)

California: Anaheim, Can keep 3 chickens on a 5,000 square foot lot, 6 chickens on a 10,000 on a square foot lot (*handcraftedcoops.com*)

Colorado: Colorado Springs, A property can contain a maximum of 10 fowl, as long as they have adequate outdoor space and at least 4 feet of square feet coop area. No roosters permitted within the city limits. (*www.home.centurytel.net*)

Connecticut: Danbury, No chickens and no roosters allowed. (City of Danbury, CT. Office of Legislative Assistant)

Delaware: New Castle County, Chickens are not allowed unless you have over 1 acre of land. (*www.home.centurytel.net*)

Florida: Miami, May have up to 15 hens, no roosters. Must be 100 feet from neighboring structures. No breeding. Do not use droppings for fertilizer. At lease two times weekly, all droppings must be collected. Wrap droppings in paper, and placed in a covered garbage can for pick up. (*www.home.centurytel.net*)

Georgia: Augusta, Chickens allowed. No permit is required. Coop restrictions apply including noise, sanitation, proximity, zoning, and building restrictions. (*www.augustaga.gov*)

Hawaii: Honolulu, Two chickens are permitted. No roosters are allowed. A permit is required. Must not make noise for 10 continuous minutes or intermittently for one-half hour or more to the disturbance of any person any time of day or night. (*honolulu.gov*)

Idaho: Idaho Falls, No permit required. Chickens are allowed. No cock or animal fighting. Anyone involved with cock fighting, including instigating, aiding, being present at, or permitting on his or her premises is guilty of a misdemeanor. (*www.amlegal.com/idaho_falls_id/*)

Illinois: Chicago, Chickens are allowed and an unlimited number of chickens are allowed to be kept at a residence but only as a pet or for egg purposes. No slaughtering permitted. Coops must be of a "humane" and adequate size for the animals and must be clean and sanitary. (*www.backyardchickens.com*)

Indiana: Lafayette, No livestock is permitted in this city. (*www.home.centurytel.net*)

Iowa: West Des Moines, Chickens may not "run at large." (*www.home.centurytel.net*)

Kansas: Lawrence, A homeowner can own up to 20 chickens, no roosters. (*www.home.centurytel.net*)

Kentucky: Louisville, If your lot of land is less than half of one acre, then you can own up to 5 hens or "non-crowing poultry." (*www.thecitychicken.com*)

Louisiana: New Orleans, No selling or donating chicks under 4 weeks of age, unless there is a quantity of 12. Fowl may not be given away as a prize or as advertising. (*www.home.centurytel.net*)

Maine: Camden, Allows up to 9 hens or other small animals such as rabbits even if your lot is less than 2.5 acres. (*www.home.centurytel.net*)

Maryland: Frederick, Bans livestock and chickens in residential areas. (*www.fredericknewspost.com*)

Massachusetts: Brocton, Hens are allowed, but roosters are not. (*www.home.centurytel.net*)

Michigan: Ann Arbor, Up to four chickens are allowed at a residence. A permit is required. No coop restrictions known. (*www.a2gov.org*)

Minnesota: Minneapolis, Unlimited amount of chickens allowed. Applicants must get 80% consent from neighbors with 100 feet of real estate. Chickens must be penned. (*www.handcraftedcoops.com*)

Mississippi: Columbus, Chickens are allowed. No maximum number restricted. Coop restrictions include zoning, noise and sanitation. (*www.thecityofcolumbusms.org*)

Missouri: Fallon, Chickens are permitted. Roosters are allowed. No permit required. Coop restrictions include proximity, noise, sanitation, and zoning. (*www.sccmo.org*)

Montana: Billings, Chickens are allowed. Roosters are not permitted. Livestock shall not be maintained in any zoning district located within the limits of the city. (*library1.municode.com*)

Nebraska: Grand Island, Chickens are allowed, 4 hens per acre with a minimum of one acre to keep chickens. No permit required. No roosters allowed. Coops need to be 15 feet away from any privately owned property abutting the owner's property. (*www.city.grand-island.com*)

Nevada: Las Vegas, Chickens are allowed; roosters are not. Must file written and unrevoked consent of any and all neighbors dwelling within 350 feet. Poultry must be contained at all times within a suitable, clean, and odor-free outbuilding or coop or runway that is free of animal wastes, and does not house unwanted rodents, flies, or any other offensive condition; and no poultry within any dwelling house, basement, or subbasement, or cellar. (*www.library.municode.com*)

New Hampshire: Rochester, Chickens and roosters are allowed. No maximum stated. No permit required. No person shall keep a pigpen, chicken coop, goat pen, or barn yard so near to any highway, park, or public place as to be offensive or a menace to the public health or offensive or a menace to any person residing on an adjoining or abutting lot nor shall a pigpen, chicken coop, goat pen, or barnyard be kept in such a condition as to allow the contents there from to be discharged upon any adjacent or abutting lot or upon any street, lane, park, alley or public place. (*www.rochesternh.net*)

New Jersey: Red Bank, No poultry or fowl inside the house, or within 40 feet of houses, dwellings, or stores. You may not have more than 12 of any fowl or poultry without a permit. A pen, coop, yard, or enclosure must be used to house and maintain fowl and poultry. (*www.home.centurytel.net*)

New Mexico: Albuquerque, Zoning allows the raising of unlimited chickens if penned at least 20 feet from the nearest residence. (*www.handcraftedcoops.com*)

New York: New York City, Chickens are allowed and roosters are not. No permit is required. If you keep poultry for sale, your coop must be whitewashed twice a year and be kept clean. (*www.nyc.gov*)

North Carolina: Greensboro, Chickens are allowed. Roosters are not. No permit required. Coops and shelters for poultry will be located behind the rear wall of the principal building. No poultry will be permitted to run loose. (*www.backyardchickens.com*)

North Dakota: Grand Forks, Owning poultry is not allowed unless it is for commercial use. Keeping any animal or fowl in violation of any provision of this section is hereby declared a nuisance. (*www.backyardchickens.com*)

Ohio: Cincinnati, Chickens are allowed. Roosters are not allowed. For coops, manure must be cleaned out daily. No person shall confine any fowl in a crate, box, or other receptacle in a cramped or unnatural position or shall overcrowd any crate, box, or other receptacle with fowl or fail to provide proper food, water, shelter, or sanitation for fowl confined in any receptacle. Dyeing is prohibited. (*www.library.municode.com*)

Oklahoma: Ponca City, Chickens must be kept 100 feet from neighbor's homes. (*www.handcraftedcoops.com*)

Oregon: Permit is not required if you own three or less chickens. Permit required if you own more than three chickens. Permits cost $31. (*www.mchealth.org*)

Pennsylvannia: Allentown, Chickens and roosters are not allowed. It shall be unlawful for any person to keep or maintain any cattle, swine, sheep, goats, or fowl in the city except at such places as are provided for slaughtering or laboratory purposes. (*www.allentownpa.gov*)

Rhode Island: Providence, No chickens or roosters are permitted. No fowl are permitted in houses or cellars. (*www.libarymunicode.com*)

South Carolina: Aiken, Chickens must be penned, and the pen kept 40 feet from neighboring residences. (*www.handcraftedcoops.com*)

South Dakota: Aberdeen, Chickens are allowed. Roosters are not allowed. No coop restrictions. Chickens cannot be kept free ranging nor in coops 125 feet of any building be it a home, (other than the home of the said owner of the chicken) library, store, etc. No building at all (except the owner) should have chickens within 25 feet. (*www.aberdeen.sd.us*)

Tennessee: Nashville, Chickens are allowed. Roosters are not allowed. Permit is required. Coops must be 25 feet away from any residence and 10 feet from any property line. (*www.nashville.gov*)

Texas: Austin, Up to 10 chickens allowed, but must be kept in an enclosure that is 50 feet away from neighbors. (*www.home.centurytel.net*)

Utah: Salt Lake City, Up to 15 chickens are allowed. Roosters not allowed. Permit is required. Chickens shall be confined within a secure, outdoor, enclosed area that shall be covered, ventilated, and predator-resistant. The coop shall have a minimum of 2 square feet of space per chicken. (*www.ci.slc.ut.us*)

Vermont: Burlington, Up to 3 chickens permitted. (*www.handcraftedcoops.com*)

Virginia: Falls Church, No livestock permitted. (*www.handcraftedcoops.com*)

Washington: Spokane, Up to 3 chickens are allowed. No roosters. (*www.home.centurytel.net*)

West Virginia: Montgomery, No chicken or roosters permitted. (*www.backyardchickens.com*)

Wisconsin: Green Bay, Chickens are permitted on parcels exceeding 10 acres in size and only on property zoned RR. Animal feedlot operations and pig farms not permitted. Barns and pens for domestic animals are permitted. (*ci.green-bay.wi.us*)

Wyoming: Cheyenne, Chickens are permitted. Roosters are unknown. Keeping or slaughtering of certain animals-restrictions within city. (*library4.municode.com*)

Appendix B: *Shopping for Your Flock*

Chicken feed, equipment, and supplies

Local stores:

Tractor Supply – This co-op can be found across the country. They provide starter mash and a variety of feed for adult chickens. They also provide other supplies that you may need for your flock. Check online at Google (*www.google.com*) to help locate your nearest store.

Alabama: Holley True Valley LLC, Selma, Alabama

Alaska: Alaska Garden and Pet Supply, Anchorage, Alaska

Arizona: Yuma Feed and Livestock, Yuma, Arizona

Arkansas: Farmers Association, Inc., Little Rock, Arkansas

California: Ranch Feed and Supply, Spring Valley, California

Colorado: American Pride Co-op Brighton, Colorado

Connecticut: The Feed Barn, New Millford, Connecticut

Delaware: Tractor Supply Company, Dover, Delaware

Florida: Tractor Supply Company, Sebring, Florida

Georgia: A G Daniel Company LLC, Eastman, Georgia

Hawaii: Waimea Feed Supply, Kamuela, Hawaii

Idaho: Franklin County Grain Growers, Preston, Idaho

Illinois: Tractor Supply Company, Washington, Illinois

Indiana: North Central Cooperative Inc, Wabash, Indiana

Iowa: Heartland Co-op, Waukee, Iowa

Kansas: Tractor Supply Company, Lansing, Kansas

Kentucky: Winchester Feed and Supply Company, Winchester, Kentucky

Louisiana: Austin Agriculture and Supply LLC, Pineville, Louisiana

Maine: Tractor Supply Company, Skowhegan, Maine

Maryland: The Feed Store LLC, Glen Dale, Maryland

Massachusetts: Ferestien Feed And Farm Supply, Inc., Foxboro, Massachusetts

Michigan: McBain Grain Company, Inc. McBain, Michigan

Minnesota: Tractor Supply Company, Elk River, Minnesota

Mississippi: Tractor Supply Company, Tupelo, Mississippi

Missouri: Tractor Supply Company, Jackson City, Missouri

Montana: Tractor Supply Company, Billings, Montana

Nebraska: Farmer's Cooperative Grain Company, Merna, Nebraska

Nevada: Inter-Mountain Farmers Association, Las Vegas, Nevada

New Hampshire: Cloverdale Feed and Farm Supply, Contoocook, New Hampshire

New Jersey: Rick's Saddle Shop Englishtown, Englishtown, New Jersey

New Mexico: Tractor Supply Company, Roswell, New Mexico

New York: Delaware Valley Farm and Garden Inc., Callicoon, New York

North Carolina: Boon's Farm Supplies, Jackson, North Carolina

North Dakota: Organic Feed Company, Dawson, North Dakota

Ohio: Champion Feed and Pet Food, Delaware, Ohio

Oklahoma: Farmers Union Coop Gin, Wayne, Oklahoma

Oregon: Wilco Co-op, Oregon City, Oregon

Pennsylvania: Calico Creek Feed and Pet Supply, Mill Hall, Pennsylvania

Rhode Island: Tractor Supply Company, Coventry, Rhode Island

South Carolina: Consumer Feed and Seed Store, Lexington, South Carolina

South Dakota: Tractor Supply Company, Sioux City, South Dakota

Tennessee: Garr's Rental and Feed Inc., Mount Juliet, Tennessee

Texas: K N Feed Inc., Ballinger, Texas

Utah: Inter-Mountain Famer's Association, Price, Utah

Vermont: Blue Seal AT Taft Corner Inc. DBA, Williston, Vermont

Virginia: Augusta Cooperative Farm Bureau Inc., Scottsville, Virginia

Washington: Country Farm and Feed Company, Enumclaw, Washington

West Virginia: Liggetts Supply, Mill Creek, West Virginia

Wisconsin: Waupun Feed and Seed Inc., Waupun, Wisconsin

Wyoming: Keith's Feed and Farm Supply, Evanstan, Wyoming

Shopping for day old chicks and eggs online

Murray McMurray Hatchery — *www.mcmurrayhatchery.com*

Natural Chicken Hatchery — *www.naturalchickenhatchery.info*

My Pet Chicken — *www.mypetchicken.com*

BackYard Chickens — *www.backyardchickens.com*

Omlet — *www.omlet.us*

Cackle Hatchery — *www.cacklehatchery.com*

Estes Farm Hatchery — *www.esteshatchery.com*

Places to purchase coops online

Green Chicken Coop — *www.greenchickencoop.com*

Omlet — *www.omlet.us*

Henspa — *www.henspa.com*

Petco — *www.petco.com*

Chickencoopsource.com — *www.chickencoopsource.com*

Shop the Coop — *www.shopthecoop.com*

Appendix C: *Organizations for Chicken Owners*

American Poultry Association — *www.amerpoultryassn.com*

American Bantam Association — *www.bantamclub.com*

4-H Poultry Program — *www.4-H.org*

Ameraucana Breeders Club — *www.ameraucana.org*

The New England Bantam Club — *www.newenglandbantamclub.org*

American Silkie Bantam Club — *www.americansilkiebantamclub.org*

Chicken Run Rescue site — *www.brittonclouse.com/chickenrunrescue*

Heritage Poultry Breeders of America — *www.hpbaa.com*

Appendix D: *Project/Show Forms*

Poultry Project Financial Records

Financial Agreement

_____ Ownership (you own and show the birds).

_____ Partnership (you and someone else share the ownership and expenses of showing the birds).

_____ Managerial (someone else owns the birds and you manage it).

I have the following agreement with the other person/party involved in ownership:

_____

_____

_____

Signature _____

Partners/Owner's Signature _____

1. Beginning Inventory: List all items on hand at the beginning of the project: all birds, equipment, feed, etc.

Date	Items and Description	Value Per Bird	Total Value
1. = Total Value Beginning Inventory			

2. Project Expenses

Includes the purchase of chickens, food, equipment, medication, utilities, etc. and also entry fees, or costs connected with attending a show.

Date	Items Purchased	Amount Purchased #/lb	Total Value Per Item/lb	Amount Paid
	2. = Total Expenses			

3. Project Income

Includes the sale of chickens, food, equipment, prize money won, etc.

Date	Items Sold	Amount Purchased #/lb	Total Value Per Item/lb	Amount Paid
		3. = Total Income		

4. Closing Inventory

List all items in possession **at the end** of the project year. List all chickens, equipment, food, etc.

Date	Items and Description	Value Per Item/Bird	Value
4. = Total Value Closing Inventory			

5. FInancial Summary

Income

Total income from project (#3) $ _____

Total value of closing inventory (#4) _____

Total Receipts $ _____

Expenses

Total project expenses (from #2) _____

Total value of beginning inventory (from #1) _____

Total Expenses $ _____

Project/Loss

Net gain or loss on project (check) $ _____

❏ Gain: Receipts minus expenses | ❏ Loss: Expenses minus receipts

Poultry Management Records

1. Labor Record - Work done by hours per month doing the following:

	Feeding/ Watering	Cleaning Barn	Repairing Equip.	Culling/ Selecting Birds	Preparing for Show	Other
Jan						
Feb						
Mar						
Apr						
May						
Jun						
Jul						
Aug						
Sept						
Oct						
Nov						
Dec						
Total Hrs						

2. Incubation Records-

Date	# of Egg Sets	Date Hatched	# Eggs Fertile	% Fertil-ity	# Hatched	% Hatched	% Hatchibil-ity	Comments

* % Fertility = # eggs fertile/ # of eggs set | % Hatchability = # eggs fertile/ # eggs hatched | % Hatched = # eggs set/ # hatched

3. Health Maintenance Records

Record procedures done for flock's health (medicating, vaccinating, worming, lice treatment, disinfecting, etc.).

Date	Description	Reason

4. Inventory and Mortality Records

At the beginning of each year, write the number of chickens in your flock in the beginning inventory column.

	Jan	Feb	Mar	Apr	May	Jun
Beginning Inventory						
# of Birds Added						
# Died						
# Sold						
# For Home Use						
# Remaining						
	Jul	Aug	Sept	Oct	Nov	Dec
Beginning Inventory						
# of Birds Added						
# Died						
# Sold						
# For Home Use						
# Remaining						

* % Mortality = Total # dead/ Total starting #

5. Exhibition Record

Date	Name of Show	# of Birds	Entry Fee	Prize Money	Extra Costs

5. Breed Show Record

Date	Name of Show	Variety Entered	Breed/Band #	# in Class	Placing

Bibliography

Websites

CBS News, *www.cbsnews.com/stories/2010/07/14/tech/main6676542.shtml*

Purdue University, *http://ag.ansc.purdue.edu/poultry/publication/commegg*

USDA, *www.ams.usda.gov*

University of Florida, *www.edis.ifas.ufl.edu*

Orlando Weekly, *www.orlandoweekly.com/features/story.asp?id=14165*

Organic Farming Research Foundation, *www.ofrf.org/resources/organicfaqs*

Chicken Keeping Secrets, *www.chickenkeepingsecrets.com/keeping-chickens/clipping-chicken-wings-why-when-how/*

Animal Corner, *www.animalcorner.co.uk/farm/chickens/chicken_anatomy*

The Humane Society of the United States, *www.hsus.org/farm/resources/research/practices/comparison_hen_welfare_cages_vs_cage_free*

United States Postal Service, *www.usps.org*

Stromberg's Chicks and Gamebirds Unlimited, *www.strombergschickens.com/stock/shipping_birds*

The Modern Homestead, *www.themodernhomestead.us/article/Butchering-Killing.html*

Shop the Coop, *www.shopthecoop.com*

Backyard Chickens, *www.backyardchickens.com*

My Pet Chicken, *www.mypetchicken.com*

Omelet, *www.omelet.us*

McMurray Hatchery, *www.mcmurrayhatchery.com*

Estes Farm Hatchery, *www.esteshatchery.com*

Lions Grip, *www.lionsgrip.com*

Funding Universe, *www.fundinguniverse.com*

Best Farm Buys, *www.bestfarmbuys.com*

Ideal Poultry, *www.idealpoultry.com*

Sustainable Echo, *www.sustainableecho.com*

Animal Rights Encyclopedia, *www.zoosavvy.com*

American Livestock Breeds Conservatory, *www.albc-usa.org*

So Po Coops, *www.sailzora.com/coops*

National Association of State Department of Agriculture, *www.nasda.org*

Chicken Keeping Secrets, *www.chickenkeepingsecrets.com*

Urban Chickens, *www.urbanchickens.org*

Home Grown Evolution, *www.homegrownevolution.com*

National Chicken Council, *www.nationalchickencouncil.com/aboutNCC*

Poultry One, *www.poultryone.com/atricles/stress*

Dummies.com, *www.dummies.com*

Bird Hobbyist, *www.birdhobbyist.com/articles*

Los Angeles Times, *www.latimes.com/features*

Books

Damerow, Gail. Storey's Guide to Raising Chickens. Massachusetts: Storey Publishing, 1995

Graham, Chris. Choosing and Keeping Chickens.New York: Octopus Publishing Group, 2006

Damerow, Gail. The Chicken Health Handbook. Massachuesetts: Storey Publishing, 1994

Megyesi, Jennifer. The Joy of Keeping Chickens, The Ultimate Guide To Raising Poultry For Fun Or Profit. New York: Skyhorse Publishing, 2009

Nelson, Melissa. The Complete Guide to Small-Scale Farming. Ocala: Atlantic Publishing Group, 2010

Verhoef, Ester. The Complete Encyclopedia of Chickens. Netherlands:Rebo International b. v.2009

Willis, Kimberly. Raising Chickens for Dummies. New Jersey: Wiley Publishing, 2009

Index